WITHDRAWN

McIVER OF NORTH CAROLINA

Charles D. McIver.

McIVER

OF NORTH CAROLINA

BY

ROSE HOWELL HOLDER

CHAPEL HILL

THE UNIVERSITY OF NORTH CAROLINA PRESS

FOR

ANNE, GLENDA, AND MELINDA

who benefit beyond their knowledge
by the life of
CHARLES DUNCAN MCIVER

Foreword

CHARLES DUNCAN MCIVER was a battling, story-telling, irrepressible Scot, North Carolina born, who saw a strange vision and dreamed a strange dream. His vision projected a system of free public schools providing every child with the fundamentals of learning. His dream portrayed a college in which young women could secure higher education, both liberal and practical, that they would pass on as mothers and teachers to make the vision of universal education a reality. Both ideas were revolutionary in his early professional life almost to the point of suggesting madness, but it was true then, as it was when Pope said it, that "A decent boldness ever meets with friends." McIver had the boldness of unshakable conviction; he was able, therefore, to oppose the current of public opinion, and in time to change and re-direct it. The largest residential woman's college in America, Woman's College of the University of North Carolina, exists as chief monument to the success of his dual purpose.

This chronicle of his life is based in large part on his personal letters and papers. Moreover, the record contained in his private papers is remarkably complete. His letters to Mrs. McIver alone furnish a running account of some of the most important periods of his life. He wrote her daily when he was away from home, and that was often; she kept the letters—all of them. She preserved along with the rest those containing trenchant comment on prominent persons and current affairs which he sometimes suggested she destroy.

His mother, bless her Scottish heart, never threw anything away either. Thus one is able to trace through Charles McIver's earliest grade school compositions a pattern of thought in process of formation. The educator kept a diary, too, at one time, and twice he started to write his autobiography. Since he was consistently in the public eye, frequent newspaper accounts contribute to completeness of his story.

Fortunately, however, it has been unnecessary to rely entirely on yellowed papers in a file for the warmth and energy and humor of a forceful personality. In spite of the lapse of half a century since his death, many persons are living who remember Dr. McIver well, and who have been generous with interviews and letters that round out his biography. They include relatives, a college classmate, members of the early Woman's College faculty and of every class during the fourteen years of his presidency, three women who served him as secretary, and numerous others who knew him as fellow townsman and co-worker in a variety of civic enterprises.

In order that the story may proceed without interruption by footnotes, sources other than those indicated in the narrative will be found in notes at the back of the book.

Perhaps one other consideration needs to be stressed. Dr. McIver's two daughters, who made their father's papers available as a basis for this biography, made them fully available. In the interest of objective reporting, they declined to impose any restrictions whatever on use of the material. Feeling as well that any possibility of censorship on their part would preclude unbiased writing, they volunteered an agreement to suggest neither changes nor deletions in the finished product. They have kept that bargain to the letter.

Rose Howell Holder.

January, 1957
Long Covert
Monkton, Maryland

Acknowledgments

MANY PROBLEMS have presented themselves in the writing of this book, the majority of which have reached eventual solution. Now, at the end, I am face to face with an obstacle that is insurmountable—a wish to make adequate acknowledgment of the help that has been freely and generously given. There is no adequate way to express an appreciation deeply and honestly felt. A mere list of persons who have been of service would run to pages. It is, regrettably, not possible.

A few of the many, however, must be mentioned. First of all, there are Dr. McIver's daughters, Mrs. James R. Young and Mrs. John Dickinson, who entrusted me with the telling of their father's story. There are no means to acknowledge the gratitude, born of humility, with which I received their permission to make unrestricted use of their father's papers. In a like category of those to whom I am a permanent debtor I must also place the late John Dickinson, whose belief that I would do a thorough and workmanlike job on the biography of his father-in-law persuaded others to that point of view.

As indicated elsewhere (notes on chapters three and four), other members of the family who were unfailing sources of information included Mrs. Minnie McIver Brown and Dr. McIver's youngest brother, Mr. James Henry McIver. And difficult as it is to single out any one person not within the family circle, I cannot fail to thank Mr. John H. Monger, of Sanford, who has held various offices in the North Carolina Society of County Historians. Mr. Monger is so steeped in the background of his locality that talking with him is like reading a footnote to history. Whenever a fact has proved elusive, a record has not been readily obtainable, the address of a person having information has not been immediately ascertainable, he has produced, with the dexterity of a magician, data and document and reliable informant.

Then there are librarians. I think there must be a special dispensation in Valhalla for all librarians, and especially for those of the Woman's College Library—under direction of Mr. Charles Adams—which naturally contained much of the specialized information which this record required. Miss Marjorie Hood, with whom I worked most closely, is the library staff member who has earned my very special and limitless gratitude. Others who have been helpful include personnel of the excellent Ferguson Library of Stamford, Connecticut, the incomparable New York Public Library, and Enoch Pratt Free Library of Baltimore, the National Archives, Washington, and the State Department of Archives and History, Raleigh. I have found only courtesy and helpfulness in libraries. Indeed I have a higher opinion of the whole human race than when I began research on this volume four years ago.

A newspaper woman once said of a famous actress that she had made growing old seem glorious. Many of the living McIver contemporaries I have encountered, vital and alert and young in everything but years, have made it seem unnecessary. There was one woman among those no longer young who insisted, in spite of an arthritic condition, on taking an automobile trip that must have been agonizing in order to put in my hands some McIver letters to which she had access. There were others—people who had never seen me before—who lent invaluable out-of-print books and irreplaceable manuscripts. How does one say thank you to persons like that? I do not know, I swear; I wish I did. Neither do I know how to say thank you to a trio whose answers to requests for information were prompt, complete, and reliable: Mrs. Carlton Jester, Jr. (Betty Brown), former secretary of the Woman's College Alumnae; Miss Barbara Parrish, her successor; and Mr. J. Maryon Saunders, secretary of the General Alumni Association, University of North Carolina.

The list grows long, does it not? It could as well contain the names of countless others who had no information to give and no material to lend, who were nevertheless helpful in their fashion.

An automobile was almost a necessity for research trips throughout every part of North Carolina, but once when weather did not permit driving from my former Connecticut home, I set out by train to keep appointments. Upon arriving at Greensboro, I discovered that one apartment, two typewriters, and three cars had been placed at my disposal. I used the lot before returning home. I'm sorry, my friends. I don't have words for the thoughtful likes of you.

Moreover, if I had all the words, there is a certain gentleman, one Glenn Holder by name, for which they would not be sufficient. My husband not only cheerfully paid the bills for numerous research trips and long distance telephone calls (suggesting additional ones now and then), but he contributed skills I do not have. I cannot read copy, especially when trying to correct something I have written; I cannot read proof. Glenn, on the other hand, perhaps as a surviving accomplishment of his editing days, can do both. In fact, a wrong font letter, a transposition, an unclosed quote, seem to leap at him across the room from a printed page. Yet, those are small matters, if worth mentioning at all. On the more important questions of content and presentation, I relied on his judgment. Indeed, I quite happily reverted to a practice I followed during my newspaper days—and other reporters with me—of laying my copy before him with a thought so comfortable it did not need to be finished: "If it gets by Glenn. . . ." This paragraph alone, which almost certainly would not "get by Glenn," has not been his to edit as the most uncompromising critic of them all. Thank you, Sir. Thank you very much.

Contents

		PAGE
Foreword		vii
Acknowledgments		ix
I.	A New Life	3
II.	War and Defeat	14
III.	The Old Order Changeth	24
IV.	The Child Is Father of the Man	34
V.	Young Ambition's Ladder	46
VI.	The Happiest Bond	57
VII.	One Bright Particular Star	69
VIII.	The Law and the Prophets of Education	80
IX.	Highways and Hedges	94
X.	Dream and Substance	110
XI.	All Things Wise and Wonderful	127
XII.	Battle's Stern Array	143
XIII.	Double Row of Tracks	162
XIV.	Horseman of the Apocalypse	178
XV.	"Free Schools for All the People"	195
XVI.	High Road to Parnassus	212
XVII.	Widening Horizons	232
XVIII.	And lo! McIver's Name Led All the Rest	251
	Epilogue	260
	Notes	264
	Index	277

Illustrations

Charles Duncan McIver   Frontispiece

                                                     Facing page

Evander McIver, "Scotch Iver"   96

Dr. John E. Kelly   96

Rev. William S. Lacy   96

Dr. James Y. Joyner   96

Mr. and Mrs. Charles Duncan McIver   97

Charles Duncan McIver and Edwin A. Alderman   112

A group of teachers at a county Institute   112

Administration Building, State Normal School   113

Library of the Woman's College   113

Ezekiel (Zeke) Robinson   192

Early President's Office at Woman's College   192

Early Students' Union at the Woman's College   193

Elliott Hall, Woman's College   193

President's Home at the Woman's College   208

Dr. and Mrs. Charles Duncan McIver and Family   208

Mrs. Charles Duncan McIver   209

McIVER OF NORTH CAROLINA

> The generations of men are but relays in civilization's march
> from savagery to the millennium.   —*Charles Duncan McIver*

1—

A New Life

As a rule, Evander McIver was deeply responsive to a North Carolina spring. His manner of speaking, plain and economical at all other times, reflected a seasonally poetic turn of mind when he remarked on wild plum blossoms or a pear tree in bloom. He also derived a special satisfaction from cultivated fields that were much more extensive than any he had known in early childhood. Evander had been born on the mountainous Isle of Skye, which had little tillable land. There Highland Scots raised Highland cattle, quarried some marble, and did some fishing, but agriculture was both primitive and unprofitable. Farming on his more abundant land was neither, hence Evander always had fresh interest in the spring panorama of green fields and flowering orchards.

Yet, the twenty-first of April, 1834, found him unmindful alike of scene or season. That ordinarily indomitable Scot was feeling awed by the power—aye, and the glory—of a frail woman engaged in the final processes of creating new life.

Nevertheless, his sense of inadequacy would pass with the moment at hand since Evander was unquestionably a person of consequence. He had been just under eight years old in the summer of 1802 when he sailed from Liverpool with his parents, Duncan and Catherine (Robertson) McIver, and their other six children. In the nearly thirty-two years since then he had given a good account of himself.

Already he had accumulated seven hundred acres of land and the slaves to tend them. He was an Elder in the church. He had married well. His wife, Margaret, was the only child of that Duncan McIver who was called, with strict accuracy, "Wealthy

Miller" Duncan. There were a confusing number of Duncan McIvers in the vicinity, as well as a confusing number of other people with names exactly alike. Relatives regularly intermarried, and family namesakes increased in such profusion that a distinctive nickname frequently became a necessity. His occupation had not only served to set the miller apart, but had given him a further advantage. Grain in the early 1800's was one of the state's leading cash crops, and the owner of a grist mill collected a fair amount of it in his toll bins. Miller Duncan converted his share into flour, sold the flour in Fayetteville, and proceeded to get rich. In time the word "wealthy" was attached to his name as naturally as the original "miller" had been.

By the spring in question the wealthy miller's son-in-law and daughter had provided him with four grandchildren, not counting the one whose birth was imminent. By any standard Evander McIver, who would not be forty until September, was a very substantial citizen.

It had been clear from the start to the lad and his family that the climate of their new home was all they had been led to expect of it. They had left their native Skye on a humid day in August. They had landed in Wilmington on the thirtieth day of North Carolina's crisp October. They missed, it is true, the striking scenery of their wild and lovely island, but then giant live oaks festooned with Spanish moss had a curious and eerie charm. Nor had they gone far before the children were almost hypnotized by deep white sand which traveled to the top of a turning wagon wheel before slithering off. Even so, the most notable difference of all was the land. To persons accustomed to island limitations there seemed an incredible amount of it.

If the country was strange, however, the people were not. The Cape Fear River region was largely populated by good Scotch Presbyterians like themselves. Some were there before 1729 when the Carolina territory was partitioned into north and south portions, but the tide of migration reached its flood between the battle of Culloden in 1746 and outbreak of the Revolutionary War. The disastrous rout which ended Stuart hopes for regaining the throne of England, plus subsequent harsh treatment accorded followers of the Pretender, Prince Charles Edward, disposed thousands of clansmen to comply with British terms. When the king offered a pardon to all Highland rebels who would take the oath of allegiance and emigrate to America, Highlanders accepted by the shipload. A trickle from that main stream would not be entirely dried up for another fifty-odd years. There were five hundred Highlanders on the "Duke of Kent" which brought the youthful Evander's family.

As early as 1775 there had been McIvers among the Scots who moved up the Cape Fear and fanned out along the tributaries of its upper reaches. Indeed, Evander and his family were the last of the clan to arrive. A twenty-year-old cousin of the boy's, John Ban McIver, Jr., met the late comers at Wilmington and served as their escort to Chatham County.

Mysterious forests of whispering long leaf pines encroached on both sides of the road and in them, according to the guide, fierce wild hogs made their home. "Piney-wood rooters" they were called because of the elongated snout with which they searched out an existence. The animals were too tough and stringy to be edible, if caught, but they gave immediacy to the philosophy of every frontier, "Root, hog, or die." And in spite of the fact that roads of a sort had been cut and houses, some of them imposing, had been built, North Carolina was essentially a frontier at the turn of the nineteenth century.

Yet none of this daunted the new arrivals. They were people of strong character with a firm belief in the dignity of labor, and its benefits. They had every intention of working hard and reaping a just reward, God willing, in plenty and security of their own making.

At length, the rutted sandy roads gave way to rutted clay roads, and the latest McIvers reached a destination resplendent with autumn. Chatham County's woods and hills had the appearance of a rich tapestry, bright with fall leaves of many varieties and shot through with the constant green of the pine. It was a "likely" spot. Duncan of Skye and his Catherine found it "to their notion."

All of North Carolina's Scotch conformed in large measure to a general pattern. Whether they were Highlanders who peopled the Cape Fear region or Scots who came from the north of Ireland (and were erroneously called Scotch-Irish for that reason) to settle in the Piedmont section, they had several characteristics in common. On the whole, they were a thoroughly democratic lot; their church had seen to that. They professed, Highlander and Scotch-Irish alike, the same Presbyterian religion. They had the same passion for education. Wherever they came from they brought along parson and schoolmaster, usually the same man. Wherever they settled, a "regular stated pastor" was the first concern of a new community, and church and school either rose simultaneously or, more often than not, one building served both purposes. They quite possibly held human rights in higher value than any other people of their century anywhere in the world.

The last McIver arrivals found a church already thriving. Buffalo Church had been founded in 1797 with the help of their own kin. For five years, therefore, it had been striving to serve the spiritual needs of all its people, the "new Scotch" as well as the old. In those early years whenever it could be managed a sermon was delivered in English at Sunday morning meeting, in Gaelic at afternoon service. Balconies afforded the slaves a chance to worship with their masters.

While church and school were warp and woof of their social fabric, the Scots had other definite requirements for the good life. These included houses that were stout and comfortable and clean, food that was good as well as plentiful, and—with certain exceptions—fine Scotch whiskey. Officers of the church, forewarned by the Scriptures that "wine is a mocker and strong drink is raging," naturally abstained, but they were a minority. For the most part, the others liked their little nip. Even some of the ladies would take a dram in the privacy of their own homes if they were not feeling sprightly, and a hot toddy was the essential first step in warding off a cold.

What they had they loved to share. Their open-handed hospitality was scarcely less warming than the "bleezing" fires they insisted upon. The Bible was guide and stay. Its language and its allusions were a part of everyday speech and found their way onto maps as place names. The hamlet near which the family from Skye located had a name that was Biblical in origin. Once when crops had failed in the Piedmont some of its people, like Joseph's brothers of old, had come seeking grain. As it was Egypt to which the brothers had gone, so Egypt (later Cumnock) the place was called. There was an Endor not far away, too, and a creek that quarreled across one of the McIver fields was called Purgatory.

As a young man, Evander had begun buying land, the first tracts paid for with English money—thirty shillings per hundred acres, fifty shillings per hundred acres. The times were auspicious for acquiring good cleared farms. North Carolina had its share of the restless breed that pushed back a nation's horizon from one ocean to another, and Evander's first year in the new country became memorable for the added grandeur of its vision. Toward the end of 1803 President Jefferson's Louisiana Purchase provided a vast new frame for the spacious American dream. Then no sooner was the War of 1812 over than the westward fever mounted in Chatham County as everywhere else. Family after family moved on—sure that faraway fields were richer, that far-off pastures were greener, that in some distant valley their particular rainbow would dip to its golden end.

Evander bought up vacated lands among others, generally for a fair price, occasionally for a mere token payment. At one time he purchased a tract from the State of North Carolina for five cents the hundred acres.

His introspection, therefore, could not have been entirely unpleasant as he awaited the birth of his fifth child.

He was waiting alone. The children, as was customary when a baby was born, had been sent elsewhere. Time enough for them to learn there was no truth in the picturesque explanations they heard from the slave quarters. They would discover in due course that the doctor did not find the baby in a hollow stump, nor under a collard leaf, although their parents had not troubled to contradict the reports. He did not even bring it to the house in his black bag. On the other hand, the facts of life were considered unseemly knowledge for the very young, and Jane, Evander's oldest, was only nine. Finally, an infant's cry from the inner room gave notice to the waiting father that his child had been born.

Still Evander did not budge. He would stick to the procedure he had followed with the arrival of Jane and Flora Ann and Duncan and Donald. He would pay the doctor before he took a look at his baby.

Evander never volunteered an explanation for that singular behavior, and it is altogether unlikely that anybody ever asked for one. Was it that he disliked to stay beholden to any person, or did he have, as some believed with reasonable cause, a special antipathy to doctor bills? Certainly he had been known to tell a doctor whose visits grew numerous that a person might as well die of sickness as to be charged to death. (The statement sounded little as it would have if somebody else had made it. Neither the mildness of the climate nor the softness of the speech around him ever took the edge off his Scottish burr.) Or was it just that he found parting with money disagreeable and wanted to get the unpleasantness finished? There was also support for that point of view. Significantly, in that day of appropriate nicknames, Evander was called "Scotch Iver," and "Scotch" referred to a person of excessive thrift as well as one of Scottish antecedents. Thus the appellative was manifestly fitting on both counts.

Still, Scotch Iver was not stingy. His acquaintances never said of him, as they sometimes did of miserly neighbors, that "He would skin a flea for its hide and tallow." Rather, it seemed to them that Evander practiced his own brand of thrift to make possible his own brand of generosity, and one was as well known as the other.

At length the doctor appeared, told Scotch Iver he had a fine boy, and got paid for his part in the proceedings. Then and only then did Evander go in to give his wife such commendation, and congratulation, as an undemonstrative Scot thought proper under the circumstances. There were individuals in the earth in those days.

The first Sunday there was a baptizing at Buffalo Church, Elder McIver carried his son and had him christened Matthew Henry. He and his wife, Scotch Iver said, "had concluded to call the baby Henry."

Henry was a satisfactory child, industrious and obedient, but then parents thereabouts were accustomed to exact obedience. He was a studious boy, too, and got only one whipping in school. That was for insisting on studying to himself when the established practice was to study out loud. Naturally anybody that queer—"quare" Scotch Iver would have said—could expect a thrashing.

Like his father, Henry was kind to the slaves and was never known to whip one. Unlike his older brothers, he did not complete his education. By the time he had finished his preparatory schooling, Scotch Iver made it plain, without actually saying so, that Henry was needed at home. Three children had been born after him, but the one boy of the trio had not survived his second year.

Therefore, Henry was the last son at home, and at a time when his father's responsibilities were heavy. Scotch Iver's lands had grown to approximately three thousand acres—twice that amount if one counted the land his wife Margaret had inherited from Wealthy Miller Duncan—and his slaves numbered over a hundred.

In deference to his father's need, Henry decided to forego college. It was a decision he regretted for the rest of his life and one that his neighbors, believing that God works in a mysterious way His wonders to perform, could well have deemed providential. Henry, having missed the "advantages" of higher education, endowed college training with transcendent value. As a result, his children were brought up to include college in their plans.

Until Henry reached his twenty-fifth year he attracted no particular notice to himself. Then suddenly he became the center of attention for visitors spending the day, and "spending the day" was a custom so enthusiastically practiced that it became something of an institution. On any fine morning when householders were not away on a visit themselves, they could expect company to begin arriving by ten o'clock. In a period when there was no public entertainment people invented their own, and good food accompanied by interesting talk comprised one of the most popular of their pastimes.

The food was no problem. There was all the variety of farm and orchard and stream to choose from; smokehouses bulged with meat, the well house held crocks of cream and butter, and there were skillful cooks in the kitchen to prepare a meal. Sometimes, if a visit were prearranged, there might be roast turkey or a saddle of mutton, but fried chicken became, and remained, a favorite company dish, served as it was with cream gravy and feather-light buttermilk biscuits. The baking soda required for bread made with sour milk also served another useful function. It was relief for the indigestion which occasionally followed.

No hard and fast set of rules governed spending the day, but callers did not come again until their visit was paid back!

The lively interest centered on Henry when he began courting William Dalrymple Harrington's daughter, Sarah. Sarah was a black-haired, gray-eyed slip of a girl with a fun-loving, prank-playing disposition. "Devilish," her friends said of her in affectionate compliment, or "mischievous." It was fully agreed that Henry McIver was "foolish" about the girl.

"Pretty Sallie" she was called to distinguish her from another Sallie Harrington, and if the distinction was unkind to the less-favored young woman, at least it had the virtue of accuracy. Moreover, both girls would long since have heard from their mothers, either in comfort or warning, that "handsome is as handsome does" and "beauty is only skin deep." True, Pretty Sallie's mother, the former Lydia Margaret McNeill, was dead. She had been Mr. Harrington's third wife.

Sallie was not only petite and pretty, she was stylish in the bargain. She considered it her bounden duty to dress well, and whatever was a duty one did without question. Duty came close to being the primary motivation of her life, as it was of all the lives about her. "I think it our duty to dress neatly," she summed it up, "and even genteelly if we can afford it, that we may feel at ease in company."

She could afford it. Her father was the richest planter for miles around; in fact, he was one of the largest taxpayers on land and slaves in the whole state. His large plantation lay on both sides of Deep River in Moore County.

Sallie was, even as Henry, largely Scottish in background. Indeed, they were second cousins. Their grandmothers, the Dalrymple girl who had married Sion Harrington (William's father) and the one who had become Wealthy Miller Duncan's wife, were sisters. Sallie, however, was part Irish, and that Celtic strain was apparently sufficient to account for her spontaneous gaiety and infectious humor—attributes she would bequeath in full measure to her first-born.

Henry, who understood his people well, knew what was going on, but their talk did not bother him a particle. They were merely amusing themselves, with no thought of meddling. The doings at the church, politics in season, the lives and loves of kinfolks and neighbors were the stock in trade of their conversation, and, of all the subjects in the human drama, romance lent itself more readily than any other to continued discussion. A courtship could go on indefinitely. Its outcome could well be a lifetime contract. For marriage was just that. What God had joined together they had been commanded not to put asunder, and what was more, the deliberate breaking of a solemn vow was the worst sort of disgrace—a downright affront to human decency. Consequently, divorce was both a sin and a shame and not to be countenanced on either score.

Actually, there was warm approval of the match. In spite of her father's wealth, Sallie was not in the least haughty or aloof, and surely a more capable young woman could not be found. After the death of her mother, the reins of her father's large household had fallen into her hands and she had proved her competence from the start. It was her job to "give out" food from the locked pantry to the cooks, to direct the preserving of food for winter use, and to maintain the orderly routine of a well-run home. Twice a year she laid out patterns and cloth, called in cutters and sewers, and supervised the wholesale making of clothes for the slaves. Although she was accustomed to plenty, she understood the first creed of the pioneer, "Waste not, want not," and practiced it rigorously. As for the food, Sallie was insistent upon good seasoning. The sage and bay leaf and thyme she valued for cooking were never neglected, but then neither were the balsam and lavender that perfumed the linens. On top of that, she was determined to air the bedding every day of the world.

Oh, Sallie was a "mighty fine housekeeper" all right enough.

Besides, she was a good age for marrying. Sallie was just turning seventeen.

Henry, the interested visitors noted, was a bit on the sober side for a girl who was "merry as a lark," but nobody, they hastened to add, nobody at all enjoyed a joke as much as Henry. He was "quick-spoken," the appraisal went on, "but he didn't mean anything by it," and it was much more important that he was a fair man—"a whole-souled person and honest as the day is long." He had great energy, too, and would make a good provider for the well-to-do Harrington daughter. Accordingly, they had no fault to find with his intentions.

It would have been a waste of time if they had, as far as Henry was concerned. He had made up his mind to marry Sallie if she would have him.

She would. They were married November 22, 1859, by her pastor, the Reverend George A. Russell. Their honeymoon consisted of a two-week visit with Scotch Iver and a return to the Harrington home for a week. Then they took up residence not far from Jonesboro at the former Wealthy Miller Duncan place which had come to Margaret McIver's children from their grandfather. Mr. Harrington gave his daughter for a wedding present her choice of one from among three trained cooks, and she had enough foresight to take the youngest, who would presumably give the longest service.

Shortly after the wedding a judge who was one of Henry's kinsmen went to call on the bride. He found that blithe spirit out in the grove skipping rope, with one end of the rope tied to the trunk of a tree and the other in the hands of her wedding present slave. Henry was not at home, but Sallie discharged her duty as a young matron admirably. The judge found her house in perfect order—orderliness was another of her lifelong traits— and took pleasure in reporting that Henry's wife was "very clever." As the word "clever" was understood in that community to mean gracious, friendly, hospitable, His Honor's visit added nothing to the common knowledge.

It was at the Moore County homestead of the late miller that the Henry McIvers' first child was born. There, on the twenty-seventh of September, 1860, while Sallie was still a month short of her eighteenth birthday, she bore a son. His name was Charles Duncan McIver.

2–

War and Defeat

THE WAR CLOUD that had appeared to be far off during the political
campaign of 1860 loomed nearer and blacker with its conclusion.
Or so Henry McIver thought. Within a month of Mr. Lincoln's
election he had moved his wife and son to a farm only half a
dozen miles from the Harrington plantation. Then, if worse
came to worst, his family would be somewhat better off near
Sallie's father.

The baby, just two months old at the time, had not yet been
baptized, and the christening took place at a Presbyterian church
in Carthage. His parents had determined earlier to use his first
name instead of the esteemed but overworked "Duncan," and the
decision had merit. Their Scottish relatives had a way of cor-
rupting some of the finest names into unattractive short form.
Thus Elizabeth became "Lizzie" and Augusta became "Gus" or
"Gussie." Malcolm was known as "Make" and Duncan was
almost invariably shortened to "Dunk," a name inconsistent with
the dignity which a boy born into the dominant group of his
section—socially, economically, and politically—could hope to
achieve. As it was he was called Charlie.

The house to which the McIvers moved was not impressive.
Certainly it was not comparable to the Miller Duncan place, which
had been the first painted house in all the country round, nor
the handsomely furnished Harrington home. The land, however,
was the best to be had. Lying along two streams, Richland and
McLendon's creeks, it was of such excellence that Ulster Scots had
cleared and occupied it long years before Highlanders began to
arrive in the 1770's.

North Carolina on the whole did not share Henry's prescience in regard to a coming conflict. True, there was excitement after the election, and even some clamor to follow the lead of its hot-headed neighbor when South Carolina pulled out of the Union in December. But sentiment was generally against secession, and the press was largely of the same mind as the people. The state had been in no great hurry to join the Union, being next to the last of the original thirteen colonies to ratify the constitution, and was in no hurry to leave.

The question was not one of the "right" to secede. The sovereign State of North Carolina had gone of its own free will into a confederation of other sovereign states, and held with the advocates of states' rights that it could withdraw of the same volition. Nor was the doctrine native to the South alone. All sections of the country had proposed secession at one time or another. It was only when separation would no longer serve their most vital interests that its proponents found the identical suggestion "unconstitutional" or "treasonable" on other tongues. The sympathy of North Carolinians was with the southern states but their common sense rejected dissolution of the Union as inadvisable.

The state did not act, indeed, until its only alternative was a choice of sides in the war. When President Lincoln called for troops in April of 1861 after Fort Sumter had been fired on, North Carolina's governor considered the levy "in violation of the Constitution and a usurpation of power," and so informed Mr. Lincoln, adding "You can get no troops from North Carolina." On May 20, there was not a dissenting vote in the convention which took the state into the Confederacy.

If North Carolina was slow, it was thorough. It put into the field over 120,000 troops, a larger number than any other southern state, and a number that exceeded its voting strength. It lost more than any other southern state, too, and contributed heavily to the commissary supplies of the Confederate armies.

Little Charlie McIver's family had all the "necessaries," as they wrote to the men at the front. It was mental anguish, not privation, that took the greatest toll of those at home in that particular community. Medicine was at a premium, but they were accustomed to rely a great deal on home remedies anyway. Salt was inadequate. Sugar soared to seventy-five cents and a dollar a pound, when obtainable at all, and people who liked their coffee strong and black, spurning anything else as "punished water," had to resort to such substitutes as they could make of parched corn-meal, rye, and potatoes.

Still, these were not matters to trouble a little boy, for whom there was even enough of sweets. There were sweet potatoes so bursting with juice that the skin would split in baking, and some of the sugary liquid blacken on the outside. There was home-made syrup. There was honey from the domestic hives, and some of the women were quite adept at robbing a wild bee tree and adding to the supply from their own bee gums.

One of the boy's permanently vivid recollections of the period concerned the day his father, a cavalry volunteer, left for the war. "I remember how," Charles wrote autobiographically, "when he was telling my mother goodbye, I begged him not to go. I didn't know what war was, but it was not hard for me to realize that there was someting awful in that separation." Finally, Henry put an end to his entreaties by declaring, "If I don't go they'll make me," thus shattering for a brief interval the security of his small son's world, in which father had been the supreme authority.

Henry's slaves, loyal as many others were, stayed on to work the farm, and Sallie's Uncle Make McNeill, too old for military service, stayed with his niece at least part of the time. The fore-man was a Negro about forty years old, known to Charlie as "Uncle Sam," who acted as master to the other slaves. Once the small boy saw Sam whip a recalcitrant worker, and the incident stuck in his mind for a couple of reasons. Sam was not harsh, and whipping a slave was something Charlie had never seen his father do.

Sam was kindness itself to the child. He humored the boy, carried him everywhere he himself had to go, let him ride the horses, and generally stood between him and any harm whatever.

Little Charlie's special companion was a Negro child named Dick, a cunning, cruel boy a few years older than his white playmate. Charles recalled afterwards that "It was Dick's delight to spread hot coals in the fireplace of a cabin, climb to the roof, and drop a cat down the chimney." He was left below to watch the cat jump when it struck the fire. After seeing the geese picked the colored boy suggested that he and Charlie pick the guineas. They did. Once, fear of punishment for some particularly monstrous piece of deviltry kept him in hiding under the front doorstep for well over a day—until hunger drove him out.

Still, Dick had his good points. He knew where the muscadine grapes grew wild and sweet. He could push a little fellow so high in the swing, fastened to a branch of the tall oak, that bare toes would touch the leafy branches, and he would have time to "run under" before the swing came down. He could climb a persimmon tree and shake down fruit sweetened by frost. That young sadist would have much preferred to see somebody pucker the mouth with a green persimmon, if he could have found a person so unwary, but not his small white charge. His genuine affection for Charlie outweighed a multitude of faults in the estimation of Sallie McIver and Uncle Make McNeill. It also relieved Sallie of keeping an eye on her son for a large part of the time, and she had another baby, William Donald, who was born early in September of 1862.

The white and colored boy had a sweet potato patch that was their own. Although the sweet potato plant was comparatively easy to grow, Charlie McIver was still too small to be anything but a nominal owner of the enterprise. Nevertheless, his sense of proprietorship was strong. Then one afternoon the boys discovered to their consternation that a neighbor's bull they greatly feared had jumped the low fence around their prized patch, and was just finishing it off, root and vine. For a time they stood stock-still and stared. At length Dick turned and said, as if he had a triumphant solution, "Charlie, let's cuss him."

Whether he would have or not Charlie never knew, for Uncle Sam came along at the crucial moment and carried him out of harm's way. He supposed he would have, since he usually did what Dick suggested, but his attempt would have shown a mortifying lack of practice. Sallie would have no nonsense about taking the Lord's name in vain, and the devil was also due his meed of respect as a very powerful adversary. Just as "hell," a place that preachers of emotional sects thundered against in the pulpit, became the "bad place" in genteel household conversation, so the devil was referred to as Old Scratch or Old Nick. Even "Satan" was considered a bad word.

"Pshaw" or "Shucks" would have been as near an oath as Charlie McIver had heard from his mother. Sallie not only thought strong language unseemly, she found it unnecessary. It was gratifying how much surprise a person could put into "Great day in the morning," and how much dismissal or disdain into "Fiddlesticks." But swearing! If she had heard her young son taking part in Dick's profane scheme, rather than spare the rod and spoil the child, she would have reached into the nearest tree for a "good keen switch"—the kind that would sing when swished through the air and sting when it landed on plump freckled legs. Thus it was double jeopardy from which Uncle Sam saved the lad.

Years later, when Charles Duncan McIver had become one of the most effective public speakers of his time, an audience of Negro youths at Tuskegee Institute would sit motionless and entranced while he talked to them. A wealthy northern philanthropist would ask, "How can you speak to them like that, with such understanding?" "I know them," Charles McIver would reply. "I played with them when I was a boy."

Although his character apparently suffered no permanent injury from it, the association with Dick did give him some decided opinions about suitable companions for the young. "It is unfortunate," he came to believe, "that so many children in their early and impressionable years should be most intimately associated with ignorance and wickedness. Nurses and playmates for children ought to be intelligent people, who use good English and are clean and respectable in every way."

Nevertheless, his recollections of both Dick and Sam remained, in his words, "tender and affectionate," and led to "a compassionate sympathy and friendliness" for their whole race. He was impressed forever after with the loyalty of people who faithfully served the wife and children of a man who was away fighting to perpetuate their slavery. The Negroes were legion who would profit by his attitude.

The war years that were so carefree for little Charlie McIver were a tense and anxious time for his elders at home. Even if War did not come close enough for them to see its savage face, they walked in its shadow from the earliest months of conflict. It was August 8, 1861, that Duncan, Scotch Iver's oldest son, died of fever in the army, and his body was returned for burial in the family graveyard across the red clay road from his father's house. Scotch Iver, unfit by age for duty at the front, was fighting none the less in his fashion. He was contributing to the Confederacy huge amounts of money, food, and coal from the rich outcropping —an extension of the Cumnock Mine vein—just back of his house. There were Scotch Covenanters among his forebears. He could sacrifice enormously for a Cause. And Sallie could pretend a gaiety she did not feel long enough for a romp about the farmyard with a laughing small Charles riding piggy-back. Day in and day out she lived in dread that the next bad news might be of her husband.

Then, suddenly, her most urgent prayer was answered. Henry returned. He was a ninety-seven-pound wraith of the two-hundred-pound man who had gone away, but he was back and that, for the time being, was enough.

Henry had been ill of typhoid fever. He had spent two of the blistering hot summer months of 1864 in a military hospital at Raleigh, and finally had been "given up to die." Thereupon, as was the practice in such cases, he was moved to a tent. The treatment roused his Gaelic ire to such a pitch that it gave him strength to take action. He and another soldier in the same predicament hired a man to take them home in a wagon, spent and weakened as they were, on a bed of straw.

During his recuperation, some of the neighbors persuaded Henry to teach the public school near his home on McLendon's Creek for a few months. His son, Charles, was not old enough to go to school, but he was permitted to attend, since his father could look after him as well there as anywhere, and Sallie had baby Evander, born October 1, 1864, on her hands. Even Will, two years younger than Charles and still in dresses, was allowed as a special reward for good behavior to accompany them once in a while. He promptly showed his appreciation of the privilege by going to sleep, a fact that astonished his older brother because the benches were hard, rough, and backless, and the din was deafening.

Henry, who remembered the whipping he once got for not studying out loud, bowed to the knowledge that he would be considered a tyrant if he tried to enforce silence, and let custom have its tumultuous sway. A few days of teaching were enough to convince him that his first school would be his last, and he could not hope, as his oldest son noted in an autobiographical account of the school, to revolutionize public sentiment in two or three months. Elsewhere in the state more progressive schools were trying out the theory that quiet, orderly study was not only possible, it was practical. The novel idea had not reached Moore County.

Thus, Charles McIver's most distinct recollection of his first school was "the constant hum and hubbub" made by the voices of pupils as "they ran races to see who 'could get over the lesson' first or who could go over it oftenest. If you could have visited our school when it was busy," he wrote, "you would not have seen many faces. Instead you would have beheld a grand array of blue back spellers (Webster) held near the faces of pupils whose mingled voices, like the sound of many waters, would have poured into your ears, and, if you had caught any definite sound, it would have probably been b-a, ba, k-e-r, ker, baker; s-h-a, sha, d-y, dy, shady; l-a, la, d-y, dy, lady; etc."

In March of 1865 a growing uneasiness was felt along the Cape Fear tributaries with word that Sherman had captured Fayetteville. That they did not fall victim to his scorched earth policy, people in the Deep River section were inclined to credit to an act of God. Spring freshets—and spring came unusually early that year —sent rivers on a rampage, and floods kept the general from coming their way, if that had been his intention.

Then it was April. The ninth of April. Appomattox, where the tattered remnant of a still gallant force laid down its arms, passed into history as a shrine to Unity that had been dearly bought. Men gray of face and gray of ragged form and outlook turned homeward at last.

Henry McIver, from beginning to end, had considered the war a tragic and avoidable blunder, and hoped, in spite of the shooting he had been required to do, that he had killed nobody. He was, however, acutely aware of his good fortune. He had not come back, as many would do, to find a blackened chimney standing as lone sentinel over what had been his home. Nor would he be without seeds and food supply, as his farm had been continuously cultivated. The state's property loss he knew to be staggering, but the loss of life was more grievous still.

His own private roll of honor was headed by his brother Duncan—handsome, beautifully educated, vital Duncan—and his sister Elizabeth's husband, together with numerous other relatives. The list was long and contained as well the names of many he had known, or knew of. Over in the next county of Montgomery the spirited Chauncey family had lost all its sons, the five brothers having died in a single battle. The parents were not entirely bereft; they still had their extraordinarily lovely and gifted Melinda. But five irrepressible young men could have given quite a lift to the dispirited home folks—to their beaten, bankrupt, bitter people.

Evander McIver, as he had done once before, looked to Henry for help. The war had left him a poor man. Duncan's death had been a mortal blow. He knew in his Scotch Presbyterian heart that Right had got the best of it in freeing human beings from the degradation of slavery, but he could question, as other ruined southerners were questioning, whether the government exercised "just powers" in snatching away a man's property without making restitution. Scotch Iver's loss from emancipation had been no trifle, even if his numerous slaves were reckoned at their lowest possible value—and "a prime field hand" was bringing around $1,500 just before the war. Acquaintances were struck by the change in the old gentleman. "Scotch Iver," they said, was "breaking fast."

So Henry and Sallie and their three small boys moved to Scotch Iver's house. It was a strong house, built to endure a hundred years and more, and, with a porch running all the way around, it looked a much more pretentious place than it was. Actually, there were only four large rooms, two downstairs and two upstairs, with a fireplace in each, and a kitchen off the back porch. The interior was finished in wide heart-of-pine boards, and the main downstairs room had a mantel of real beauty. The house was pleasantly situated, too, in a grove of white oaks, but for all that it had not been a happy home. The wife for whom it was intended did not live to enjoy it. Margaret McIver died in 1853, the year the house was built.

The Scotch Iver lands formed a wide crescent with the house in the center, and standing there the owner could not see, in any direction, to the end of his property. It was past all belief, but he had lived to see that half-moon of valuable land become a liability.

The year after the war the McIver family lost both Evanders. The baby boy named for Scotch Iver died in June. Scotch Iver lived until autumn. He was buried in the family burying ground to which Margaret and three of their children, Duncan and a boy and girl who died in infancy, had preceded him. One event in his life span shared importance on his tombstone with its beginning and end. It was noted that he was born in Isle of Skye, Scotland, September 15, 1794, emigrated in 1802, died September 22, 1866.

In the five-way division of Scotch Iver's property, Henry got a tract of six hundred acres on Buffalo Creek, partly in Chatham County and partly in Moore, and a fifth interest in the undivided mineral rights. Immediately following his father's death he built on that land the house in which his boys, Charles and Will, together with children born later, would grow up.

The house was twice as large as his father's. There were two stories with four rooms each, delightfully cool in summer in a grove of oak trees, and warmed to a fine degree of winter comfort by a fireplace in every room. A one-story kitchen was joined to the back porch. A front porch where the family liked to sit on warm evenings was broad and inviting and had a smaller over-hanging porch at the second-story level. There was also a servants' kitchen back of the house where the farm laborers got their meals and the household servants preferred to carry on certain prolonged tasks such as rendering lard or making preserves.

This was the place that became Charles McIver's home when he was six.

3—

The Old Order Changeth

Two YEARS LATER, the Henry McIver place looked exactly what
it was, a going concern. The pleasant house, in a setting of
shrubs and flower gardens, gave an impression of order and plenty.
The extensive complement of farm buildings suggested completeness. Surely an owner who had his own grist mill and blacksmith
shop, not to mention a wood-working shop that furnished a majority of the farm implements, intended his plantation to be
chiefly self-sustaining. Moreover, cotton gin and tobacco barns
indicated that cash crops were grown to supply the price of any
item it was not possible or practical to produce at home.

In addition, the farm itself had many natural advantages.
Buffalo Creek, cutting across the McIver fields, powered the gin
and grist mill and provided abundant fish for the table. Coal
from the Scotch Iver home place was fuel for use of smith and
wheelwright, and timber in great variety afforded the kind of
wood needed for every type of farm equipment. There was even
a natural salt lick for the cattle.

In short, self-reliant people possessed a stronghold in the Mc-
Iver homestead. Their security, as long as they worked, could
be threatened only by unpredictable forces, and concerning those
—whether hail or cloudburst or killing frost—they were serene.
Had it not been promised that God tempers the wind to the shorn
lamb? Scotch industry and the resources at hand added up to a
very real independence.

Yet handwriting was beginning to appear on their self-sufficient
walls. More and more they were going to the store in Sanford,
which Henry owned in partnership with two other McIver men,

for products that had once been made at home, for cloth, for
cheese, for plow points. Transportation was still needed to place
manufactured goods within reach, but it had begun to appear
that the factory, making better articles at lower cost, would eventually turn the self-contained plantation into an anachronism.

In the meantime, the McIver family would enjoy what it had,
and only one requirement in the Scottish scheme of good living
was missing. There were no schools.

Before the war North Carolina had the best public school
system in the southern states, and one of the most creditable in
the entire country. Its educational fund, however, had been
largely invested in banks that had in turn bought Confederate
securities, entirely worthless when the war ended. The schools,
therefore, collapsed with the Confederacy.

The system had been in existence only a score of years as it
was. In Colonial North Carolina it had not occurred to anybody
that the state was responsible for educating its citizens. The
early authorities had not heard so much as a whisper of that
revolutionary doctrine in the country they had left. Education in
seventeenth-century England was considered a privilege of the
well-born, and all but those precious few had to get along without
it as well as they could. If it was necessary at all, it was necessary
for the ruling class alone, and as a consequence the majority could
not properly be said to need it. Their function was to obey, not
govern.

Many liked the prospect so little they set out hopefully for the
colonies. In the new world, by all accounts, free men could make
a place for themselves, and not have to accept a social status fixed
for them before they were born, and for their children after them.
Yet, oddly enough they brought along the belief that education
was a luxury for the few. That aristocratic concept prevailed
throughout Colonial North Carolina in the early days as it did in
Virginia, where a governor condemned learning as the source of
disobedience and heresies. The gentleman thanked God there
were no free schools in Virginia.

Accordingly, the early North Carolinians who could afford
luxuries for their children provided education through a tutor

or small private school and often sent their sons back to England to be educated. Those who aspired to the crafts made apprenticeship arrangements if they could, and the "free school" was for paupers only. Thus, reeking of charity, it was wholly unacceptable to a fiercely proud and highly individualistic people. The situation remained unchanged until late in the Colonial period when the Scottish migration occurred, introducing the idea that a school must have its place alongside the church in every civilized community.

North Carolina started its life as a state with provision for a public school system of sorts—a fact that some historians credit to the large number of Scotch Presbyterians in its constitutional convention. At any rate, framers of its constitution wrote into the document "That a school or schools shall be established by the Legislature for the convenient Instruction of Youth, with such salaries to the masters paid by the Public, as may enable them to instruct at low prices; and all useful learning shall be duly encouraged in one or more universities."

Apparently the Legislature believed in starting at the top. It chartered a university in 1789. (The university was opened in 1795; its first class was graduated in 1798.) That goal accomplished, over three decades passed before it took the next step toward public education by instituting a Literary Fund in 1825. The Fund, no part of which came from taxes, would be applied to education when sufficiently accumulated, and in 1839 a law made its proceeds available for schools. By the following autumn nearly all of the counties had voted for a free school under its provision.

For the hundred years preceding, Scotch Presbyterians wrote the brightest chapter in North Carolina's educational history. The academy they established in every settlement in connection with the church was usually taught by the pastor as a part of his ministry, although he did invariably charge tuition. Those preachers were stern disciplinarians to a man, their drill in mathematics and the classics remarkably thorough. It has been argued that the number and excellence of the academies delayed state provision for schools, but it is just as likely that a demand for education would have been lacking if the academy system had

not created it. In the first years of statehood the people were dead
set against taxes for any purpose, having recently achieved a
victory over King George the Third on that thorny issue. Besides, they were accustomed to have their denominations take the
lead in educational matters. Some of the smaller sects, notably
the Quakers and Moravians, were quite active along with the
Presbyterian Scotsmen.

It was one of the Scots, Calvin Henderson Wiley, who became
the state's first superintendent of common schools. Dr. Wiley
was an educator of real stature, who succeeded in gaining the
people's confidence in state-supported education, the taint of charity notwithstanding. He even managed to keep the schools going
during the war, only to see them fail to reopen when the conflict
ended.

The Negroes, who had none before, now had schools provided
by the Freedmen's Bureau and various other organizations and
church groups. But it was only in towns and cities, and chiefly
in those electing to accept help from the Peabody Fund, that any
attempt was made to carry on public schooling for white children.
In 1867 George Peabody set up a trust to aid education in the war-
prostrated South, the money being administered on the sound
principle that the Peabody Fund, like heaven, would help those
who helped themselves.

By that time the enthusiasm for public education Dr. Wiley
had generated in a campaign throughout North Carolina had no
spark of life left. It had been strangled by poverty and a fear
amounting to horror that unsegregated schools would somehow
be forced upon the people. The new state constitution adopted in
1868 was silent on the segregation question, hence did nothing to
allay uneasiness, while agitation in Congress for a civil rights bill,
on the other hand, did its part to turn apathy toward "free"
schools into open hostility.

Meanwhile, Henry McIver had two boys old enough to go to
school, and something had to be done about it. He and a pair of
other Scotsmen, his cousin Archie, who lived a short distance
down the road, and William McNeill who lived between them,
got together and decided to do what Scots had always done, pro-

vide their own. (The plan by which several families pooled resources to hire a teacher for their children became fairly general.) Henry was appointed to secure a teacher, and as soon as that chore had been successfully completed, they built a schoolhouse.

It was the kind of school Charles McIver would come to describe as having the "usual slabs with the flat sides up." It opened in October following his eighth birthday the month before.

The school was a one-room building with four windows and an open fireplace. Boys kept the fire going. Girls took turns, by twos, in sweeping the schoolhouse regularly. The students numbered more than twenty, the majority of them McIvers, and the teacher boarded a month at the time with a different family. The school was located as nearly as possible equidistant from all of them. Its first term lasted five months.

Charlie and Willie McIver walked the mile to school in scrupulously clean clothes that had been made at home; only Sunday suits were bought. The boys set out past tepee-shaped hills of sweet potatoes so numerous they resembled a miniature Indian village and scuffed new-fallen leaves with almost-new shoes that had marked the end of summer's barefoot time.

In their lunch boxes they carried sandwiches of fried ham or pork shoulder between slices of biscuits, often a sweet potato, and now and then some cheese cut in yellow wedges from the big hoop at the McIver store in Sanford. Some days there would be flapjacks—fried pies of dried apples and peaches—which they liked, and at other times there would be molasses, cookies, cakes, pies, or jams to serve as dessert.

By eight o'clock in the morning they hung their caps and coats along the wall on pegs that suited their height, and at noon they washed their hands in a basin filled with spring water. Two or more children might thrust grimy hands into the water at the same time, but one of them had to empty the basin. It was bad manners to leave dirty water for somebody else to throw out. At half-past four in the afternoon school was dismissed.

In the hours from eight to four-thirty, Charles McIver gave

his attention to reading and writing and ciphering and spelling, and in time to geography and history and grammar.

Reading was done from the McGuffey Readers, which were as much ethical code as reading book. Every McGuffey story had a moral, and in case there could be any doubt about it, sometimes, as in the *Fable of the Hare and the Tortoise,* it was printed out clearly:

> Moral. Thus, plain, plodding, people we often shall find
> Will leave hasty, confident people behind.

Contents of the Readers slipped so securely into everyday speech that reference, for instance, to the "boy who cried wolf too often" needed no explanation. Also expressions such as "Where there's a will there's a way," and "Circumstances alter cases" were widely adopted.

From the Readers the children learned pieces to speak. The First Reader had *Mary's Little Lamb* and *Twinkle, Twinkle, Little Star.* The Fourth included *Wreck of the Hesperus* and *The Old Oaken Bucket.* The Fifth, like many another collection after it, contained *The Blue and the Gray,* a poem that first appeared in the *Atlantic Monthly* in September, 1867, to commemorate the action of women at Columbus, Mississippi, who impartially decorated the graves of Union and Confederate soldiers alike. With its refrain, "Under the sod and the dew, waiting the judgment day," followed in every stanza by lines emphasizing the equalitarian aspect of death, it became one of the most-quoted poems of any time. It was credited as well with erasing some of the bitterness engendered by the fighting.

The Readers, even the advanced ones that introduced scholars to the best writers, leaned heavily on sentimentality. (The Dickens excerpt was the *Death of Little Nell.* Tennyson was represented by *Enoch Arden at the Window.*) Descendants of those students for two and three generations would be thoroughly familiar, from repeated hearing, with *Somebody's Darling,* mawkish verse about a dying soldier, and *Which,* another bit of overdone sentiment. The latter concerned a couple trying to make up their minds which child of seven to give a rich man in exchange for wealth. Finally the rich man got no child at all. Not in a McGuffey Reader!

In the Fifth Reader Charles McIver came upon a poem about Abou Ben Adhem which ended with the line, "And Lo! Ben Adhem's name led all the rest." He was so impressed that the name of a man who loved his fellow man was accorded the position of highest honor, he memorized it then and there. What is more he quoted it, and often, for the rest of his days.

Charles had learned from his parents before he came under the McGuffey influence that labor has dignity and thrift is a basic virtue, but he may have taken to heart the lesson obviously stressed by *The Village Blacksmith* and *The Rich Man's Son* that contentment is more to be desired than riches. True, his own criterion for success was usefulness, not contentment, but the conviction remained that money had no value except as a tool.

Charlie McIver studied spelling from the same blue back speller that had hidden the faces of his father's pupils, stood in a row along the wall to recite, and "turned down" the student ahead of him who missed a word he could spell. As time went on, he learned the capitals of all the thirty-seven states, the principal rivers and mountains of his country, and something of his native Carolina's preëminence in pine tar products.

The teachers who helped him most, in his estimation, were John E. Kelly, who prepared him for college, and Miss Mary Newby. The only impression left by Miss Janie Dye was that of having "a peculiar partiality." She thought "every girl a natural born angel and every boy the exact opposite," and was the only woman teacher Charles McIver ever had who was "partial to her own sex."

"Miss Mary Newby was probably not the best scholar among my female teachers," he also recalled, "but her English scholarship was good and her knowledge of subjects taught in elementary schools accurate. She showed great confidence in the character and ability of pupils who were honest and fairly studious. She was very industrious and worked hard to make her pupils so, using every legitimate means to inspire them with ambition." He took pains to note that she was a good woman, albeit she was not a Presbyterian. Miss Newby was described as a devout Episcopalian.

Charles McIver was never able to tell which of the three major institutions, home, church, and school, had the greatest influence on his upbringing, but by the time he got to school both home and church had made indelible imprints. Many of his grammar school compositions contained Bible quotations, gave a Bible reference, or sometimes, as in his essay on education, did both: "We should hear instruction and be wise and refuse it not. Prov. 8th chap. 33rd verse." He could also use his Bible knowledge as a school impertinence. When one of his teachers explained uses of the indefinite article, pointing out that "a" could be used only before singular words, as "a girl" or "a boy," "a lady" or "a man," he informed her solemnly, trying hard to keep his freckled face straight, "Teacher, you can say 'amen.'"

His compositions reveal not only a pattern of thinking in process of being formed, but something of his manner of living. And he did write on a variety of topics, big and little: Home, Winter, Industry, The Sabbath, Friendship, Education, Horses, Water, and even The Earth itself.

As hot weather always made him uncomfortable, it is not surprising that winter emerged as his favorite season: "It generally snows in the winter, and then it is pretty cold. But boys like to see it snow. They have a fine time playing snowball and catching rabbits. But the best of all Christmas comes in December, which is one of the coldest of the months. And 'Old Santa Clause' is pretty apt to bring all the children something till they get so old they know who he is, and then he does not bring so much. Sometimes he brings them a switch when they are bad, so they had better begin to be good for Christmas is most here. Farmers ought to be busy hauling leaves and straw in the winter. But still winter is the most pleasant of the seasons." The composition was dated December 19.

His composition on industry showed a staunch belief, never altered, that industry is the most fruitful virtue. It also expressed a degree of annoyance with persons who "do nothing all Summer and go around begging those who have worked hard and are bountifully supplied."

Even in that community of hardworking and provident Scots, there were a few ne'er-do-wells. One was a farmer named Clark, a ridiculous figure of a man who rode a donkey so small that the rider's feet almost touched the ground. He was always sidling up to Henry McIver with a whining plea, "Mistah Henry, give me a little piece of paper, so's I can get some meal and meat and molasses at the store." Charles could mimic him precisely.

Another who came begging was a big ex-slave, John Gilmore, who worked on the place. John was a peerless story teller, and the McIver boys liked to slip out to the servants' kitchen and listen to his "yarns." One, about a headless horseman, bore a striking resemblance to the *Legend of Sleepy Hollow,* but John did not know one letter from another and how he could have learned of Ichabod Crane's tormentor remained a mystery. But mostly he told animal stories right out of the jungle, and hair-raising tales of wild dogs right there in the heart of North Carolina. The young McIvers never knew whether there was a word of truth in his wild dog stories, but suspected John invented the beasts to keep boys at home nights.

John's family increased by a baby a year until the stair-step children finally numbered over twenty—a dirty, respectful brood, dressed largely in outgrown McIver clothing, who considered "the big house" at least an outpost of Kingdom Come. The big Negro had his own garden, a poor affair at best, and raised a hog or two, but there was never enough food for long at a time. Still, if he had no meal or bacon, Mr. McIver did, and he had "diplomacy." By skillful reference to his "rheumatiz" it was no great effort to wheedle a half-bushel of meal away from the kindly Henry. A peck was insufficient to supply his family with a supper of "flat cakes without h'isting"—corn meal mixed only with salt and water, made into thin cakes, and fried in bacon fat.

One learns from Charles's compositions, too, that the boy valued friendship of the David-Jonathan example, considered a good home a great blessing, and believed that "time is very

precious and should not be used in a foolish or trifling manner."
On none of those subjects did he ever change his mind.

He was a good student from first to last. When he was twelve
he got a diploma signed by Miss Bertha Buie which recognized
the fact: "Be it known that on the 15th day of December Charlie
D. McIver received this Diploma having been awarded the largest
number of Premiums for Good Conduct and attention to studies
during the term from Aug. 15 to Dec. 15, 1872 kept in Woodland
Green, Moore County."

Friday afternoons were marked by exercises of some sort,
usually "recitations" for the girls and "declamations" for the
boys. Or there might be a debate or a spelling match.

After school the McIver boys had their chores to attend to.
One of the earliest was bringing in wood for the fires, and a Mc-
Iver son unborn for another decade and more would one day hear
the longtime servant Angelet call: "You, Harry, you come here
and pick me up some chips. Mistah Charlie used to pick up my
chips and you no bettah than he was."

Later they moved on to the chopping block and wielded an
ax. In that community no man who wanted the esteem of his
fellows would allow his wife to chop wood. A person would
have to be shiftless indeed to leave the task to a woman, thus
incurring the stinging judgment that he was "not worth the
powder and lead it would take to blow his brains out." Even the
most genteel among his neighbors thought, and said so, that any
such lazy loafer should be tarred and feathered and ridden out of
town on a rail. Consequently, boys early inherited the task of
cutting wood.

Charlie and Willie McIver built the fires, too, and thereby
learned a lesson in providence. It was a simple matter, if one
had remembered to bring in the kindling, to set fat pine splinters
blazing under quickly laid oak logs, and scurry back across cold
floors to the warmth of a feather bed until the fire gave off a
steady glowing heat. Forgetting the kindling was not only its
own chill punishment, it was a fitting one. In that regard, virtue,
even as Mr. McGuffey taught, was its own reward.

4—

The Child Is Father of the Man

A FEW YEARS after Charles Duncan McIver's death a chief justice of North Carolina's supreme court made a commencement address at Sanford. His speech was largely concerned with the illustrious man who had grown up nearby. "Consider Charles D. McIver, the boy of sixteen years," the speaker urged oratorically. "He came in from a day's plowing in rather barren acres. As he entered the kitchen where his mother and sister were preparing their frugal meal he threw down his cap exclaiming, 'There is something better for me than pulling the rope over a mule all my days. I am through. I mean to go to college and get an education.' "

Audience reaction was of two kinds, depending on whether the hearers were McIver relations. The unrelated were amused that anybody, judge or no judge, should talk such arrant nonsense. The kinfolks were outraged, disgraced, at the notion that any McIver of the name had ever had too little to eat.

The judge's error lay in knowing general conditions of the period and not the particular case in question. The whole of North Carolina was wretchedly poor after the Civil War and went right on getting poorer by the day as Reconstruction authorities trebled and quadrupled taxes and piled up a crushing bonded debt. But Charles McIver's family, with a farm, a store, and a moderately large lumbering operation, did not fit into the prevailing pattern of destitution, although cash was frequently difficult to obtain.

Charles did plow; there was that much truth in what the justice said. From his earliest recollection, he stated himself, he had regular duties on the farm. He worked during the summer, and after school the rest of the year, until he went away to the University. Then he worked during vacations. "I have done almost every kind of unskilled labor that a farm boy or man can be called upon to do," he told more than one audience, and he came to regard "the habit of constant industry thus acquired and an abiding sympathy for all honest toilers, whether with their hands or their brains," as one of the most useful parts of his education.

He would have had to work, since his parents believed in the efficacy of labor, whether or not there was necessity. And there was necessity. The share-cropper system did not spring into existence ready-made to replace slave labor. Henry McIver cultivated as much land as he could with the regular help of two or three laborers hired by the month, and with that of his sons when they were old enough. He leased the remainder to tenants who also supplied an ample pool of day labor. Mr. McIver offered his boys scant praise for their efforts, fearing to "give them the big head," but he taught them, as he had been taught, that any honest day's work is an honorable day's work; that anything worth doing is worth doing well.

Other than that, the judge could scarcely have been more completely wrong. The idea of college was no sudden whim to teen-age Charles McIver. "Fortunately," as he put it, "my father and mother reared me to the idea that, as a matter of course, I was to go to college." As to his father's acres, far from being barren they were productive of a continuous bounty.

Nor did his mother cook. Mrs. McIver was the envy of women neighbors because her cooks stayed on the job during cotton picking time when their own had a habit of deserting for the ready cash and camaraderie of the cotton patch, and she invariably had a nurse for each of her nine babies. Colored Angelet ruled the McIver kitchen for thirty years with all the assurance of divine right, and the assisting Harriet was a good cook, too, somewhat offsetting the fact that she was a thief. It was not the part of discretion to allow Harriet a key to the smoke-house.

Actually, some of the food prepared in Sallie McIver's kitchen was not just excellent; it was epicurean. Charles's mother never lost her earlier interest in proper seasoning. At exactly the right moment, her granddaughters recall, she set all little girls about the place to picking nasturtium seeds, which she put through a complicated pickling process to make her own capers. In the non-drinking family of a Presbyterian Elder, she still made some scuppernong wine for flavoring, especially for use in syllabub, a favorite dish of her son Charles. She would whip a quart and a half of cream to a froth, not stiff, fold in a cup of wine from that bronze and luscious grape, grate a bit of nutmeg over the top and serve the resulting syllabub with fruit cake or pound cake.

Indeed, lavish dining was a part of every social occasion at home or church. In August, when the crops were laid by, a protracted meeting was held at Buffalo Church. The opening Sunday was marked, as were the quarterly communion services, by two lengthy sermons and "dinner on the grounds." Food was carried in large baskets or trunks. Each family had its own permanent table under the trees, and the social gathering around it, replete with exchange of greetings and compliments and food "receipts," gave "big meeting" time all the aspects of a festival. If Charles McIver ever ate a frugal meal from his mother's kitchen it was because he was sick.

He ate well all his life; too well, perhaps, since he became heavy. But he enjoyed food enormously and consumed it enormously.

In fact, whatever he did, young Charles did with tremendous vigor. When he played ball, he gave the thread ball with its India rubber core such a thwack he nearly always made a home run. He wanted action in his games and recreation, and he wanted company, too. Fishing with a hook and line, which required sitting quietly on the banks of Buffalo Creek, could not amuse him for long. He preferred seining. That not only kept him on the move, but it was a group endeavor. He liked to hunt —to hunt squirrels and rabbits by day, to go fox hunting and 'possum hunting and 'coon hunting at night. He liked to swim in the creek with his brother Will. Charles was eight when another McIver son, Rufus, was born; ten when the only daughter,

Elizabeth, arrived. (She was called Lizzie, of course.) Luckily he and Will were near enough the same age to be companionable.

To be sure, work and play had a way of overlapping. Fish could be fun to catch; they were also food. It was exciting to find a rabbit on a cold morning in the rabbit gums behind the house, or put on homemade leggings and boots—fashioned from old tow sacks or pieces of cotton bales—and trail the animal through fluffy snow, but eating it was also satisfying. Nor could finer food than quail reach any table, no matter how little quail hunting resembled work.

Work, real work, began at sun-up in the busy season, and even that seemed insufficient to use up the boy's explosive energy. Stock roamed free—fields, not pastures, were fenced—and if any cattle failed to follow the belled leader to the barn, it was Charlie who jumped on a mule and sought the strays until the cows came home.

While Charles was developing a capacity for hard work that he was never to lose, he was acquiring equally enduring social habits from parents who had no affectations. Not everybody who came to the McIver door was an invited guest. If heavy rains sent streams out of their banks, making fords impassable, or bad weather otherwise made travel difficult, especially at night, anybody who was on the road took refuge in the nearest house. When a chance visitor came to the home of Sallie and Henry McIver he received the genuine sort of hospitality that said, in effect: What we have is yours, share it and welcome. Friend or stranger, it made no difference, and the equal treatment of all comers constituted Charles McIver's first lesson in democracy. Moreover, his parents made it plain there would be "no putting on airs" and no unmannerly behavior either. If the visitor poured coffee into his saucer, or served himself from the wrong dish, good manners kept one from taking any notice.

The children had been well drilled in polite conduct, but service in some houses was not what it had been in the time of trained slaves, and the hospitable householder could only hope for the best. At any rate, the Henry McIvers were spared the embarrassment that came to their cousins, Archie and Augusta

McIver. When a supper guest dipped into a jelly centerpiece, moulded elaborately in the shape of a fish, the serving man said in a horrified, and horrifying, stage whisper, "Fo' God, Miss Gussie, he done et your bouquet."

The episode delighted Charles, who would remember it later on when he needed a humorous illustration.

Prophetically, that gregarious young fellow liked nothing better even then than to mix with people—all manner of people, in all quantities, under nearly all circumstances. Corn-shucking made his Octobers pleasant. Neighbors customarily gathered for the cooperative husking chore around a semicircle of corn at one farm after another, ate in relays, and accorded the boy who found a red ear a perfect right to kiss the girl next to him.

He enjoyed hog-killing time, too, in spite of the serious business at hand. For one thing, the McIvers usually had a house full of company. Family and visitors feasted on such fresh meat as they did not know how to process for later use, and, as a consequence, little went to waste. Syrup-making was another autumn function Charlie found more play than work. As a boy he liked to chew, as did other youngsters, the juicy ends of cane stalks and maybe dip them, when nobody was looking, into the vats of thickening juice, for a taste of the hot, sweet liquid.

The long farm day ended with family prayers, also long. Henry, who held the same church office his father had held, read from the Bible, and then tired, sleepy children went down on their knees while their father prayed, chiefly for certain of the Christian virtues: for patience, for fortitude, for submission to the will of God.

Farm work ceased at noon each Saturday to permit preparation for the Sabbath. On Sunday, if there was a service at Buffalo, the family went to church. In fact, any dereliction on the part of the Henry McIvers was cause for comment. Absence was uncommon enough to be noted, at least once, in a letter: "Neither Henry nor Sallie was at preaching Sunday." Father and sons dressed up in their bought Sunday suits. Sallie wore a fashionable black dress made by a Fayetteville seamstress, and Henry's white shirt, with detachable starched collar and pleated front, had been carefully "done up." It was a matter of some pride among housewives that their husbands' shirts should be exquisitely finished, and Mrs. McIver required, if a laundress had been careless, that the shirt be ironed over and over until it was satisfactory.

At the door of the church all couples separated, the women on one hand and the men on the other, like so many Biblical sheep and goats. It would likely have surprised the preacher, however, and would have dumbfounded St. Paul, to know which group one of the youthful parishioners regarded as the sheep. Young Charles McIver considered his mother the epitome of all goodness.

For that matter, if the church fathers wished to prevent distraction from the sermon by separating the sexes, they outsmarted themselves. Some of the worshippers, by their own admission, could not keep their attention on the bleak reminder that man is prone to sin as the sparks fly upward. Their thoughts were too busy flying sideways.

Charlie, however, had real affection for his church and honestly believed forever after that there was "more genuine piety and moral courage" among its people than any he had known. When Dr. John McIver, as precentor, led the singing with a flute—the first musical instrument used in a church thereabouts—the boy sang with volume and gusto. In another connection he wrote of himself, "I'm a Scotchman, I never change." Certainly in his devotion to the church he did not change. He attended church services twice on the last full day of his life.

When a man sets himself against the current of thinking dominant in his time, as Charles Duncan McIver did, and, what is more, changes the current, it is valid to inquire what forces, including the religious and educational, may have moved him to the action. Also it must be noted that both church and school introduced him to able men as he was slipping into his teens.

Dr. William Sterling Lacy, son of one college president and grandson of another, became pastor of Buffalo Church in 1873. He delivered his sermons in a beautifully mellow voice, and his flock considered them uniformly excellent, if a trifle grandiloquent in language. Scotch-like, he thought of the church as a cultural center for the community. He started a library there, largely made up of contributions from the members. He organized the Buffalo Lyceum, a club that presented monthly programs of discussion, music, and readings in the homes. Its motto was "The true, the beautiful, the good," a favorite theme of the reverend doctor's. He had a lecture on it in which he quoted Plato, Shakespeare, Virgil, Homer, Ruskin, and Edwin Atherston; made reference to Keats, Shelley, Byron, Milton, and Socrates, not to mention Madame de Stael and Josephine. Buffalo had a high proportion of college graduates for a country church, but its 250 members included numerous persons who could not fully appreciate their pastor's erudition. Still, if they did not know what he was talking about they were proud to have a preacher who did, and Dr. Lacy was on the whole extremely popular for fifteen years. Eventually Henry McIver would disagree with him and Will would call him a fool to his face, but Charles, uninfluenced by either father or brother, remained his friend. He did not withdraw his friendship once it had been given.

Neither, his friends averred, could he do enough for them. During the years when his influence was tremendous, he would often recommend one for a position about which the person had not heard, and many have liked to recall that he would travel a long ways, disregarding his own convenience, to do them any possible kindness. One such trip as a youth provided an unexpected insight into human nature. The wife of an elderly acquaintance had died, and her body was being returned to a former home for burial. The soft-hearted lad, unwilling that the bereaved husband should take that pathetic journey alone, volunteered his companionship. He rode to the funeral between the minister, who intoned a list of the woman's good deeds, and the widower, who replied with the faintest grunt of assent. Young McIver grew sick with pity for the old man grief had rendered inarticulate, and heartily wished the preacher would keep quiet. Finally, the man did run out of anything to say, but silence was worse, and desperately he started over. She had been a good woman, faithful to her home and church. She had nursed the sick. She had comforted the widow and orphan.

At length the husband interrupted. "Preacher," he said, "all you say is so. I just didn't like her."

Charles McIver would have occasion to remember, whether he did or not, that one person may admire all that another does, and still not like the doer.

No matter. He would not permit any friend, Dr. Lacy included, to be criticized in his presence, although he was quite possibly in agreement with the critic. And since it is one of the more endearing traits of the race that loyalty begets loyalty, no man could have had a more devoted circle of intimates throughout his life.

Nevertheless, it was not his pastor who turned the young man into a champion of fair play for women. Dr. Lacy preached the social philosophy of his day: "It is the father's duty to provide and to command. It is the mother's to guide and to nurture. It is the child's to learn and to obey." To be sure, he expressed overwhelming admiration for "the perfect graces of a pure and womanly nature" and had only commendation for the nobility of women's selfless service. He thought highly of self-sacrifice in women, the preacher did. But he wanted no change in their status quo as helpmeet only, tolerated no departure that would deprive their "weaker natures" of male protection. "When women are sent forth to struggle in a heartless world for a livelihood," he declared, "how soon do hard lines mark their faces and penury and care and disappointment write their traces on brows that should be smooth and fair."

Smooth and fair, indeed! Did brows remain smooth and fair when their noble owners did the unremitting labor some of the women in his congregation could not escape? From the eminence of his pulpit could he not see their work-coarsened hands? A majority of them had no maids to instruct in the proper ironing of their husbands' shirts. They did the ironing themselves with sadirons heated, summer as well as winter, on hot stoves or before huge fires, and did the washing, too, with harsh homemade soaps compounded of lye and fat and wood ashes.

After the back-breaking work of the house a wife might also join her husband in the fields if, for instance, a storm threatened winter supplies for the livestock. If there was a baby, and usually there was, the child was placed on a pallet at the end of the row while the mother, her hands chapped and torn by dry blades of corn, stripped fodder from the stalks. When the feed was in, she still had supper to cook, the cow to milk, and a variety of other tasks to do. If exposure had made the baby sick, she sat up during the night and applied home remedies, since doctoring was expensive and doctors were hard to reach. Then with the dawn, whether she had slept or not, the work began again. Were the lines exhaustion left in her face more beautiful because she had not worked regular hours for pay?

The preacher did not ask. Neither did Charles McIver, who nevertheless saw and remembered the conditions of their difficult lot. The clue to his championship of women which would have done credit to Plato, the fervent feminist Dr. Lacy liked to quote, would have a source other than his boyhood minister. It was much later that he would begin to question a chivalry that was large part condescension, to ask how women felt about their dependent status. "Galling" was the word he would use to describe their situation.

At thirteen, however, he accepted the world as he found it, and it was his pastor's social innovations that interested him most. Dr. Lacy inaugurated the moonlight picnic. The late afternoon supper was followed by a watermelon cutting, and the McIver fondness for watermelon was so notable it has taken on the proportions of legend. The subsequent ride home by moonlight was no hardship either. In that community where relative married relative as often as not, it disturbed young Charles not one whit that he was riding with "kissin' kin." Cousins or not, girls were rather more delightful than otherwise. In fact, Charlie McIver liked girls just fine.

A church picnic when he was fifteen, albeit by daylight, betokened the sort of man that the boy would become. Accompanied by his cousins, Loula and Bud McIver, and a young lady visitor, he was driving a two-horse rockaway with his customary speed and verve to the picnic grounds ten miles away. Ahead he saw with some consternation an elderly neighbor who believed in "taking care of his horses," which meant that he never got them out of a walk, and it was bad manners to pass an older acquaintance.

Charles, caring neither to loiter nor to offend, found his own solution by turning a brief encounter into a visit. He drew alongside the other vehicle, turned an ingratiating smile on Neighbor McNeill, and took a moment to "pass the time of day." On leaving, he stood up, bowed deeply, and said "Good day" as one did in parting—all of which was no more than pantomime to the old gentleman who was too deaf to understand a word. The personality facets thus revealed proved to be permanent. All his life Charles was in a hurry; all his life he was unfailingly courteous. The incident was of a kind to make Angelet exclaim, arms akimbo and dusky face aglow with pleasure, "Hain't that boy got manners? Hain't he been raised?"

Insistence on courtesy, in all truth, was just another service the better Scottish families rendered their state. The rural inhabitants, not as concerned at best with the amenities as an urban people, had not only suffered the general let-down in manners that was part of war's aftermath, but they had lost what example they previously had in the slave-holding gentry. The whole country population might have degenerated into a tobacco-chewing, snuff-dipping peasantry (and more than a few did) if some segments had not clung stubbornly to the belief that polite behavior was essential.

The school man, John E. Kelly, who opened a school nearby at which the young McIvers—and others—could prepare for college, kept the vital education job in the family. He was a grandson of Scotch Iver's sister Catherine. His own higher education was obtained at the Presbyterian-sponsored Davidson College, and his school, if judged by the extraordinary record of its pupils, was altogether excellent.

Charles walked to school with his cousin Alton, son of his father's sister Flora Ann and Dr. John McIver, who was also his dearest friend. Their close relationship lasted, too. One day Alton would describe Charles in a letter as "he whom my soul loves"; being a Scot who restrained any show of emotion he naturally put the statement in quotes. Charles, on his part, would remark without apparent self-consciousness to the young woman he was about to marry, "I love Alt."

The boys enjoyed their walks to and from school, as Alt reminded him later in a letter. "We thought we were nearly killing ourselves studying at night," he wrote, "while the only things that kept us from getting eight to ten hours of good sleep were William Rowan and the owls." Alt maintained that the only time Charles showed any evidence of serious thought was the day he tried to persuade one of the local characters it was a sin to swap knives on Sunday.

Yet, study he must, and behave himself, too, for the alternative under Mr. Kelly's chalk-line discipline and high work standards was pulling up stumps. For the girls, it was scrubbing desks and windows.

Also at the end of three years he could meet the entrance requirements at the University of North Carolina. They included: "A competent knowledge of the elements of the English language, Geography, and Algebra through equations of the second degree; Latin grammar, Prosody and composition, four books of Caesar, five books of Virgil's Aeneid, or the equivalent in Ovid, Sallust, or Cicero's orations; of Greek Grammar and Composition, four books of Xenophon's Anabasis, or Memorabilia, and two books of the Iliad."

The fact that Charlie, therefore Alton, was planning to attend a school other than Davidson, which had educated his pastor, his teacher, and a majority of his male relatives, created a temporary disturbance. He argued plausibly that he wanted more change of atmosphere than the denominational college would afford, but more importantly he was swayed by the University's record in producing leaders. Already its alumni had numbered a president and vice president of the United States, seven cabinet members, five foreign ministers, eight United States senators, assorted bishops, chief justices, and House members, together with thirteen out of twenty-odd North Carolina governors since 1814 when the first alumnus was elected chief executive of the state.

That oldest of state universities, which had ridden out the

vicissitudes of Civil War only to fall into the hands of political spoilsmen, had been closed by its own board of trustees a scant half-dozen years after fighting ended—and could as well have closed, for all the patronage it had, three years before that. It reopened just in time to catch Charlie McIver's interest as he made plans for college. The renaissance, culmination of a campaign largely sparked by a gifted woman, Mrs. Cornelia Phillips Spencer, came in September of 1875.

Henry McIver did not argue against Charles's choice; he proposed instead that he and his son go to Chapel Hill and see what the University had to offer. They attended the commencement of 1877, and for the sixteen-year-old youth the visit was a case of love at first sight. Moreover, it was a love affair that he carried on from that day forward, missing only one subsequent commencement throughout the whole of his life. He was duly impressed by the procession, the address of the popular Zebulon B. Vance, who was serving his third term as governor, the crowds that taxed commercial and private accommodations, and the distinguished graduates who had returned for the exercises.

He entered the University that fall while he was still sixteen, the minimum entrance age.

The year he became sixteen, 1876, saw the end of a Reconstruction program that had been more desolating than the war itself. Hence, while Charles McIver was growing up his state was going to wrack and ruin in the hands of its most vicious elements, imported and domestic. The greedy and unscrupulous Carpetbagger was hardly more despised than the native Scalawag who became his partner in unabashed corruption, and the bewildered Negro, having had citizenship thrust upon him without any preparation for it, was the unwitting tool of both. The unholy combination proceeded to rob the state without let or hindrance from its former white leaders, who were disfranchised and helpless.

Yet, in spite of the inglorious period of financial riot, political license, and social upheaval which was coincident with his early years, Charles McIver had a healthy happy boyhood, and one, moreover, that was well supplied with everything except money. And that he scarcely missed at all.

Education cannot be given to any one. It cannot be bought or
sold. It is as personal as religion. Each one must work out his
own mental and spiritual salvation. This is the fact that makes
democracy possible. It is the salt that saves the world.

—*Charles Duncan McIver*

5—

Young Ambition's Ladder

THE UNIVERSITY OF NORTH CAROLINA opened early, August 30, in
1877, and new students were required to be on hand the two preceding days for examinations. Thus Charles McIver left for
Chapel Hill while late summer heat shimmered over the landscape.

The boy kept much too busy that August morning, laughed
much too much, in order to disguise mounting dread of the goodbye he must shortly say to his closely knit family, which by then
included a winsome small brother, Cyrus, not quite three, and infant Wesley, born the month before and said to be the image of
his oldest brother.

By the time he reached the University, however, Charles had
regained his natural exuberance. He stepped from the hack with
supreme good humor and a contagiously expectant grin to face the
sophomores who had, for purposes of their own, constituted themselves a welcoming committee.

There had still been insufficient money, when the time came,
to defray his college expenses, small as they would be. Tuition in
the reopened University had been set at sixty dollars. Room rent
had been fixed at the insignificant sum of ten dollars a year, if any
sum could be considered insignificant in a deadbroke state. But
board and clothes and other costs still had to be reckoned, and
there was not enough ready cash to meet the requirements. That
fact, however, did not change by jot or tittle his parents' premise
that he must go to college. They had not reverted with the greater

part of North Carolina to the old thesis, never quite abandoned, that education was a luxury and therefore out of reach for an impoverished people. It was a necessity, and one patently did not forego necessities. Besides, their son had cut his wisdom teeth on the McGuffey Readers and knew that having the will, he would find the way. His father would provide what he could, of course. The remainder Charles arranged to borrow from his uncle—Alton's father, Dr. John McIver—whom he and the rest of the young McIvers, regardless of relationship, called "Uncle Doc."

The University buildings, eight in number, had been in a disreputable state from disuse and neglect two years earlier when the school reopened, and dormitory equipment was still meager and uncomfortable when Charles entered. Indeed, it was suggested in some quarters that cheap rental would have been insufficient to induce boys from good homes to occupy the accomodations provided, except for the fact that out-of-town students, as well as unmarried professors, were required to live in the dormitories. One of his contemporaries later declared "the note of life was simple, rugged—even primitive."

Lacking as it was in luxury, campus living was primitive only in comparison with a later day. In 1877, young Tom Edison's incandescent light was two years in the future, and a boy studying by an oil lamp could hardly feel deprived of something that did not exist. Likewise, plumbing and central heating had not yet become essential to an acceptable standard of living. If the young men had to get water from the well and warm themselves by open fires it was no more and no less than they had done all their lives. It might not have been a laughing matter to feel bed slats through thin mattresses, but they point-blank refused to be grim about it.

Charles McIver roomed in Old West, a three-story brick building which contained twenty-eight sleeping rooms. He boarded with a widow whose house backed up to the campus—a woman of estimable family who was earning her living in one of the few ways open to women and "set a good table."

Eighty-eight freshmen entered the University that term, bringing the student body to a total of 160. Given such a small group

Charles soon knew everybody in the school, as well as a number of those who lived in the academic village, also small.

One of the latter was Mrs. Cornelia Spencer, the same Mrs. Spencer who had worked tirelessly and effectively to get the University going again. Nor was that extraordinary individual concerned with the education of men alone. For some years she had been advocating through her "Young Lady's Column" in the *N. C. Presbyterian* that young women have "every facility to acquire an education such as the culture of the day demands. If the state educates its boys, I am for having it educate its girls also. Why not?" She had no wish to see girls at the University, however; in fact, she distrusted the whole idea of coeducation, but she hoped for the day "when the higher education of women also will be felt to be a necessity" and the girls could have a university of their own. She particularly saw the need of a school to train them as teachers. In her opinion a woman's first business was to be womanly, and from time to time she expressed concern that women might seek employment in unfeminine pursuits, but teaching she explicitly regarded as a profession becoming to her sex. "Women are born teachers," she maintained, and upon hearing that women had been excluded from a teacher organization exclaimed, "Not admit woman into an Educational Association! Why she is herself an educational association . . . created man's earliest and best teacher by God himself." Charles McIver grew very fond of Mrs. Spencer, and she, in turn, called him one of her boys.

Also everybody on the campus came quickly to know the new student, engagingly friendly and completely devoid of snobbery, whom they called Mac.

Entering at the same time as Mac was another Charles— Charles Brantley Aycock. They were two young men whose achievements would be minted as different sides of the same coin, who would be bracketed in the history books as benefactors, each in his different fashion, of the same cause.

The two Charleses shared more than a first name. They had in common a conviction that education is one of the great indispensables, but for reasons as far apart as prestige and pathos. The young Scottish Carolinian, in the long-established tradition of his kind, believed in it because he had enjoyed its advantages. Young Aycock, on the other hand, had seen the tragedy of its absence. He had watched his mother, a woman of much natural intelligence, go through the humiliating experience of "touching the pen" with which some one else signed a deed for her, since she could only make her mark.

The two boys were not classmates. Aycock entered as a sophomore, thus joining a class that would enable the University to carry on its habit of educating future governors by graduating two of them (Locke Craig and Charles Aycock) at the same time.

Mac threw an exhaustless amount of energy into campus activity, curricular and extracurricular. The lad who had grown accustomed to home runs in Moore County could also "bat a ball the farthest and holler the loudest" of anybody at a college baseball game. Having enrolled for the classical course leading to an A.B. degree, he found his subjects—Latin, Greek, mathematics, rhetoric—but an extension of the same studies Mr. Kelly had propounded for him. He proceeded to do as well in them as might have been expected of one who had received the excellent Kelly training. In fact, students who excelled in the University of that day were largely those who had undergone the relentless drill of a private academy.

Two literary societies, the Dialectic and the Philanthropic, were dominant factors in every phase of campus life—literary, political, and social. Membership in one or the other was required of all students, and Mac joined the Dialectics, later served as treasurer.

He entered as wholeheartedly into the society program as if it had been a watermelon cutting, with the exception of one part. Great emphasis was placed on debate and oratory, and while no student could surpass him when it came to sprightly and amusing conversation, he became tongue-tied and incoherent when he tried to think before an audience. Proceedings of the societies were secret, but it was known that students who refused to speak had to pay a fine. The fact partly explains a statement McIver made in an address at the University some years after his graduation:

"During my four years at this institution I made no appearance
before the public as a speaker when the payment of fines . . . could
relieve me from that duty." So in a literary organization celebrated for the training it gave future statesmen in debate and
parliamentary procedure, he held his tongue.

Otherwise, Chapel Hill measured up to his expectation. His
only sadness that autumn came from back home when Cyrus died
of diphtheria in November.

During the fall semester, he was absent from recitations just
twice, and his grades were good: Greek, 96; Latin, 94 1/3;
Rhetoric, 92; Mathematics, 91. Attendance at religious services
was required, and he was absent from prayers not at all. Charles
McIver was never "pious," certainly never in the connotation of
excess or pretended goodness. Orthodox he was and remained.
He did not question the fundamentals his church had taught him
and retained a sense of obligation to it. Neither did he—and that
the church had taught him, too—sit in judgment on his fellows.
For instance, he did not drink, but he declined to be a damper on
the revelry of drinking students. Instead he would carouse with
the noisiest of them and be the most jovial "drunk" in the crowd
while staying cold sober. His nearest approach to intolerance
appeared in a sharp antipathy toward fraternities, which he considered group embodiments of snobbery. The aversion apparently
had no basis other than a feeling that they were undemocratic.
His friends argued that no sense of rejection or exclusion could
have influenced his attitude. No doors had been shut in the face
of that companionable young man.

His December report card noted that Mr. McIver had paid
thirty-five dollars for tuition, room rent, and servant hire for the
fall term.

During the spring term he improved his grades somewhat,
adding four points to his math grade and making 97 on the history
he had substituted for rhetoric. His Greek rating remained the
same commendable 96, and his Latin mark (dropping a third of
a point) came out an even 94. School closed June 6, and, with his
bills paid up in the identical amount as in the fall, he went home,

picked up a cradle, and stepped into a wheat field to lend a hand with the harvest.

When school opened in the autumn of 1878 he was present with the other sophomores to welcome a beginning class of sixty-six new students, including two who would be among the closest of his lifelong friends and associates. One of the boys, James Y. Joyner, would complete the course in three years and get his degree at the same time as McIver. The other was Edwin A. Alderman.

McIver and Alderman were a pair of diametrical opposites. Mac was a burly boy—big in body and voice and enthusiasm. Alderman was slight. Mac was breezy, jolly, thoroughly democratic. Alderman was dignified, inclined to be pretentious, and leaned toward the aristocratic, although he admitted he had come from just such a "simple home of sacrifice and self-denial" as all the rest.

"All of us were poor boys," Alderman would note, and it was characteristic that he should add, "Those who came from the towns looked perhaps a trifle more modish to the experienced eye." That fact gave Charles's mother some concern, too. Writing to him in the spring of his sophomore year about a new coat and vest his father was having made to his measure, she added: "If they are not quite as good as you would like, don't grieve about it, but put them neatly on and wear them with all the ease and dignity you can."

Put them neatly on is just what he did. Neatness became something of a McIver trademark. Many persons, when asked years later to describe the McIver they knew, would reply with the identical beginning: "He was the neatest man I ever saw."

Yet, in spite of their dissimilarity, McIver and Alderman would become as close as men are ever apt to, and their lives would follow a curiously parallel course, touching at frequent intervals for a renewal of the old-time camaraderie.

From the start "there was no mistaking," Alderman later declared, "the quality of this great, big country boy, eager, restless, purposeful, hopeful, with a face and an eye wherein humor and sympathy and shrewd discernment struggled for mastery. He had already become a leader among his fellows."

The conclusion was inescapable. Whenever Mac stopped at the Old Well he was quickly surrounded by a crowd. He loved to talk; he talked well. Others liked to listen because he made everything funny in the telling, gave even the most serious matter a humorous fillip, and convulsed them with his mimicry, whether of farmer Clark on his donkey or an august university professor.

Up in "Ol' Mac's" room the same sort of jocularity often prevailed, but with a difference. There it was a preliminary to habitual earnestness when a few kindred souls settled down for spirited talk after the comings and goings were over for an evening. One of the regulars was Alderman, whose pretenses fell away when he was with friends, and whose usually precise speech slipped into the vernacular as he presented an effective argument. The straight-thinking Joyner would be there, and sometimes the straight-talking Aycock. Also for a couple of years there was among them a young man with the merriest of dispositions and the mouth-filling name of Marcus Cicero Stephens Noble, which his acquaintances ignored in its entirety. They called him Billy.

In his own room McIver participated in the sort of debate in which he could not bring himself to engage publicly. There he and his intimates were not concerned with affairs of the nation or the world at large, but with the imperative needs of their own world, which roughly had the bounds of North Carolina. There was not much one could do, or even learn, about current happenings elsewhere in a day of slow and inadequate communication. Anyway, calling first and foremost for attention was their own arrested, still backward-looking commonwealth. No matter how discussion ranged over the whole of the state's problems, it came back to the same starting point. North Carolina could make no progress whatever until it had thrown off the shackles of illiteracy.

And they were just the boys who could strike off the chains. Indeed, it has been truly said that the renaissance in North Carolina education began then and there in that very group. For surprisingly enough, with the exception of Aycock (who would nevertheless be education's servant), every one of them was headed for the schoolroom—and that in a time when universities were largely the stamping ground of young men planning to enter the ministry, medicine, or the law. Theirs were the names—McIver and Alderman and Aycock and Joyner and Noble—that would be written high across the page of a more enlightened North Carolina. Theirs was a tight little circle, and it would remain so—the hard inner core of a large undertaking. Others, many others, would appear on the circle's periphery, notable among them the distinguished Walter Hines Page. But those few names would run through the chronicle of renascence like a singing chord.

Meanwhile, they were a group of young men who spiced their seriousness with hilarity, but never lost sight of the job at hand. They were genuinely in earnest about getting an education.

McIver's second-year course expanded beyond the previous narrow limits of its classicism to include the concrete sciences. Those he undertook with good results, achieving a 98 on physiology and a 99 on botany. In zoology he rated in the 90's, and only a lower mathematics grade, 80, was a disappointment. (He was a "whiz at math," in the estimate of his youngest brother.) He continued to do so well in Greek that he won the Greek medal in the spring of his sophomore year, and took honors in Latin with grades of 95½ and 96 under a favorite teacher, George T. Winston. In Dr. Winston he found the capacity "to inspire in all the youths he touches self-reliance and the audacity to undertake large tasks." Theirs, too, would be a continuously satisfying relationship. Mac's personal popularity was reflected in his election as a commencement marshal, a top social honor.

His amiability, popular as it made him, was no part spinelessness, as the other students were quick to learn. No Covenanter among his ancestors could have made a more impulsive assault on anything that contravened his standard of justice or sportsmanship. Coppery glints in his brown hair gave friends an excuse to remark "The red in Mac's hair isn't there for nothing." In later years an acquaintance would put the sentiment much more grandly. "His temper," that one stated, "flashed like summer lightning, and was as quickly gone."

Once at least it flashed like summer lightning, and what is more to the point, hit its mark. A mountain boy determined to educate himself against all odds had arrived at the University after walking all the way from his home in western North Carolina, a five-day carriage trip. There was one story, unconfirmed but not necessarily apocryphal, to the effect that he walked barefoot to the very edge of the campus to preserve the only pair of shoes he owned. Mac had made up his mind on sight to help the youth in every way he could. William George Randall was a sensitive lad. He would make a sensitive artist. His shyness was both painful and apparent.

The University authorities, aware that boys will be boys, had "thought best to notify the public," in the words of the school head, "that hazing was absolutely prohibited." In spite of the interdiction boys continued to be boys, and the hazing devised for young Randall was fiendishly made to order for the timorous, artistic lad. When Mac came upon the scene Randall was being forced to dance naked on a barrel to the ribald raillery of his tormentors. He intervened, apoplectic with anger, and put an immediate stop to the other's agonizing situation—thereby winning a devotion that went beyond ordinary friendship. In countless ways thereafter Randall "tried to pay back," McIver said, "what he thought I had done for him." There are those who maintain that Randall's portrait of the ebullient McIver caught better than any other the essence of his friend's character. It revealed the artist's knowledge that McIver's surface affability concealed an inflexible will.

Mac left the University the spring of his sophomore year owing for his "tuition, etc.," according to a note from the bursar on his report card. No amount was mentioned, but similar notations afterward indicate that University costs had gone up. Instead of $35.00 for tuition, room rent, and servant hire, the charge per semester was $42.50, which Mr. McIver was requested to remit at his earliest convenience.

By his junior year McIver's attainments had begun to impress themselves upon President Kemp Plummer Battle, another University notable for whom the student had an abiding respect. His first semester record in political economy, French, general chemistry, logic, and physics (averaging above 90) would appear to warrant the initialed comment Dr. Battle wrote in ink on his term report: "Mr. McIver's record speaks for itself. He deserves credit for progress, diligence, and conduct. K.P.B."

"An excellent student," Dr. Battle noted on the basis of his spring work which included rhetoric, constitutional and international law, French, chemistry, and physics. Actually, that spring his science grades in both physics and chemistry fell to a level barely above passing, and were the only poor record, except in "mechanics," that he made during his entire four years. His astronomy grade in the fall of his senior year was not as high as that on subjects which interested him more, such as English literature, French, and metaphysics, but Dr. Battle affirmed that he was "A truly exemplary student in all respects." The notation on his final report read, "An excellent student, good scholar."

Yet, this outstanding student had no part in the commencement of his graduation year. On that score he parted company with the rest of his group of intimates. His friend Jim Joyner made a speech on commencement day. The previous year Charles Aycock had won the Mangum medal for oratory; the following year Ed Alderman would win it. Aycock, with an awkward manner, unmusical voice, and forthright language, was nevertheless a compelling speaker. Alderman, with a beautiful voice, an urbane stage presence, and a style of speech that tended to be ornate, attained another kind of eloquence. Charles McIver, graduating the year between, attained none at all. Still quaking at the idea of facing the public, he was excused from a commencement appearance by his own request.

The 1881 commencement drew the usual large crowd, followed the traditional pattern. General M. W. Ransom got the public speaking off to a good start by outlining the "Duties of the Young Men of the State to the State," and urged the thirty-one graduates to cultivate patriotism, education, and justice. Thomas Malvern Vance, as befitted a son of the spell-binding Zeb (senator, former governor), raised an intriguing question during the evening devoted to addresses by representatives of the two literary societies. "Has the Time Come for Universal Suffrage?" he asked. The word "universal," in his bright lexicon, did not include women or Negroes.

The University of North Carolina gave Charles McIver a diploma and a Bible, both of which were presented by Governor Thomas J. Jarvis. His father gave him a gold watch. For the formal education thus brought to a close, much as he abhorred owing money, he had accumulated a large liability. He would never again his whole life through be free of debt's hated shadow.

6—

The Happiest Bond

CHARLES MCIVER'S DEBT for his University years amounted to
$1,200. As the best available means of paying it off he took a
teaching position in Durham at forty-five dollars a month. He
became assistant to the headmaster of a small private school, the
Presbyterian Male Academy.

On the thirteenth of October following his graduation he obtained a teacher's certificate signed by George W. Jones, Durham
County's superintendent of public instruction. It was "first grade"
too, as he had "furnished satisfactory evidence of good moral character and his scholarship was represented by the following grades:
spelling, 95; defining, 95; writing, 90; arithmetic (mental and
written), 100; English grammar, 100; geography, 95."

Since grades of 100 were obtainable it is surprising that he did
not get a perfect mark in spelling. He was an excellent speller.
His writing would appear to deserve better than a 90 as well. He
did join words frequently, giving a flowing, hurried appearance to
his handwriting, but it was readily legible at all times.

School had scarcely got under way when the headmaster was
summoned to other duties by the death of his father, and his assistant inherited the academy, lock, stock, and barrel. Aside from
uncollected tuition bills and good will, he fell heir to little besides a number of dilapidated desks, a few battered maps and
globes, a blackboard, and some "philosophical apparatus."

By then a movement was gaining ground in North Carolina to
provide free public graded schools—called "graded" to distinguish
them from one-room, one-teacher establishments attended by
children of all ages. The aim was to classify students both by age
and educational attainment, and supply a teacher for each grade.

Progress was slow, depending as it did on the willingness of an individual community to raise the necessary funds. Greensboro, acting in 1875, was the first town to establish a graded school, with Raleigh taking a similar step two years later and Salisbury three years after that. When Goldsboro followed suit by voting special local taxes for a school, Dr. J. L. M. Curry, a power on the whole southern educational scene as agent of the Peabody trust and the Slater Fund (for Negroes), persuaded Edward P. Moses to come from Knoxville, Tennessee, to take charge. The Goldsboro school opened in 1881 in good time to afford Edwin Alderman his first teaching assignment upon his graduation the following year.

By the time McIver reached Durham the graded school idea was beginning to emerge there also. A special act was being agitated to levy taxes—twenty cents on the hundred dollars' worth of property—for support of the proposed school. Durham business men, in impressive majority, wanted no part of the scheme and said so volubly in handbills entitled "As We See It." As they saw it the town's well-being lay in keeping taxes low, as "We all know that high taxes make high rents; and high rents and low wages bring poverty to the working man, and will drive him to seek employment elsewhere." They made out a case that sounded very high-minded and a part of it—the need to improve streets and increase manufacturing—was politically unassailable as a rule. But their chief argument was to the effect that establishment of a graded school would destroy existing private academies, *"with no hope"* of getting their equal.

They could truthfully boast, they maintained, "of the best educational advantages of any town in the State, numbering as we do two first class Male Academies with *growing* tendencies. Also two Female Seminaries, where, as in the male schools, a full corps of competent teachers, with all the late appliances and advantages, make them inferior to none and where over 100 young ladies are now going to school, merry as birds." They felt sure if boys and girls were thrown together in school the best families would send their daughters elsewhere. In short, they were opposed to a tax raise that would put an end to private schools with "more refinement and classical education than the most ardent friends of the graded school claim for theirs."

Although it was his livelihood being threatened, Headmaster McIver explained to the gentlemen that he was in disagreement with their position. Private institutions were reaching only a small proportion of Durham's school population; they had never reached more than 7 per cent of school-age children anywhere in the state. Since he believed instruction was every child's right, he was duty bound to support the Special Act and take a chance on finding another place.

He did just that. In May of 1882 he cast his first vote, having reached his majority the preceding September, in the interest of public education. Nor was the vote wasted. The measure passed.

At the end of the academy year, the young schoolmaster attended school-breaking at the Methodist Male Academy and, in recognition of the courtesy, the minister who was its head called on McIver, along with several other well-known people, to "say a few words." The prospect of speaking in public made McIver feel like a trapped animal, and his face, since he always blushed easily, flamed a painful crimson, but he got to his feet and set out to say that he sympathized with the aims of his fellow educator. "I sympathize with Dr. Deans," he began. "I sympathize with Dr. Deans," he repeated. He stammered the words another time or two, and gave the whole business up as a bad job, while an otherwise kindly audience could not restrain its mirth. It was the first of many crowds that laughed uproariously (although the reason was different) at a speech by Charles McIver.

McIver liked Durham. He had enjoyed a satisfactory year. Nevertheless, when he went home nothing had happened to change an earlier resolve that he would never make a speech or teach a woman.

Abridgement of the resolution was forecast shortly afterward, however, when he was elected principal of the newly authorized high school in which he would teach male and female alike.

As a matter of fact, the new public system, contrary to the predictions of its detractors, absorbed all of Durham's private school teachers.

His second year in Durham found McIver interested in obtaining a higher degree at Chapel Hill, and his good friend Professor Winston outlined for him the requirements for an A.M. and Ph.D. It is interesting to note that his inquiries concerned academic, not legal, training. He did read some law later on, but only in desultory fashion, and his interest in becoming an attorney was no more than lukewarm at best.

The personable bachelor teacher was popular in Durham, and, in the opinion of his friend Dicky Dalton, who had gone on to study medicine in New York after a year at the University, and his brother Will, then a law student at Chapel Hill, he was quite a gallant. Dicky chided Charles for "taking away from me and then turning footloose again every young lady I set my eye on (should have said heart)." Before the middle of January, 1883, Will was demanding to know how many girls he had promised to marry since Christmas. Another letter from his brother spoke of a "bust-up," and added "I am glad of it. I did not believe the girl would suit you. Your disposition to court any girl you want to and then feel good over it, whether you get kicked or no, may be a very happy one; but I agree with you in not admiring it very much. I would rather see a fellow more in earnest on such matters."

Apparently he did not take his school duties as lightly, for his services were shortly in demand by a new and larger school at Winston. According to a recently started Raleigh publication, *The North Carolina Teacher,* the new Winston Graded School building would be the best in the state. The periodical was a house organ of Alfred Williams and Co., booksellers, but Editor Eugene G. Harrell envisioned it as a journal of progressive education with a much wider scope than the mere selling of books. In columns that had been dedicated to all matters of education, *The Teacher* gave a detailed description of the projected school, which would contain fourteen classrooms and an assembly hall.

When Mr. McIver resigned his Durham position in January of 1884 a local paper described him as one of "the first educators of the state"—not a slight accolade for a teacher less than three years out of college.

He left Durham for Winston on Monday, February 4, and got to his destination at three o'clock in the morning. A few days later Editor Edward A. Oldham of the *Western Sentinel* looked up to see a young man "with a smile on his rounded, apple-cheeked countenance," who had come to present a note of introduction from M. C. S. Noble. (Letters of introduction were highly valued, and McIver not only made habitual use of them, but wrote them by the score. It became his habit as well to enlist editorial support on what he believed to be the side of the angels.) Moreover, if Billy Noble's was the first name from the old Chapel Hill coterie to pop up in Winston, it was not the last. The new school was determined to secure teachers of superior qualification, and James Joyner was added to the faculty on the recommendation of his friend Mac.

During much of his first year in Winston Mr. McIver kept a standard diary, which he had received as a gift. A more uninspired chronicle could hardly have been found in a day's journey. As he said himself, when he had anything to write at the end of the day he was too busy to bother, and when he had the time there was nothing to write.

McIver's social life fell into much the same pattern it had followed at Durham. Shortly after his arrival in Winston he made a diary entry that set the tone of it: "Met two Winston ladies. Like 'em." He met many ladies. He liked 'em. Various feminine names dot the diary in connection with teas, weddings, walks, and calls, with musicals, church services, and the theater. His usual Sunday schedule was church, Sunday school, and church again. He was elected president of a social club. Occasionally, there was something to denote that he was in Winston to be principal of a high school: Made out teachers' examinations. Helped examine teachers for positions in graded school. Made out courses of study for the board. Went to teachers' meeting.

His work was more demanding than the record indicated. The school building had not been completed when he arrived, and the superintendent, J. L. Tomlinson, had taken advantage of the lull to make a study tour of northern schools. Many of his duties consequently devolved upon Mr. McIver until his return in March.

There were, even so, two noteworthy entries among the trivia. On a rainy Tuesday night in March he went to see *Enoch Arden,* and little as he enjoyed the play, the evening was nevertheless productive. He "met W. H. Page, editor of the State Chronicle."

Mr. Page was indeed editor of the *State Chronicle,* a paper he had started a year earlier in the capital city of Raleigh. His emphatic journalism was a bellows with which he hoped to kindle some spark of progress in a static society. He was trying to needle his state into action, urging North Carolina to realize the potential of its rich resources—climate, soil, materials, and sound population; to devote its energies to becoming agriculturally, economically, and industrially self-sufficient; to turn its back on a past with which it was too much preoccupied. Mr. Page could not consider as "lost" a war that had preserved the union, but his readers adhered to an opposite point of view. Their nostalgia for a vanquished era had become a mirror, however distorted, which reflected the heroic aspects of their recent history. The voters continued to choose for important positions only those persons who had earned (or assumed) positions of high rank in the ex-Confederate army. Mr. Page turned his biting satire on one such individual whose farm plan the editor considered obsolete. His paper conferred upon the official a name that once distinguished an ancient Egyptian king, thus associating the man's agricultural program with practices that had been antiquated for centuries. When the gentleman learned his namesake ruler had been a mummy for some two thousand years, he was not amused. A Carolina editor who was Page's contemporary, reminiscing a half-century later, declared "Page made people mad—with him and with themselves." His readers did not like to be reminded that their heroes were beaten heroes.

McIver and Page, who was five years his senior, became friends, fast and lifelong friends as it turned out. Perhaps that was inevitable; the goals they had set for their native state were similar. It was their method of crusade that differed. Walter Hines Page was an iconoclast. Charles Duncan McIver was not.

McIver was able to adapt himself to the truth that North Carolina could be persuaded, but could not be prodded, out of its
inertia.

Mr. Page, on the other hand, was convinced in another year
that he could not earn a living as an editor on his home grounds,
and permanently shook their dust from his feet to live in the
northeast.

A combination of circumstances under which Mr. Page went
and Mr. McIver stayed was responsible for a correspondence
quite possibly as delightful as any that has been entrusted to the
mails. The McIver letters were not as good as Page's. Few have
been. Indeed, Mr. Page would achieve no greater claim to distinction than that afforded by his letters, eminent though he would
become as editor, author, publisher, and Ambassador to the Court
of St. James. Still, McIver held up his end admirably enough
with documents that were readable and refreshing, as well as a
commentary on conditions in the state both men loved. Also,
when McIver was engaged in "concocting his revolution" (to use
a Page phrase), the expatriate Carolinian would be found aiding
and abetting from his northern sanctums.

Another entry, significant in the light of later events, was
made on April 14, 1884—Easter Monday. It read, in its entirety:
"Day was cool and weather threatening. Frank Hanes carried me
to ride in the p.m. Stopped with a picnic crowd for a while and
enjoyed it. Didn't go to the dance at night. Board decided on
books."

Nothing of great import was indicated, to be sure, yet in that
picnic crowd was a tall, slender brunette whose mobile features
were distinguished by a truly beautiful mouth. Shortly thereafter
entries that were meaningful began to appear: Called on Miss
Lula Martin. Called on Miss L. M. at night. Took tea at the
Martins'.

Miss Martin was an extraordinary young woman, an articulate
feminist who could speak her piece on the rights of women with
telling effect. Her home was in Winston, destined to become a
single entity with the quaint old Moravian village of Salem in
which she had attended Salem Academy, and where she had

imbibed much of the church belief in the equality of persons. Her father was a doctor, and she never quite recovered from the shock of learning, when she proposed to take up medicine, that being a woman was a well nigh insurmountable obstacle. The church fathers, her own father, had believed in opportunity for all who were able to use it, but the world at large was illogical enough to ignore her keen intelligence because she was a girl. It was intolerable, she asserted, and remedial steps ought to be taken. Surprisingly enough, the attractive young man she met at the Easter picnic agreed with her. In fact, he considered her one of the "most sensible" young women he had ever met. Since she was first grade teacher in the new school, their work, as well as the social scene, threw them together, and before the summer was over Superintendent Tomlinson was writing McIver, "I have heard it is an 'open secret' that you and Miss Martin are engaged to be married."

McIver divided his summer more or less evenly between devotion to Miss Lula—he never in his life omitted the Miss from an unmarried woman's name—and devotion to his profession. He went to summer Normal school at the University, but so did she, and they preempted a spot in the middle of the campus for carrying on their courtship. When he went to his home near Sanford for vacation, he put into long letters to Miss Martin his happiness at having for the first time a love that would "bear the test" and which, more importantly, he returned without any doubt of himself. But he also tried out some theories of elementary teaching on a group of small boys who had never been to school.

Heavy as he found time on his hands without Miss Lula, he was nevertheless glad to be with his family, which was all together, "three children on each side of the table," for the first time in a year. Small Wesley had died at the age of five. Claude, who looked like Charles minus freckles, and Harry the baby, a smaller version of Will, had been born while Charles was in college. The other four were Charles, Will, Rufus, and Elizabeth.

Charles wrote at length of his family to the young woman who would become a part of it. Stronger ties than brotherly affection were growing up between him and Will. His sister, of whom he was proud, he found quiet and gentle like his mother, a pretty girl with musical talent, "who seems to have inherited all of Ma's goodness." His father was compared to Aristides the Just. Rufus, then fifteen, was described as having a fine intellect, although absent-minded and meditative, and given to reading theology and other subjects too deep for him. (Rufus, like his oldest brother who had loved the colored boy Dick, wickedness and all, had been deeply attached to a Negro companion, whom he had fatally injured in the accidental discharge of a shot-gun. In time, brooding on that unfortunate occurrence permanently clouded his reason.) Claude and Harry the vacationing Charles was teaching to read by the word method.

Another reference to Claude also disclosed one of his own traits. Quite candidly he admitted a common human failing more often denied than acknowledged: "Claude and I love praise." It was a statement he could have made of himself with equal truth for the rest of his life, although the McIver fondness for flattery, apparent as it was, afforded no benefit to the sycophant. "You couldn't get him to do anything by it," a friend summed it up. "He just loved to hear it."

In one letter he skimmed lightly over the thorny fact that Miss Martin belonged to a different church. "Ma has been lecturing Will about his Methodist sweetheart," he wrote. "I haven't told her about mine yet. I mean about her being a Methodist."

In all truth, Miss Martin had not been a Methodist very long, having been born into the Moravian faith and having accepted it without reservation until her early teens. Then she learned of an obscure incident involving Moravian pioneers who had chosen wives by lot and became so incensed that the church had sanctified any marriage of the sort she resigned forthwith. Neither bishop nor family could dissuade her. The Methodist church was her choice because certain favorite members of her mother's family were Methodists.

Her church affiliation did become known before too long, for Charles wrote "Miss Lula" of having seen his pastor, Dr. Lacy, and of the ensuing conversation. The Reverend Mr. Lacy asked

"How are you and that teacher getting on? The tall one, the pretty one."

"Pretty well," was the answer.

"But Charlie," protested the Presbyterian divine, "she's a Methodist."

Charles replied jokingly that he hoped the pastor was "not going to be selfish enough to want to keep all his Presbyterian boys from helping out the denominations not so fortunate as to believe as we do." Still, a difference of denomination was not a question for levity in his community. It was considered only a little less divisive than a difference of political belief, which was a monstrous matter altogether even if the woman could not vote. The good Scots claimed to have learned from experience, as they opined the cave man had, that a man could choose the woman he would take into his home, but whether or not it was a pleasant place thereafter was more her choice than his. At any rate, the man and wife who had a different church or political affiliation were considered the "house divided" which the Scriptures inveighed against. Besides, it was sad to see children separate on Sunday morning, one group going with the father, one with the mother.

Charles's lyrical accounts of Miss Martin were sufficient at length to tip the scales of family approval in her favor. Before their marriage the following summer he was able to tell her, "All the folks at home seem to be perfectly satisfied about my prospective future."

The wedding of Mr. McIver and his Methodist sweetheart took place in a Presbyterian church after all, because her own was closed for repairs. They were married July 29, 1885, at six o'clock in the evening.

The church was suffocatingly hot and was jammed with so many student and teacher friends of the couple it resembled a school convention. Miss Martin wished no wedding ring. The bridegroom thought her entirely right. The ring was a nice sentimental idea for those who regarded the circle, being without end, as a symbol of undying love, but would never do for a young woman who knew its history as a badge of slavery.

They concurred, too, in an opinion that psychologists and marriage counselors would be expressing freely in another three-score years: The good marriage must be a complete and equal partnership. It was arranged, therefore, that her pastor would omit the word obey from the ceremony.

But, lo and behold, the preacher who appeared before them at the altar was not the bride's own, but the Presbyterian minister who had not been properly coached. Charles sensed her consternation, and she in turn caught his flicker of amusement at her predicament, together with some curiosity as to what she was going to do.

Lula Martin did not know. She could scarcely answer "I will not" when asked if she would take that man for her lawfully wedded husband, since she intended to do precisely that. Besides it would baffle a considerable number of little children if teacher broke up her own wedding. Her tension eased somewhat in amusement at Charles. In the midst of the solemnity he took out a handkerchief and mopped his brow, the traditional gesture of a harassed man, when she knew full well he was nothing of the sort. He was merely suffering from the heat. "It was *so* hot," she would say feelingly to explain somewhat her defection from high principle, for she did answer the vital questions affirmatively. In fact, her account of the wedding would always be hilarious in the telling.

The newlyweds went first to Greensboro and continued the following morning to the bridegroom's old home. There, Methodist or no Methodist, Lula became an immediate favorite with the McIver family. One warm gesture she especially appreciated. Charles's Grandfather Harrington had not yet gone to his last sleep under the staunch hickory which he, a great lover of trees, had selected as the only marker for his final resting place. He came by horseback from his home near Carthage, erect and dignified in the saddle, although he was nearing ninety then, to welcome his new granddaughter.

Somewhat later in the year Will wrote his sister-in-law tactlessly, if teasingly: "Can you keep Charles at home nights? Does he not want to get up a flirtation with every new girl he comes across? One thing I always noticed on him is somewhat peculiar, I think. It is not so much beauty as novelty in women that attracts him."

"Sister Lula" was not perturbed, believing herself to be greatly loved. She did not question her husband's constancy then, and afterwards came to regard it as irreproachable. In time she also came to appreciate more fully that she was one of the fortunate wives who can count on a lifelong devotion. The traces of recurring seasons were not frightening for Lula McIver, since her husband showed little awareness of them. He would bring back from New York or Chicago or Paris a piece of apparel that would scarcely have fitted her youthful slenderness, much less the stout and matronly figure she would become with the accumulating years. He would be surprised, and she would enjoy his surprise, which she interpreted as a flattering indication that he still saw in her something of the girl she had been.

It would be supposed that other women were in love with Charles McIver. It would not be supposed that he was in love with any other woman.

The chief factors of any civilization are its homes and its primary schools. Homes and primary schools are made by women rather than by men.   *—Charles Duncan McIver*

7—

One Bright Particular Star

WHILE HE WAS at home that summer before his marriage, McIver made a couple of discoveries concerning himself. In the first place, he found that he was news. Although he was not quite twenty-four, anything he did as an educator was beginning to attract attention. *The Teacher,* as a case in point, reported on his practice work with little boys and commended the idea to others.

In the second place, he found that teaching was not something he could take or leave alone. There were just too many people, as his mother often remarked, who "didn't know B from bull's foot." In his state, where 20 per cent of all white people over ten years of age and fully 70 per cent of the colored population were illiterate, schools became the only means by which the commonwealth could propel itself out of backwardness. Unfortunately, there were appallingly few teachers to operate the lever, since the schoolmaster was disdained in every community as a member of the lowest professional caste. The immediate first step, then, the vital starting point toward transformation of his retarded section was the training of teachers.

In accordance with that conclusion the Winston Graded School offered a Normal course that fall.

By the following spring, when he became vice president of the Teachers' Assembly at its meeting in western North Carolina, McIver was convinced that education was "the supreme issue with which the South must cope." It was important anywhere, in his view, but in areas hamstrung by retrogression, it was fundamental. The educators in attendance were a goodly group, some six hundred strong; it was heartening that they showed a growing concern for a teacher-training school, but one fact was disturbing nevertheless. The woman teacher, whom he considered along with Mrs. Spencer to be the "natural" instructor of primary children, constituted an appreciable minority.

Moreover, it was stern truth that the girls were apt to stay a minority. Much as young women were needed as teachers, and much as some of them would have welcomed a chance to teach, as he knew from Miss Martin's indignant testimony, they had small hope of getting the necessary preparation.

McIver knew the reasons, too—the first of which was prohibitive cost. Existing institutions for girls were private and expensive. Besides, they were chiefly of the finishing school variety and offered a girl little if any practical education. In North Carolina, where the good strong word *woman* was thought insufficiently respectful unless it had "noble" in front of it, the word *lady* was held in high repute. Schools which daughters of the well-to-do attended in pursuit of social prestige rather than knowledge naturally were intent on turning out Ladies. The state, to which young men looked for higher education at moderate cost, offered its white girls nothing, expensive or otherwise. Just nothing.

McIver was beginning to feel a surging impatience with such flagrant waste of talent—especially talent that was imperatively needed in the schoolroom. Also, he was beginning to feel shame for North Carolina men whose vaunted chivalry toward their women folk spent itself in pretty speeches, shut its eyes to the "callousness of neglect." The dual affront to his sense of the rightness of things was a gauntlet he was unable to ignore for long. Once he had accepted its challenge he had a shining goal from that time on: "Just and liberal treatment for women in the matter of higher education." It became the one bright particular star he would follow unswervingly for the rest of his life.

Rather abruptly he took up a verbal weapon on behalf of women immediately after the teachers' meeting. During a summer Normal session at Winston various persons were being called on to make impromptu talks, and, since he was secretary of the school and its instructor in methods of teaching Latin, he could hardly hope to escape. With familiar stage fright beginning to constrict his throat, he appealed for help in a hurried note to Miss Martin, who would in a few weeks more be Mrs. McIver. "I'm afraid lightning is going to strike me," he wrote. "What shall I talk about?"

Her answer was not hesitant. It had no ifs or ands or buts. It said "Talk about women's education."

Thus a public speaker was born, and born in the only fashion, two of his close associates maintained, that could have enabled McIver to become a speaker. He had to have a subject in which he could lose himself in order to overcome his paralyzing fear of an audience. Having that engrossing subject, he became for Joyner "the most irresistible and convincing speaker I ever heard"; for Alderman "the most effective speaker for public education that I have known in America."

Thanks to Miss Martin's adroit priming of his mental artillery, McIver was ready, when called on, to fire away, and his ammunition was more than ample. He had the Martin bill of particulars about the plight of women, and he had, in addition, considerable ammunition of his own. His sister Lizzie would shortly be through prep school and he had been investigating schools she might attend.

"When I began to examine catalogues of what are usually called female colleges," McIver told his listeners, "I found certain facts staring me in the face." Wherever his sister decided to go in North Carolina the cost of her education would be twice as much as his own had been, and as a result she would probably go half as long. Even if she should have the unlikely affluence to stay four years, her education "would not be of the kind to make her an independent and self-supporting factor in life."

And therein lay the rub, as he saw it. The education a girl got in boarding school, where she learned to play a little on the piano or paint a little on canvas, added no more to her earning capacity than the training for household tasks she had already mastered. The noble woman who lost her husband or never had one would find a seminary education of little account when she came to support herself. Domestic drudgery would still be her portion, as it was the portion of women who could neither read nor write their names. She could take in boarders. She could take in sewing. She could not, at the respectable level, so much as take in washing. The washer-woman was nearly always colored, or if white, had been ostracized for improper conduct.

That first speech, naturally enough, was not the sort of address that came to be associated with McIver, but it was a good start. The typical McIver product at its best was amusing, anecdotal, hard hitting. Furthermore, if the leading newspapers of the day were to be believed, it was characterized by a cogent earnestness. One daily, the Charlotte *Observer,* went so far as to say that "McIver's chief charm as a speaker lies in his earnestness, which makes his words doubly effective." It pointed out further that "he attempts no flights of oratorical powers, but the manner of the man is eloquence itself."

In respect to its earnestness, the maiden effort resembled his later oratory. And it had a little of the later product's sledgehammer quality as well.

For nearly a hundred years, he declared heatedly, the State of North Carolina had provided and partly supported a university for white men and had never spent a dollar on higher education for its white girls. For almost a decade it had provided Normal schools for its Negro youth, both men and women, so that a Negro girl setting out from the McIver farm at the same time as his sister would have a school within reach to prepare her for something other than menial labor. His sister would have none, and where was the fairness of that?

The state, the church, the philanthropist were in partnership with him, he asserted, to see that he got an education he could not otherwise afford, not to mention northern philanthropy that was supplying handsomely equipped institutions in which colored boys and girls could secure an education at a fifth of its actual cost. But "government and religion and private generosity all say by their acts that they have no concern or interest in the education of my sister." Without rhyme or reason the white girl had been overlooked, and she was the very person who would use education most creatively for everybody's advantage.

What first engaged his attention as a personal matter concerning his sister, McIver wrote later, he soon recognized as "the greatest question in education."

Indeed, the two major problems in his line of vision—the public school's unarguable need for more teachers and the young woman's unjustifiable lack of useful education—had a single solution: Educate the girls. Teaching was about the only profession open to women. If they had education, the teacher supply would take care of itself.

It was said of McIver during his lifetime that he was always in a hurry, although Alderman was quick to explain that he was "never mentally in a hurry." In all truth, his habit of rushing headlong at the nearest obstacle was not an example of precipitate haste. It was rather the full-steam-ahead of a man who knew exactly where he was going.

In the beginning he had chosen a road that had common education as its goal, and he was still following the same road, but he now saw as its further aim a wider horizon for women. Actually, the two objectives were largely indistinguishable at that stage, as he proposed to elevate the state's whole level of literacy by enabling its women to educate themselves and others. Since he was following a clear course there was not much excuse for dallying.

He finished the school year at Winston, but before it was ended he had arranged to take a positive, if limited, step forward. Early in 1886 he accepted an offer from Peace Institute, a girls' school at Raleigh, to head its literary department, and forthwith proposed to Peace's John B. Burwell that the school initiate a course in teacher education.

Mr. Burwell's reaction to the idea was enthusiastic. "I have long wanted," he wrote McIver in March, "to introduce, as you suggest, a Normal Course: *It is very desirable indeed,* and I know of nothing which would give more satisfaction. Let us by all means work this up. I have now a dozen or more fine young ladies who are preparing to teach and to whom this would be of great advantage." He meant to award the prospective teachers a Certificate of Graduation in the Normal School Course, which

would be a big help in getting them positions in the Graded
School.

"I am now," the letter went on, "and have ever been, much
perplexed as to what course to pursue in regard to what we call
special course pupils, and what is commonly known as 'parlor
Boarders.' We have now three or four who take nothing but
music and *painting*: this means that they are engaged about five
hours a day and the rest of the time loaf and demoralize others.
Our school has always been noted for advantage in Art and Music,
and I wish and intend to keep up the high standard, but there is
no reason why young ladies should not accomplish all they can in
this line and at the same time employ their time profitably in
other studies. . . . Can you make up a course that will remedy the
evil?"

The Teacher, in its April announcement that McIver had
been elected to a professorship at Peace, referred to him as "one
of the foremost teachers in the State."

The year, thus satisfactorily under way, continued to go well.
In May the McIvers' first child—a daughter, Annie Martin—was
born. Shortly thereafter McIver attended a Teachers' Assembly
at Black Mountain which made him chairman of a committee to
petition the Legislature for a teacher training school.

He also did one of the best day's work of his career in persuading Ed Alderman to share his point of view about education for
women. Mr. Alderman came to agree that women's lack of
consideration from the body politic was "an inherited wrong"
that must not be allowed to continue.

The breathless McIver arguments for a Normal school were
in the main arguments in favor of educational facilities for young
women. If North Carolina would only establish a school which
its girls could attend inexpensively, for around one hundred dollars a year, the public school system would soon have teachers
worthy of the name. Such a school was no more than the girls'
due anyway. Founders of the state had been foresighted enough
to incorporate in the constitution a provision for the Instruction
of Youth, but judging by the fact that illiterate females outnumbered illiterate males in the state by 23,000 souls, neither they nor

their descendants had taken much cognizance of an elemental fact of life: Not all of the Youth was male.

The original idea of the training school, Alderman asserted after the institution became a reality, "was born in the brain of Charles McIver. He did not borrow the idea from Massachusetts or New York. The whole scheme forced itself upon him out of the dust of injustice and negligence right under his eyes. I recall the day at Black Mountain when he spoke of it to me in his compelling way, and won my quick sympathy and interest in the idea. His busy brain and unwearying energy rapidly drew friends to the movement, for no one who met him failed to hear of it. Together we drew up the memorial to the Legislature in its behalf, and I remember the day in 1886 that he, as chairman, and George T. Winston, Edward P. Moses, and myself, presented this matter to the Committee on Education. We knew that it was doomed, but came away elated and somewhat excited over our first contact with legislative responsibility and greatness."

"Doomed" was not the word McIver would have used. For him, it was merely postponed. He could temporize. He could compromise. He could not retreat. And if he had to halt temporarily he would continue the battle where he stood. The man had enough Irish in him to make fighting a pleasure, even a necessity if he could find an injustice to get angry about. He was so overwhelmingly Scottish that education seemed a matter above all others worth fighting for. When he found injustice in education, therefore, he had a Cause—and he called it that—which was irresistible. "Fight" was a word he often used in connection with his uphill struggle to get a "square deal" for women in education.

McIver was also constitutionally unable to stay idle; he worked that summer, and every other summer, from a compulsion to be about important business as well as a need for money. Before going to Raleigh, he conducted at Yadkinville a Normal School for Yadkin County, one of several regional sessions which superseded the Summer Normal at Chapel Hill. Although the University summer school had been enormously effective for seven successive summers after its inauguration in 1877, the previous

Legislature had discontinued it in favor of short Normals at points of greater accessibility to teachers. McIver approved of the change. The "average" teacher taught sixty days out of the year for around seventy-five dollars in pay—a bit of history that would seem preposterous and incredible to North Carolinians a few brief generations later—and could not afford to travel any distance to summer school.

The Yadkin school opened with seventy-five teachers (from five counties), increased in attendance each day, and closed with over two hundred, as noted by a couple of newspapers, *The Landmark* and *The Outlook*. Similar reports of small beginnings, impressive endings, would become commonplace with repetition as the McIver reputation grew. The school was not as financially profitable to the conductor as it might have been. He had to stay at a hotel which cost a dollar a day when he could have stayed for half that in a home which took paying guests, but the home was unsuitable. Both the man of the house and his wife retailed liquor.

Of that session he wrote Mrs. McIver on July 23, "I gave this p.m. the nearest to a set lecture I ever did. I spoke on Female Education for three quarters of an hour to about 125 people."

Professor McIver disliked the condescending word "Female" and in a short time changed the title of his main theme to "Women's Education."

Meanwhile, he was beginning to marshal the arguments that North Carolina would hear for years to come, along with many other parts of the country: The state or nation that would once educate its mothers need have no fear of illiteracy forever after; an educated woman did not bring up illiterate children.

An educated man might have illiterate children. Fathers were frequently too busy at other pursuits to spend much time with their children, to say nothing of educating them, but a woman in the constant company of questing young minds "necessarily propagates whatever education she has." There was no teacher who could not, on the first day of school, select the children of cultured mothers, nor could all of the teacher's work offset for less fortunate students their close daily association with an uneducated mother. Therefore, money spent on the education of a woman would yield a better educational return than that spent on the education of a man.

Investment in a man's education paid fine dividends, to be sure, but it was a short-term investment. Ordinarily, the dividend did not extend beyond his lifetime and was largely of the material kind. On the other hand, "If it be admitted, as it must be, that woman is by nature the chief educator of children, her proper training is the strategic point in the education of the race." As the central figure in the home, the woman created its atmosphere, both intellectual and moral; set its standards; determined its ideals.

"The chief factors in any civilization," he went on, "are its homes and primary schools, and homes and primary schools are made by women rather than by men."

The conclusion? It seemed inescapable to McIver. "The cheapest, easiest, surest road to universal education" was the education of those who "would be the mothers and teachers of future generations."

The last three days of the two-week session were given over to Negro teachers, and absence of church service on his final Sunday in Yadkinville spared McIver a day devoid of occupation. Sunday schools had problems, too. Then he would conduct a "Sunday School Normal." He made two forty-minute speeches on the duties of superintendents, means of securing regular attendance, and ways to maintain good behavior.

Yet, he still considered himself an inexperienced speaker, and one aspect of the Sunday session flustered him acutely. It was due, ironically enough, to some of the mothers in his audience.

Women naturally went, whether they were Sunday school workers or not, for want of anything else to do on a Sabbath without preaching. A common sight on the road that morning, as it was on any Sunday, was a woman beside her husband on the buggy seat, holding the smallest child on her lap, while a couple of older children rode in the box at the rear of the buggy, facing backward. Or if there were too many youngsters for the buggy, a family took the wagon. Then the numerous progeny rode in the wagon bed, with the exception of the baby, who customarily went in his mother's arms.

If, in the course of the church program, the infant began to cry, an older sister might take him outside, but it was more likely that the mother would quiet him on the spot with a breast-feeding. For McIver, accustomed to greater modesty in his well-bred women relatives, the situation was almost his undoing. There were three women on the front seat, he wailed to his wife, in that embarrassing state of exposure at the same time.

Following the Normal, he did some further teaching at Graham and some recruiting of students, which he called "electioneering," for Peace. It was arranged that his wife and baby would join him, when school opened, in quarters provided by the Institute.

In Greensboro, on the way to his new work, he was shaken up by the "Charleston earthquake," so called because of the enormous damage it did to the historic South Carolina town. His account of the experience was given to Mrs. McIver with a characteristic light touch.

"Did you think the world was coming to an end last night?" he wrote her on August 11, 1886. "Here in Raleigh there seems to have been general panic, especially among the colored brethren. Chimneys were thrown down and the strongest houses shook, windows rattled, etc. Rev. Mr. Watkins thought somebody was trying to break in his house and went to the door and threatened to shoot whoever it was. But he found he couldn't intimidate an earthquake. I accounted for the little disturbance at Greensboro very naturally when I heard there was a meeting of Republicans there. Several amusing things are told of the earthquake everywhere. It did no damage to me except that it broke a bottle of Gates hair restorer in my trunk."

At Raleigh, Professor McIver began to hear from many sources that Captain Burwell was delighted with him, and most particularly with his enthusiasm. He found, too, that "The idea of putting in the normal feature is exceedingly popular, among teachers and people. The majority of the patrons of female colleges, I think, are getting tired of paying big prices for butterfly accomplishments and nothing besides. There is a demand for something practical, and I think we may congratulate ourselves on being the first to inaugurate so progressive a movement in North Carolina."

No matter that the new place represented a reversal of his original stand on teaching. His determination to teach no women had been abandoned for a position in which he would teach women only, and it looked as if it might turn out all right!

8—

The Law and the Prophets of Education

THE RALEIGH move represented more than a departure from original intent for McIver. It represented opportunity to become a sort of one-man lobby for his educational program in the state Legislature, on a person-to-person basis. And there McIver was in his element.

He sought out the lawmakers—no mistake about that—and almost to a man they liked him. It was difficult not to like anyone so genial. That was the word, genial, they used again and again to describe him. He showed such unmistakable pleasure in their company they would have been less than human if they had failed to respond in kind. He looked a man straight in the eye, talked to him with the profound concentration due a person whose opinion was invaluable. Naturally, the individual thus singled out found it easy to listen, even when hearing an idea he ordinarily dismissed as the brain child of a crank—some crackpot scheme, say, for universal tax-supported education.

Anyway, McIver was no crank. The man was the very essence of sanity and good will and reasonableness.

In addition to which he was grand fun. He had an inexhaustible fund of entertaining stories which contained for his listeners the piquant extra of surprise. It was downright astonishing that a "thorough-going Scotchman" could be a funny man. He enjoyed their stories, too. He would chuckle and chuckle and chuckle over a good one.

So McIver got to know the lawmakers well when the General Assembly convened. He went often to their hotel rooms, and however much an evening was enlivened by laughter, sometime before it was over he prodded their consciousness with his two-tined fork. The state needs teachers. The girls need teaching.

The situation was the same when they went to his home, where Mrs. McIver was already becoming the incomparable hostess North Carolina would long remember. The atmosphere of the place was unmistakable to the most casual guest. It also saturated the McIver children early. The pampered little daughter Annie would go to her father's bookcase, pretend she was going to remove a book, and then, spreading her hands protectively behind her small self, would shake her head vigorously and say, "No, no. Papa 'pank." Papa would have done nothing of the sort—he was said to be "an out-and-out softy" with his children—but the bit of play-acting was a straw to show which way the wind blew in that house. Anything to do with Education had to be respected.

The visitors knew that. They could count on a lively discussion, probably a spirited argument, in which both Mr. and Mrs. McIver would seek to set them straight on school questions. Afterward, they admitted, they were apt to have a period of self-examination. Men who honestly believed themselves gallant came to question whether they, as keepers of the state's purse, could so much as call themselves just. After all, they were appropriating money for improvement of their own sex and never a farthing for the ladies. McIver's insistent voice was becoming the Legislature's conscience in regard to women, as it would later become the conscience of a whole state.

No matter. The legislators had a good time with McIver whether they agreed with him or not, and some who liked him most agreed with him least—in the beginning.

He liked them, too, genuinely and sincerely. "If I were asked," Alderman once stated, "what was the greatest thing about Charles McIver, I would say that it was his interest in and sympathy and love for men and women, not attractive men and women alone, or good men and women, or great men and women—but men and women." Many persons expressed the same idea variously. McIver, Josephus Daniels said, had a genius for friendship.

Mr. Daniels preceded him to Raleigh by one year. In October

of 1885 he obtained a license to practice law and on that same date stepped into the old *State Chronicle* office to fit himself into the editorial shoes vacated by Wat Page. In time, he said, he came to feel closer to McIver than any man he knew with the exception of Charles Aycock.

McIver made it a habit to drop into the *Chronicle* office after his classes at Peace and talk for an hour or so. There was rarely a day for months on end, Mr. Daniels reported in his autobiography, that they did not spend some time together. In April of 1887, when McIver had been in Raleigh some eight months, Daniels offered to sell him a half-interest in the *Chronicle,* either to keep it as a weekly and form a law partnership, or to turn it into a daily. With the suggested partnership in mind, McIver read some law when he could find the time, or thought about it, although as he told Mrs. McIver, "We could do nothing at law if we kept up a daily."

Actually, Mr. Daniels managed to do both insofar as law was a springboard into the political stream. He became, after acquiring possession of the *News and Observer,* an outstandingly successful practitioner of personal, politically spiced journalism. He also garnered some political plums, chief among them appointment as Secretary of the Navy under Wilson and Ambassador to Mexico under Franklin D. Roosevelt, his assistant in the earlier Navy post.

Apparently Mr. Daniels knew his own mind all along. "The kind words in your breezy letter," he wrote McIver in August following the April offer, "were among the pleasantest things that ever blotted paper. . . . I am determined about having a daily and I want to talk with you about it."

McIver wrote breezy letters to his wife, too. In early July he went to Sparta to conduct one of the State Normals and the trip, admittedly, was "long and tiresome," but he gave a light-hearted account of it: "Well, we had bad luck yesterday. One of our horses seemed to have a sort of colic. Swelled, dropped as if she was dead in the harness and rolled and tumbled until 1 o'clock last night. There was a big crowd around as there always is about a sick horse. All gave remedies various and different, and we tried enough of them to kill the horse." Finally, it was Professor McIver himself who suggested the effective remedy and he added puckishly he thought he had better turn horse doctor. Even so, he had to hire another horse before proceeding the next day.

The Sparta interlude was pleasant. He had an excellent place to stay, the fare was good, the mountain air delightful. The Normal opened the day after his arrival with 150 teachers in attendance and the prospects good. President Battle of the University came by to help out with a lecture one week and Jo Daniels the next. And during the final week of the session he received word that he had a son. Charles Duncan McIver, Jr., was born on July 23 at the home of Mrs. McIver's parents, Dr. and Mrs. Samuel Martin, in Winston. He was delivered, as his sister Annie had been, by Dr. David Nicholas Dalton—the same "Dicky" who had accused the infant's father of purloining the Dalton girl friends, Lula Martin among them.

The following summer, 1888, McIver was principal of two State Normals, one at Wilson in the eastern part of the state from July 2 to July 20, and one at Sparta in the west from July 30 to August 17. (Ed Alderman and Billy Noble were engaged in the Normal program, too, that summer.)

Meanwhile, by reason of his relation to public and private schools, McIver reported to his wife, he was easily a leader of the Teachers' Assembly which met at Morehead City in June, exchanging mountains for seashore as a convention point.

Assembly proceedings bore out the statement. He made a speech on how to educate the future woman of North Carolina. He nominated for president his one-time professor, all-time friend, George T. Winston. He was elected chairman of the Executive Committee which had among its members his superior at Peace, Mr. Burwell, and his cronies Alderman, Winston, and Noble. He constituted with Peace's Burwell and *The Teacher's* Harrell an editing committee to see, as he explained it, that nothing improper went into the printed proceedings.

McIver was also chosen chairman of another committee that would have much more significance than any of the rest. It was a committee to petition the Legislature, for a third time, to establish a training school for teachers. Serving with him were Alderman, Harrell, E. P. Moses, Winston, D. Matt Thompson, and Mrs. J. A. McDonald. McIver, Harrell, and Moses, it was decided, would draw up the memorializing paper.

McIver's friends thought of him as a person who remained cheerful and undiscouraged, but Mrs. McIver knew better. She was with him at Morehead City for a part of the teachers' meeting, and she was no more than gone when he began writing to urge that she leave the children with Dr. and Mrs. Martin and spend at least a week with him. "I feel sick and disheartened," he pleaded, "and need your encouragement and yourself." He felt, in spite of her objection to the cost, that he could not afford *not* to have her with him, since "you are more to me than either of us know."

The importunate letters continued. He was lonely that summer for his family. "How is my little Annie?" he wrote. "She is spoilt but I love her little badnesses even." He was often "tired, tired, tired." He spent his energy recklessly. After full days of teaching teachers there were full evenings of public lectures and debates. It would shortly be said of him, as it was of another great American (Webster) that he was a steam engine in trousers, a figure of speech appropriate to its time. In another age McIver's energy would likely have been called atomic. That summer foreshadowed, too, in one instance, the privation that would frequently be his portion in months to come. The example was a hardship Mrs. McIver shared.

She could not arrange to leave the children, but in view of his continual insistence, she did go with him to Sparta, taking the children along. They stopped overnight in the mountains in a two-room cottage. One room was sleeping quarters, which the hosts hospitably turned over to the guests while they retired to the kitchen, presumably to sleep on a pallet there, or in the loft above it.

The accommodation was all the mountaineers had and the McIvers were grateful, but the bed, once the reasonably clean counterpane had been thrown back, was found to be slimy with dirt. A doctor's daughter, herself a would-be doctor, Lula McIver spontaneously devised measures to elude the unsanitary bedding. She stripped off the dirty pillow cases, placed the pillows on the floor, and covering each of them with one of her own clean petticoats, made beds of sorts for her two-year-old girl and year-old boy. She napped as best she could sitting upright in a rocking chair. Only Charles, too spent to care, threw himself fully clothed across the bed and slept as the exhausted must.

That summer, with its foretaste of the fatigue and discomfort and homesickness that the future held in store for him, also brought an offer, as if inescapable destiny were manifesting itself, to head a girls' college.

While he was at Wilson the Trustees of Floral College (Robeson County) wrote to ask if he would consider a proposition to become principal of their institution.

A letter from Alex McIver at Pittsboro gave more particulars. "Floral College wishes to give you the college and grounds and their good will for five years free of charge if you will go there, select your teachers, and start a first class school for girls on an economical basis. When I knew Floral College in 1884 it was the best girls' school in the state. I want to send two girls to you there. Peace Institute is too costly. Its patrons complain of its extravagance. They want something more to the point and for less money."

Manifest destiny or not, McIver turned down the offer. Turning down offers came to be something he did rather well.

Following the Wilson Normal he stopped off in Goldsboro, before going to Sparta, to do some prospecting for Peace students, and incidentally to throw a little light, in a letter to Mrs. McIver, on the political mores of the times. The Democratic party, it will be remembered, was in control. The Negroes, identifying themselves still with the party of their liberation, were Republican. He wrote with his usual tongue-in-cheek levity of a Democratic rally.

"They had a big jollification here last night. The town was ablaze with illumination, tar barrels, etc. Long torch light procession. Up till 1 o'clock.

"One man killed with a brick bat and the murderer put in jail. There was a big crowd in the jail, among others a young white man named Lynch from Greene County. Some Greene men broke into the jail and put in some crowbars to the Negroes, whom they could reach, and tried to hire them to help Lynch out. The Negroes just got their own cells broken open about day and without helping Lynch, skipped. So to sum up the Democratic proceeds—Big jubilee, one Democrat killed and another put in jail. Four Republicans turned out. . . . Joyner and Mrs. Joyner are cordiality itself."

As indicated, he visited Joyner, who had turned to the practice of law and set up shop in Goldsboro. Alderman was the school's superintendent. Aycock, also a practicing attorney in town, was a speaker at the rally. Too bad Billy Noble did not show up. They could have had a plenary reunion of their Chapel Hill gang.

His summer's work, which ended at Graham, earned McIver nearly three hundred dollars. Protracted meetings cut into the Graham attendance, and he missed the Sparta breezes. Consequently, he was glad enough to get back to Raleigh and start "doing business at the same old stand."

Or stands, since he worked as hard at educating the state Legislature as he did the girls at Peace. When the law-making body reconvened he was on hand to greet its members. He would meet a returning legislator, hand outstretched, face actually beaming with pleasure, and say "I am *so glad* to see you." He would call the man by name; he took pride in remembering people. Soon he was back in the assemblymen's hotel rooms, joking, arguing, pleading for his double-barreled program: adequate schools for everybody, better education for women. Other forces were at work in the state toward the same end; the politicians were not unaware of them. But it was McIver, there in their midst, who was an exclamation point drawing them sharply to attention. One by one, and rapidly, he beguiled them into his corner. They could not resist the dynamic McIver personality, reinforced as it was by both pixie grin and persuasive tongue.

Unfortunately, the state as a whole was not keeping step with the McIver-indoctrinated Legislature. There was stubborn, widespread objection to public education throughout the social order, from top to bottom, and not, as might have been expected, among the ignorant alone. Now and then McIver found occasion to remonstrate, for example, with an editor who was giving aid and comfort to the enemies of educational progress.

The answer to one of his protests—from J. P. Caldwell, of Statesville, editor and proprietor of *The Landmark*—is quoted for a couple of reasons. It reflects some of the sentiment prevalent at the time on questions of education. It came from an editor who gave McIver credit for his complete change of heart on the subject, and who, as publisher of the Charlotte *Observer* somewhat later, drew a large and influential paper into the educators' camp.

"What is writ is writ," he declared in a letter dated August 6, 1888, "and I do declare to you that I take no stock in many of the educational methods of the day. I am opposed to the whole graded school idea and system, for instance. . . . I do not believe in educating people in the higher branches at the public expense. After a child has been taught the elementary branches in the common school, he and his parents should scuffle for the balance— that's what I had to do. I believe with you in the teachers' institutes. I am strongly impressed that the teachers who go to the normal schools and the Assembly go for a frolic and that few are really benefited. You speak of the Teachers' Assembly becoming 'a power' in the State. That is one of the things I object to. It is getting to be dictatorial; its tone (pardon me) is becoming insolent . . . I am not one of those who are opposed to popular education at the public expense, but I would carry it just as far as I have indicated and no further. As for the children of the *elite* I would shut them out of the public schools entirely. A man who is able to educate his children ought to be made to do it or else live to see them grow up in ignorance. And by this I don't mean to advocate any system of compulsory education. God forbid; that idea is a nightmare to me. I would like to see the common schools filled with the shirt-tail children, and to see the basis for an education laid in them—No Algebra, no language, no painting, drawing, or any such business at the public expense."

Toward the end of the legislative session of 1889, the Training School bill came before the General Assembly. It had not discarded the coeducational status of its predecessors, but the memorial paper prepared by McIver and his committee bore down hardest on one point: the bill's importance to the education of girls ought to pass it if the measure had no other merit.

That paper asked some pertinent questions. How, its draftsmen wanted to know, if it had been wise for a century to provide a university for boys, could "any man consistently refuse to allow a small amount from the public school fund (not enough to shorten the school term one-half a day) to establish a Training School where *girls* can prepare for almost the only work by which our social conditions allow them to earn a livelihood?" If one sex had to get along without education, would not men be better able to get along without it than women? Why for a hundred years had the state been helping the stronger and letting the weaker take care of themselves? Was there any good reason that they should make annual appropriations for their sons and disregard the modest, the only, request their daughters had ever made? Should the state help her sons to develop their intellectual and industrial powers and do absolutely nothing for those who were to be the mothers of the next generation of men?

The petition reiterated the old McIver plaint that the state's female colleges, being without endowment, were too expensive for the average well-to-do citizen to patronize. The family of moderate means could afford, however, to send its daughters to the proposed training school for an education that would make them selfsupporting, and without the adoption of some such measure the girls "were doomed to live and drudge and die without ever having known the blessing of being independent." At the same time, the memorial concluded, the state was losing much of its best teaching talent, and self-interest, as well as justice, demanded passage of the bill.

The Speaker of the House was McIver's personal friend and, like King Agrippa under the spell of St. Paul, was "almost persuaded" to desert the opposition. He was altogether persuaded, on the other hand, that affirmative action on the Training School proposal would arouse the political wrath of his constituents. Nevertheless, he did promise McIver if the measure passed the Senate, an eventuality he did not for a moment consider likely, he would not oppose it in the House.

The Speaker's wife had arrived in Raleigh to spend the closing days of the legislative session with her husband, and the McIvers asked the couple to supper. "Don't mention the bill," Charles McIver warned Lula. "He feels terrible about it." She reminded him that it was not her custom to embarrass a guest, but the evening did not go entirely according to custom. After the meal when everybody was sitting in mellow mood before the library fire the Speaker said, "Mrs. McIver, since you think so much of education, you will heartily approve of something we did today. We passed a bill establishing a school for the Indians."

In spite of Charles's glance, which plainly said, "Now, Lula," the remark strained Mrs. McIver's habitually impeccable manners to the snapping point. "If I only could be an Indian or a Negro," she replied with no little asperity, "I might expect something from this Legislature."

When McIver appeared before the Assembly to make a plea for the school, one opponent urged that his colleagues should not be moved to foolish waste of the state's money by one who came among them "clothed in purple and fine linen." Mrs. McIver, from her position in the gallery, dropped a note to her husband. "Pull up your coattail, Charles," it advised, "and show them your purple and fine linen." He might have created something of a stir if he had; he was wearing a patch on his britches. His deceptively expensive appearance was due to the skill with a needle of Mrs. McIver, who had applied the patch, and the skill with an iron of one Ezekiel Robinson, an exemplary colored servant who had pressed the pants. Zeke's devotion was the sort McIver could not use up in a lifetime. The slight dark man would keep dignified watch over his casket when he was dead.

North Carolina's educational leaders in general, Charles McIver in particular, had done their work well. The Senate passed their bill by a whopping majority, to the surprise of a great many persons other than the House Speaker. But they had not done well enough. It failed, by sixteen votes, to survive the House.

Nonetheless, the Legislature could not make up its mind to have done with the educators once and for all. At the suggestion of the State Superintendent of Public Instruction, Major Sidney M. Finger, it discontinued the eight Summer Normals and provided in their place a system of county institutes that would not, in the intent of the act, be content with teacher training alone. The measure called for instructing teachers in the methods and meaning of their job, to be sure, but it also called for educating the public concerning school needs and ways to meet them. The institute conductors would thus seek to create and mould a sentiment favorable to public education. While they were about it, they would, in effect, conduct an educational canvass as well, since one of their duties, as defined by the Legislature, was to make suggestions for improving the school system.

The institutes were unique in all the annals of education. The two men chosen to conduct them did a monumental service for their state. They were Charles McIver and Edwin Alderman.

On March 22, 1889, State Superintendent Finger wrote McIver:

"At a meeting of the State Board of Education held today, you were selected to conduct institute work, in accordance with a recent act of Assembly which abolishes the white normal schools. Your annual salary will be $2000, you bearing your travelling expenses, and the details of the work will be left mainly to your judgment subject to the advice of the State Supt. of Pub. Ins. and the specific requirements of the statute. I trust you will signify your acceptance at an early day."

Alderman was ill when he got his notification, and did not reply until April 4, but his answer was an acceptance as McIver's had been.

The two young men, still under thirty, discussed the plans and purposes and difficulties of their assignment when the 1889 commencement brought them together at Chapel Hill. They had given up their jobs—McIver at Raleigh, Alderman at Goldsboro; they had wives and young children at home; and they still could not curb their flaming enthusiasm for the undertaking.

There was no precedent, as Alderman recalled, for what they were trying to do "except Horace Mann, and he seemed so far off and so great that each of us would have laughed at the other for mentioning the comparison." Finally, at cockcrow, Alderman asked McIver to let him have one more word and then they would both go to sleep. McIver replied "in his hearty, wholesome way" that he did not propose to let Alderman have the last word and be put to sleep at the same time, so they talked on until sun-up. They might have been less blithe if they could have seen more clearly the way ahead.

North Carolina's attitude toward education was a paradox. The people reserved their highest esteem for a man who understood Latin and Greek and even acclaimed the person without much formal training if he were "a well-read man." Yet they showed on the whole a towering indifference to getting the benefits of education for themselves.

Old ghosts of the idea that education was a luxury for the privileged and public schooling a public charity accounted in part for the situation, but not in preponderant part. The Carolinians offered many excuses for their opposition to public education. Some objected that the "free schools" were too inferior to support; others that, being secular, they could not teach morality. Many celebrated when the State Supreme Court declared unconstitutional an 1881 statute which permitted school districts to levy local taxes—the law under which the Durham and Goldsboro schools had been established, giving McIver and Alderman, respectively, their first teaching posts.

The people objected, too, that the Negro, under the dual school system, shared tax benefits although his taxable property was negligible, and summed up the objection in the often-heard expression, "Educate a Negro and spoil a field hand." (There was just enough truth in the remark to make it harmful. Some of the colored people, misinterpreting the promises that accompanied their freedom, had thought education meant release from labor, and a smattering of learning had made them "no-'count.") The electorate objected most vehemently of all that it was robbery

to tax Brown to educate Jones's children. And that came close
to being the heart of the matter.

On that score McIver and Alderman, far from being wide-eyed
visionaries, were not fooling themselves. From their experience
with the Legislature they had learned that the word "tax" could
chill a politician to the marrow, and with understandable reason.
The entire populace had a low boiling point on the subject with
the result that, as McIver often phrased it, "Agin' taxes equals politics." The people's hostility to taxation was no less intense than
that of a French revolutionary who had seen his substance diverted
to the upper classes. It was no less determined than that of their
forefathers who defied the arrogant assumption of a British
monarch that free men could be taxed without their say. The
aversion had got a double dip in the distilled bitterness of Reconstruction abuses. Taxes, for whatever purpose, were an evil.
There was no such thing as a good tax.

A man needed missionary zeal to broach the subject of increased taxation to a North Carolina voter. Fortunately McIver
and Alderman, who understood the matter well, had the zeal in
good measure.

They had an equal amount, and were aware they would need
it, to direct toward accomplishing their additional purpose, the
establishment of an institution chiefly beneficial to women. If
North Carolina could be persuaded to support public education
at all, it would almost surely balk at giving girls any training beyond the grade school level. Since nothing, nothing at all, is
harder to dislodge than a social concept that has been fully
accepted, they found themselves confronted by a deeply embedded
stumblingblock. The idea that women had no function in the
work-a-day world, hence could not benefit from college courses
preparatory to the professions, was too ingrained to provoke discussion, much less argument. One man, and a public school teacher
at that, stated the prevailing view, if ridiculously, when he declared in a debate with McIver, "It is not women's hemisphere to
be educated."

Assuming that women would continue to occupy their restricted orbit—and the probability of change was beyond popular

conception—the men had a point, as higher education was synonymous in their thinking with classical education. The Latin phrase so dear to the heart of many public speakers would be of no use to the girls in wringing a chicken's neck. Nor would an equation in algebra—Algebra!—help in patching a pair of overalls. What could women possibly want with such folderol? Why could not the charming creatures, bless their contrary hearts, be content to remain a ladies' auxiliary to male enterprise?

The McIver-Alderman team, talking the night away, recognized still another obstacle to test their crusading caliber. If they got the schools, if they got women trained to staff them, there would remain the problem of endowing the teaching profession with enough respect to make it effective.

All in all, they were shouldering a prodigious task when they set out to preach a gospel to which they were thoroughly consecrated; a gospel that proclaimed, in essence, that human beings have as much right to be educated as they have to be free. The doctrine was strange and new and all but incomprehensible to their native state, to individualistic, conservative, rabidly tax-hating North Carolina. They were going out into the highways and hedges to induce that state to dig deep into its pockets to finance an institution—communal, democratic—in which it had little faith. The highways would be nearly as uninviting as the hedges.

The teacher is the seed corn of civilization. None but the best is good enough to use.   —*Charles Duncan McIver*

9—

Highways and Hedges

THE INSTITUTE WORK began on July 1, 1889. During the next three years McIver and Alderman would carry their unique campaign into every nook and cranny of North Carolina—from Cherokee to Currituck, from Murphy to Manteo. Obviously, although the brunt of the task was theirs, the pair of them could not reach every county in the state annually without help. Hence Major Finger welcomed an offer (from Dr. Curry) of Peabody funds that enabled him to employ three others—Noble and Joyner and Moses—as institute conductors during July and August. The following two summers he drew into the institute program the same trio plus several other excellent school men.

Mrs. McIver was also her husband's assistant at intervals, and he valued her help above that of anybody else, as he told Major Finger. "What I need," he wrote the state superintendent on one occasion, "is somebody to give me a breathing spell occasionally between lectures and to give variety to my work. Mrs. McIver can do both of these things, and besides, can present one or two subjects better than I can."

McIver and Alderman alike began in the western mountains and proceeded toward the seacoast. Each held a five-day institute. Each kept the other informed concerning the comedies and the errors, the hardships and the discouragements. And the progress. Travel from one county seat to another was a story in itself. Railroads were inadequate to the institute demands. They were friendly enough where they existed—an obliging engineer would hold his train while a professor finished breakfast—but their lines too often did not correspond with routes the institute instructors had to follow. To offset a leisurely breakfast, one might have to roll out of bed at a predawn four o'clock and ride twenty miles to catch a train. When there was no train to catch the men had to rely on means both sundry and surprising. Alderman crossed one stream (to the Indian reservation) in a birch bark canoe. McIver crossed another on a slippery foot log, having had to abandon a carriage that could not ford a swollen creek. It took Alderman seven hours of hard riding over a high mountain to go twelve miles in "an ordinary springless wagon used for other 'substances.'" McIver required a full weekend to go from Concord to Albermarle, a short ride as the crow flies, because Bear Creek was too flooded to cross, and he had to take refuge in the home of a Dutchman. When he finally got under way again on Monday, the water ran to the seat of a high carriage and he arrived at eleven o'clock, wet to the knees, to open his institute. Sometimes, having to pay his own way, McIver had to borrow money to proceed at all.

From the start they attracted large crowds. Naturally people went, moved by curiosity if nothing else, to hear young men who had the temerity to urge higher taxes, of all things. No speaker worth his salt had advocated anything since Reconstruction but low taxes and white supremacy.

The instructors, animated as they were by identical aims, still had completely dissimilar platform manners. Alderman, whose speech could get more than a little flamboyant, nevertheless had a genuine literary gift. His sentences were carefully formed, his diction superb, his bearing magnetic. He unquestionably talked over the heads of his country audiences at times, but they did not hold it against him. If there was anything rural North Carolina dearly loved it was resounding oratory. Anyway, his hearers got the point well enough to be impressed by the fact that this eloquent and charming young man should think highly of teachers and teaching. Consequently, he was able to do his share toward making the school a renovating force instead of "a scorn, a shaking of the head, and a hissing."

Also, on his part, he learned lessons that would be valuable to the state. He saw, along with McIver, the pathetically undernourished condition of the schools—a malnutrition deriving from too little of everything: too little equipment, too little public interest, too few teachers and they in turn having too little pay, too little training, too little pride in their work, and no morale whatever. He also learned, by his own statement, the essential open-mindedness, the justice and dignity of character of the average North Carolinian.

McIver achieved his effectiveness by methods peculiarly his own. Not greatly concerned with syntax, he jumped into the middle of a sentence and got out somehow. It scarcely mattered that his arguments were somewhat ponderous, since he clinched them with an apt illustration or a quotable aphorism. Moreover, he was invariably interesting, invariably amusing. "It was a dull and senseless audience," Alderman maintained, "that did not respond to the breathless onrush of his appeal . . . lighted with a homely humor and power of illustration, a shrewd adaptation of story and anecdote unequaled in North Carolina since young Zeb Vance won his triumphant way." In one respect he differed from the young Vance. He did not, as Zeb had been criticized for doing in his early years, tell off-color stories. He had one about petting he included occasionally in his first addresses, but Mr. Joyner, fearing he might offend the strait-laced, persuaded him to discontinue it.

It was Joyner, friend to both men, who assessed rather astutely the essential difference of their speaking results. A charmed audience, as he noted, came away from an Alderman speech nodding its head and saying, "What a wonderful address." An aroused audience came away from a McIver speech figuratively rolling up its sleeves and saying "What can we do to help Professor McIver?" Not everybody was immediately ready to help, it is true, but in every audience there were a few, almost surely a few, who took up the fight with McIver's own cudgels—the blunt, forceful arguments he had handed them.

Alderman had more polish. McIver had more "punch."

At one point in the campaign, the two conductors held joint institutes at Edenton and Camden Courthouse for six northeastern counties. At Edenton, as befitted good feminists, they were shaved by a female barber—a bright Mulatto who worked in her

Evander McIver, "Scotch Iver,"
grandfather of Charles Duncan
McIver

John E. Kelly, who prepared
Charles McIver for college

The Rev. William S. Lacy, pastor
of Buffalo Church during Charles
McIver's boyhood

Dr. James Y. Joyner, one of the
closest of McIver's lifelong friends

Mr. and Mrs. Charles D. McIver during their years
at Peace Institute in Raleigh

husband's shop. There, too, McIver faced the challenging situation of having to follow his urbane companion on the rostrum. He listened and wondered how in the wide world he was ever to gain the attention of an audience that Alderman was hypnotizing. He turned the trick by a laugh at himself. At Chapel Hill the colleagues had known a Negro barber, Tom Dunston, to whom the English language was a wild and wonderful thing. He quoted Tom: "Dat ar man McIver shore can sponsify powerful, but I tell you, he jes can't laborate, spashiate, and zaggirate like Mr. Alderman."

The curious who dropped in to hear McIver may have come to scoff, but they remained to laugh, and they returned to listen, often with reinforcements. Unlike Alderman, he spoke their language. If he wanted to impress upon them that they must work out their own salvation he told them about Old Frog. Two frogs, the story went, were knocked into a crock of milk as the cover was set in place. One splashed around frantically for a few seconds, gave up, and drowned. But not Old Frog; he kept kicking. And the next morning when the housewife lifted the crock lid, there sat Old Frog safe and sound on a firm island of butter. It was not an elegant story but it had the virtue of being understood. Every woman who had churned milk in her own kitchen and gathered butter to the top of the churn with quick, short strokes of the dasher, every male, man and boy, who had seen her do it (and that meant his entire rural public) knew he was telling them to keep toiling doggedly at problems that looked hopeless. When they came in from the fields at planting time he told them "Teachers are the seed corn of civilization." They knew about seed corn; it should be the best available. They listened and were stirred—some to opposition, some to favorable action, all to discussion.

"The very publication of some of your advanced ideas on education does occasion a discussion," he was informed by Editor D. F. St. Clair, of the *Central Express* at Sanford, who wrote to say "I am in hearty accord with you in your revolution of education in North Carolina. You have made a marked impression in Moore County. I happened to go into a crowd the other day and a fellow who had heard you talk was presenting your ideas with all his might."

Discussion was what he wanted, McIver said in a letter to Major Finger, since they were opposed by two people, the politician and the preacher, who could get the public ear. "The former is afraid," he explained, "and the latter is against us because we do not teach sectarianism."

The first four days of an institute were devoted to the teachers, whose attendance was compulsory. Schools were suspended for a week, when in session, to permit teachers to be present at the training programs. There was too little time to teach subject matter, but the conductors gave what assistance they could with methods of instruction, discipline, and proper use of textbooks. Even more importantly they supplied the teachers with that intangible and powerful quality known as inspiration.

Inspiration was a commodity for which they had plenty of need. The teacher in every community not only ranked below doctor, lawyer, merchant, chief—below the butcher, the baker, the candlestick maker, he was one of those, or something else, in the majority of places. Schools in a round dozen towns— among them the two at Winston and Durham that had felt the McIver touch, Billy Noble's school at Wilmington, Joyner's school at Goldsboro where he had succeeded Alderman to the superintendency, and of course the bellwether school at Greensboro—had sessions of nine or ten months. But the remote rural districts, mired in poverty and apathy and inaccessibility, pulled the average term down to sixty school days. The piddling pay (average: $25.80 per month for men, $22.95 for women) for teaching three months could not be spread over the other nine. In fact the man (and the institute conductors found men teachers outnumbered women nearly two to one) who left his regular occupation to teach at all was in the somewhat apologetic position of admitting publicly that he needed a little extra cash. Too often he got contempt for his pains. There was nothing to wonder at, McIver told his audience, in an old woman's answer to the census taker. When asked how many children she had, her reply had been: "Two living, two dead, and one teaching school." He was in-

furiated by shortsightedness which paid cotton pickers and tobacco
stemmers more than trainers of the young.

"It is impossible to overstate," he insisted, "the necessity for
raising in the public mind the standard of qualifications for those
who are to teach the children. The public school teacher, if
properly qualified, is our most important public official. Those
who teach the young are civilization's most powerful agents, and
society everywhere ought to set apart and consecrate to its greatest
work its bravest, its best, its strongest men and women. *The
teacher is the seed corn of civilization, and none but the best is
good enough to use.*"

A higher standard of teaching, he realized, had a necessary
corollary—a higher standard of compensation. Noting that
skilled mechanics everywhere were receiving higher pay than
teachers, he declared society ought to be more anxious to secure
competent men and women to build the social structure than to
have competent artisans to erect its buildings. *"Moulding character is of more importance than moulding iron."*

How timeless was his argument; how often it would have to
be reiterated for generations other than his own: "The public
ought to right about face. The custom of tempting the capable
and ambitious to turn away from teaching ought to give place to
a policy of financial and other rewards that will tempt the most
ambitious and strongest people in every community to enter the
field of greatest and most potential service to the world." A
teacher could lay aside his hangdog look and hold his head up on
the street after listening to McIver.

The fifth day of an institute was people's day. School committeemen and the general public were urged to attend, and
various exercises culminated in an address on taxes. It was Mc-
Iver's habit to set up and knock down again the most commonly
heard objections to taxation for education.

He saw aversion to taxation as due, in the first place, "to
ignorance of the fact that just taxation is simply an exchange
of a little money for something better—civilized government.
The savage alone is exempt from taxation. It is strange that the
man who cheerfully pays his annual insurance premium for pro-

tection against fire and death should regard it as tyranny when called upon to pay his tax, which is an annual premium to protect against arson and murder."

Since training was an essential condition of all progress, education became a legitimate tax on protected property. Far from being robbery when Brown paid tax to educate Jones's children, it was social insurance he was getting, just as it was when he paid to build jails and insane asylums. He did not expect to "participate personally" in those either.

The fraternal aspects of life as McIver knew it among a small student body at Chapel Hill had exceeded his own intimate clique. He renewed acquaintance with class and college mates, and enlisted their help, as he moved from place to place—from mountains to piedmont to seashore. He was always glad, too, when he had a chance to work among Quakers, since he had never known a Quaker or a Scotchman who was not an advocate of education.

He had reached Asheboro, which he called *the* Quaker country, by the end of September in his first eastward swing, "took dinner with McAlister, an old college friend," and looked forward to one of his most successful institutes, he wrote Mrs. McIver, who had remained in Raleigh to teach at Peace Institute. "Friday," he told her, "will probably be one of my most successful days as the County Farmers' Alliance meets here on that day." McIver and Alderman were generally credited, it should be noted, with converting the influential Alliance to their aims, including a training school for women. It was in Asheboro, too, that a "genuine Quaker" told McIver "Health seems to be thy fort." He considered the statement oddly put, but true.

The opinion was widely shared. The description "robust" was universally applied to McIver throughout his life and found its way repeatedly into books concerned with his era. Yet it was not fitting. A crowd had a tonic effect on him, and he responded with vivacity, even when tired or ill, but he sometimes had to dig deep into reserve strength to make the effort. He frequently suffered from indigestion, biliousness, and colds.

Immediately after he had impressed the Asheboro gentleman with his good health he wrote Mrs. McIver from Yanceyville:

"I was pretty sick last night. I took 20 grains of quinine and some of the meanest whiskey that I ever saw. I awoke at 12 o'clock and such a roaring I never heard. A cyclone was in my head. Cold has settled in my body but my throat is not yet affected."

Self-diagnosis and self-treatment were not uncommon in Mc-Iver's time. Accordingly, the man dosed himself mercilessly. Quinine enough to produce many tempests in the head he took in coast areas where he was fearful of malaria. Calomel—the inevitable calomel, Mrs. McIver called it—he took without geographical limitation. If the water was impure—as it was at Camden Courthouse where neither he nor Alderman had a drink of it—he either did without or bought a bottled mineral water when it was available. At such places he welcomed cold weather because the "varmints in the water are more likely to be dead and harmless." He could never bring himself to push the "wiggletails" aside and drink as if they were not there.

Indeed, the institute schedule was anything but conducive to good health. The food was incredibly bad at times, but even worse for McIver it was frequently unclean. A spotted table cloth, a smell of stale grease, food served in swarms of flies, made tough going for a man accustomed throughout his boyhood to the food prepared in Angelet's scrubbed kitchen, in which the only odors were those of cleanness and good cooking, unless one counted the occasional scent of an oilcloth table cover before the newness wore off.

It was endurable at all because the pendulum had a way of swinging wildly from famine to feast. One week he would be subsisting on oranges that he bought for a penny apiece; the next he would have the best of everything—good fresh bread, eggs, milk, butter, and perhaps excellent oysters, which he, being an inlander, considered a treat. At a time when he was relying on tomatoes to ease hunger pangs, an old college friend might come to the rescue with a splendid dinner. (He liked tomatoes best as they had come, peeled and sliced, to his mother's table, but he enjoyed them in any fashion, and carried them, in season, to eat along the interminable roads from one institute to another.)

At Chapel Hill, where he took university men sharply to task for failing to teach a spirit of universal education and declared they could not have more boys there until more were educated in lower schools, he had a weekend with the Winstons. Thus, from being almost sorry he was alive most of the week, he switched abruptly to "the simple, substantial, palatable food of Mrs. Winston's delightful table," and went on shortly after that to Henderson, arriving in time for a breakfast of strawberries, oatmeal, steak, fish, and large baked Irish potatoes. After which he added, rather unnecessarily, "I am sick with indigestion."

A saving sense of humor took the sting out of his accounts of some of the worst hardship, as in the case of a Bayboro "hotel" where the window panes were largely missing. When the wind blew out, during the night, the socks and underwear he had crammed into the openings, he was reminded of the little boy who could not recognize the word glass and the teacher told him "it is what you put in windows." Then the lad brightened up and said: "G-l-a-s-s, daddy's old britches."

Sometimes humor was not sufficient, and disgust spilled over in his letters to Mrs. McIver. "And such a place as I am stopping at," he wrote from Lillington. "I think the landlady is a widow and snuff stains ornament her mouth in wreaths. Winton coffee, no milk, messed eggs, sick-chicken, dingy grease, evergreen collards, aged butter and a spoilt child made up the bill of fare for dinner."

Nothing, of course, was withheld from Mrs. McIver, either of triumph or despair. He might tell of "extravagant praise," as at Winton, where the county superintendent got "carried away completely and overdid the compliments" until it was embarrassing. Or he might state, with equal candor, "I have never had so dead a failure as here." He included stories he enjoyed, and at least one, told by a woman at a hotel luncheon table, he could have done without. It concerned the ubiquitous Zebulon Vance. Vance, prone upon the deck with a fearful case of seasickness and incapable of lifting his head, was blocking the path of some women. "Step right over, ladies," he told them. "If I see so much as an ankle I'll never live to tell it." The story was not new, but

McIver, who remained thoroughly conventional in his social attitudes in spite of his insistence on an improved status for women, was disconcerted by the fact that a lady told it in public.

Those letters home continued to be love letters in a very real sense, even when sentiment appeared in whimsical dress: "I'm glad you still think I'm the best and smartest man in the world," he wrote Mrs. McIver from Albemarle. "I think you are too." And sometimes there crept into his daily communications the physical hunger of a virile man too much absent from his mate.

In addition, there was humanity in his letters—a humanity so overflowing that Alderman's biographer, Dr. Dumas Malone, found that McIver was reputedly the "most beloved of the educational leaders of his generation in North Carolina." It took the form of thoughtfulness of others. Without consulting his institute partner, for instance, he suggested to Major Finger that his colleague be given assignments near Chapel Hill, so that Alderman could be near his wife and child. It showed in his quick sympathy with any person making a brave struggle, one of whom was a child in a Clarkton church: "I went to Sunday school at 10 o'clock. It was an old regulation Presbyterian Sunday school. Doing good, but could do more with a few changes. Solemn, I tell you! I could catch a shorter catechism phrase now and then from those who sat near me, and when I heard a little ten or twelve-year-old boy answer the question 'What is God?' I thought of a little mule pulling a heavy load up a steep hill, and stopping now and then to blow. It was hard work."

The hardships were rare in which he could not find extenuating circumstances. At Smithfield, from which he wrote "I am uncomfortably situated in a hotel run by a dirty, old cunning looking man, who also runs a saloon nearby," the redeeming feature was that Billy Noble, at Selma that week, "runs over every day and enlivens me." At Troy, where he drew a devastating picture of a backwoods community, he had the company of his brother Will, partner in a law firm there, although how Will stood it, he could not see.

He stayed at Will's hotel, the proprietor of which was a "big fat dirty man" who looked like the "very commonest field hand" with "a half square foot of naked stomach to be seen through a hole in his dirty shirt." The business men, of whom he expected better, went without coat or vest. The one gallus fellow was plentiful, and so were the flies. But he was most distressed about the cook. "The cook is, or rather was, a white man and looks like the proprietor's twin brother except he has only one gallus and is dirtier and smells bad and wears a greasy apron and has a snuff toothbrush in his mouth when he waits on the table. I can hardly eat enough to keep alive."

There was a good courthouse, however, sitting in its own square at the top of Main Street. It did not house the jail, as its successor would, but there was a jail nearby with comfortable quarters for the jailor, ample cells for the male offenders, and even a few on a separate corridor (usually empty) for female law-breakers. There was little to suggest that Troy would shortly become, under the educational spurs of McIver and Alderman (and later Aycock), a trim, well-paved modern town with a school-proud population.

Actually, Montgomery's county seat was typical of its numerous counterparts throughout the state: "One-horse" villages with a good courthouse commanding a main street that was a series of mud holes in rainy weather, a grove near at hand where horse traders gathered when court was in session, a jail that was a better structure than the school, not to mention a density of popular ignorance that McIver found most discouraging—the kind "which blindly imagines its worst enemies to be its best friends." McIver thundered at all inhabitants of such county seats: "Education is one of the functions of the State, and it is a shame upon all of us that our school houses are not as good as our jail houses and in many cases the investment in our universities is not equal to that in our penitentiaries."

By year's end the pace had begun to tell, as he admitted in a letter to Joyner the middle of December. "I want to go on a visit to my father's Christmas. I need rest, too. I have done the hardest work since July that I've ever done or seen done by anybody. I leave at six in the morning for Louisburg where I will hold my

20th institute. After this week Alderman and I will take a good vacation."

He denied being discouraged—in a letter from Louisburg to Major Finger—but he did go on to say that he believed the fight in North Carolina would be harder and longer than he had once supposed, that it would require the courage and life of a martyr to stem the opposition, that "whoever does much in this cause must look for recompense within himself." He had resolved, too, that such a man "must be capable of pursuing the even tenor of his way, without swerving, without pausing, and without stepping from his path to notice the angry outcries which he cannot help but hear and which he is more than human if he does not long to rebuke." That was one resolve Charles McIver kept. No matter how much he was urged to refute slanderous rumors, he consistently ignored the clamor from friends and traducers alike. If the tenor of his way was not even it was undeviating to the point that any turning aside at all had the appearance of offering the other cheek.

His first full calendar year as institute conductor, 1890, got off to a good start at Warrenton, where interest reached such a surprising pitch that six hundred people jammed the courthouse and many had to remain on the outside for lack of room. Also Manifest Destiny reared its head again. A Mr. S. H. Chester wrote from Franklin, Tennessee, that a fortune could be made in a girls' school there. "We are trying to get on foot here a Presbyterian Female College," he stated in a letter dated January 29. "I write to enquire whether you can be induced to take hold for us—with proper inducements and guarantees for the first year."

But McIver had even then the singleness of purpose that was a major factor in his success. He believed and taught that "The man who seeks one thing in life and but one, may hope to achieve it before life is done." The alternative, the seeking of many things wherever one goes, the quotation continued, would result in a harvest of barren regrets. It was a college for North Carolina girls that he wanted, and in order to get it he was prepared to plow a straight furrow.

Then, still early in the new year, the institute situation began to deteriorate, particularly in regard to comfort. For example, at Jackson he was placed in a room with no carpet, no bureau, one window, a hard knotty bed, one little hanging looking glass, and a crack in the floor about an inch wide that ran from one wall to the other. To make matters worse, the waiting boy considered his cleaning duties done when he had emptied the chamber pot out the window.

It also gave the conductor a sense of frustration, but not for long, to learn that a minister was inveighing against public education. "Went to hear the Episcopal preacher," he reported to Mrs. McIver. "After seeing him and hearing him I don't care what he says against public education. A mighty mellow sham he is. Looks like a cross between a marshmallow and a mushroom."

He moved on to Plymouth, which was "no Eden," and then to Columbia, "by far the worst place" he had seen up until that time. "The courthouse is filthy," he wrote, "and there has been no attempt yet to sweep it out." He took one look at that courthouse, as he did many another like it in which he had to " 'wrastle' with quids of tobacco" and, pleading always the cause of women, startled the populace with the stinging pronouncement: "Men have had the exclusive management of courthouses and largely the management of schoolhouses, and upon both the marks of masculinity and neglect are plainly visible."

Outspoken at all times, McIver made good copy. And he had a friendly press. "I have been delighted," Joyner wrote him, "to see the complimentary reports of your work that have appeared in the papers." County superintendents of public instruction frequently expressed the identical sentiment in almost the identical words.

Truly, many editors were outdoing themselves. McIver's speeches were described as "a splendid and powerful presentation of his cause and a complete refutation of the arguments against it"; as "replete with logic and good-natured satire, and marked by that true eloquence which is born of deep conviction"; as "earnest and masterly appeals for the diffusion of intelligence."

He himself was described as "an apt and ready speaker," "a sound and logical reasoner," "an earnest advocate of the cause in which he is laboring." One paper after another noted that citizens of each town turned out in larger numbers as an institute progressed and concluded, along with the Henderson *Gold Leaf*: "He has aroused interest on the subject of education and the true character and value of the public school as never before. He has placed the public school in its proper light before the community, and made its friends and supporters men who have heretofore been careless and indifferent on the subject."

If necessary, McIver could be his own best press agent. Upon arriving at one town, he expressed concern in his daily letter to Mrs. McIver that the institute had not been "well advertised." But there was a succinct postscript to that latter: "Have been to prayer meeting. The institute is advertised now." Nor did he leave the power of the press entirely to the good impulses of editors who praised his results editorially while omitting particulars of his thesis. He sent the papers communications of his own from time to time. One was a mildly sarcastic piece in which he purported to agree with the school teacher who said "Tain't women's hemisphere to be educated nohow. It's us men's hemisphere." He was complacent concerning the discriminations which he enumerated against white girls, although admitting a twinge of conscience now and then as he saw all the other young people— white and colored boys and colored girls—going off to schools provided by church or state or philanthropy. The impact of the piece was cumulative as well as deceptive. His delineation of the shabby treatment of white girls made a telling impression before it was concluded. The expert in personal relations was becoming something of an expert in public relations, too.

The Teachers' Assembly in June rounded out a twelve-month period otherwise devoted to institutes. McIver made a speech on the training school which his friends said was the speech of his life. He was sandwiched as a speaker between Major Finger and Dr. Curry, no mean purveyors of the spoken word, and Billy Noble loyally maintained he "laid out both of them." The Assembly chose McIver as its president without a dissenting vote.

At that point also, the institute conductors took a backward look at the first year of their program and Superintendent Finger incorporated their findings in his biennial report. Institutes had been held in 84 counties, 60 of them conducted by McIver and Alderman, who had traveled well over 6,000 miles, instructed around 3,000 teachers, and made public addresses before an estimated 25,000 to 30,000 persons. In places where school terms were shortest, school taxes had not been levied to the constitutional limit. Poor pay and short terms were largely responsible for the poor quality of teaching. Both McIver and Alderman were agreed that the teaching force was incompetent, but McIver, noting that teachers were aware of their shortcomings, was kinder in his judgment than Alderman, who privately described the majority of them to his friend as "prodigiously stupid." McIver regarded them as superior to the people who hired them and discovered a few women teachers as thoroughly competent as any to be found anywhere.

Indeed, the entire institute group had a good word to say for the ladies. "Our teachers do not read much," Alderman reported. "They teach an art which they do not practice. Of course, notable exceptions exist, generally among the women." Joyner observed: "On the whole, the ladies surpassed the male teachers in intelligence."

Both full-time conductors made a strong plea for a training school to benefit the ladies.

Their report for the next biennium would find McIver and Alderman still in agreement, especially in regard to a couple of changes that were remarkable for so short a time.

First, in returning to places where they had previously held institutes, they found there had been a swift flowering of the seeds they had planted. There was a kindlier, more rational attitude toward public education, a flourishing sentiment in favor of schools that amounted to a deep-stirring grassroots impulse toward popular education.

Of equal importance, they reported after two additional years a professional pride among teachers, an esprit de corps, that had not existed when the institutes began three years earlier. The contagion of their opinions had infused the teachers not only with respect for the job, but with a self-respect that could record their place on the census rolls without apology from any mother. And if McIver and Alderman had accomplished nothing else in their three institute years, that achievement alone would have made their work epochal. They rescued the teacher from some nameless limbo between the quick and the dead.

~~~~~~

Ignorance is ignorant even of its own friends. It is the blind
Samson that destroys the temple, self and all.
—*Charles Duncan McIver*

~~~~~~

10-

Dream and Substance

IMMEDIATELY FOLLOWING the Teachers' Assembly at Morehead
City, McIver returned to the institute grind. July marked the beginning of a second institute year, and the first week of that
month found him working in wilting heat at Greensboro. He
complained to Mrs. McIver that he did not know how he was
going to get through the summer, since it took just two hours to
ruin shirt, collars, and cuffs. And tie. McIver habitually wore
white lawn bow ties that were becoming something of a trademark—"preacher ties" the Negroes called them—and they would
survive only a few launderings. But his supply stayed ample.
Mrs. McIver saw to that.

She accompanied him part of that summer, or, if feasible,
preceded him to the next institute town and astonished the county
seat by organizing a broom and pail brigade to clean the courthouse. Townspeople watched in disbelief as cartloads of debris
issued from the cleaning sprees, and courthouse corridors hardly
looked the same at all with tobacco juice missing between the
inevitable benches and the inevitable spittoons. Numerous letters
attested the satisfaction her work gave or expressed pleasure that
she would return.

The institutes continued their erratic course, from resounding
success to disheartening frustration. In reporting one of the more
pronounced failures to Major Finger, McIver stated "This is a bad
place. In fact, it is almost 'the bad place.' " The reason for his
opinion appeared in a wry summary of the situation: Attendance
of teachers thirteen (unlucky number); attendance from town,

zero; school too short to count; and the poor turned out to grass. Wire grass, at that.

Other institutes snowballed from an infinitesimal beginning to a gratifying climax as the Washington, North Carolina, *Gazette* noted in a racy editorial entitled "Are you an Idiot?" "If you are," the comment went on, "you will not be interested in the free lectures of Prof. McIver. . . . Prof. McIver is a genius. He is entertaining. Why, at one point he opened with an attendance of five. The last evening eight hundred attended. The truth is, the professor grows on you. Go once and you will go again."

Autumn brought one change from the previous year. Charlotte became "home" as Mrs. McIver, whose quiet competence was increasing her own reputation, moved to that city as Lady Principal of Charlotte Female Institute. As she had found time at Raleigh to become enthusiastic about sketching and painting, along with teaching at Peace and caring for two small children, so at Charlotte she turned with great avidity to her unfulfilled first love, medicine. No medical course was available even then, but she did have lessons with the state's first practicing woman physician, Dr. Annie Laurie Alexander. The children, when they grew older, liked to tease their mother about her enthusiasm for doctoring. She stalked them with a thermometer, they told her. She was never happier, they accused laughingly, than when they were sick!

It was a pity, in a way, that her opportunity could not have been greater, or her interest less. She gave her absent husband some unnecessarily bad moments with accounts of temperatures and stomach upsets and mustard pastes. Before a follow-up letter indicated that all was well again, he would rush off a reply in genuine fright, urging that she telegraph if the sick child got worse so that he could return home.

Education, however, continued the main topic of conversation when McIver was at home, and little Charlie, as Annie had done, showed symptoms of catching the educational mania that obsessed both his father and mother. Rising first, in the manner of children, he would bring in the Sunday paper, and Zeke or his parents would find him ensconced imitatively in his father's easy chair with the printed sheets in front of him. Although he was too small to know one letter from the other, he would be "reading" the news. "Education," he would murmur as he turned the pages. "Education, education, education."

And education was looking up. The Teachers' Assembly which made McIver president had appointed him once again as chairman of its committee to petition the Legislature for a teacher training school, and other forces were gathering in support of the project. The powerful Farmers' Alliance had endorsed the proposed school at its June meeting. The King's Daughters were petitioning for an industrial school for girls. It was getting almost fashionable, McIver remarked in a sardonic aside to Major Finger, to be in favor of public education.

For once it was his pleasure to swim with the tide, and the institution, for which one could begin to hope a little, like a pillar of cloud by day and a pillar of fire by night, directed his course. It took him far afield of the actual institute itinerary. He increasingly accepted invitations to speak at colleges, especially church schools—Trinity College (Methodist), Chowan Institute and Wake Forest College (Baptist), Guilford College (Quaker)— since denominational leaders must not misunderstand the aims of a state-supported college for women. There were times, he admitted to Mrs. McIver, when he found his mental joints as stiff as his travel-weary physical joints and had to lash himself into an appearance of life. But it was no time to let up. The Legislature was going to be asked for many unusual appropriations: among them $25,000 for the new (1889) Agricultural and Mechanical College at Raleigh, nearly as much for the industrial school being urged by the King's Daughters, and special sums to university, penitentiary, insane asylum, and nobody knew what else.

Toward the end of November, 1890, that invincible team of McIver and Alderman got together at Goldsboro to plot their strategy. On the thirtieth McIver wrote his wife: "We think it best to present our last year's bill for Training School or Normal College except that we will make it for women only and ask for $3,000 more. We have both worn ourselves down more than we have realized by this institute work and I don't think we could

Charles D. McIver and Edwin A. Alderman while they were serving as Institute conductors

A group of teachers at one of the county Institutes. Professor McIver is third from the left on the second row

Main (Administration) Building and Brick Dormitory, which comprised the Normal and Industrial School at its opening

Library of the Woman's College of the University of North Carolina

stand it much longer. I know Alderman looks five years older than when we began this work." The new institution, as projected, would supersede the existing program of local short-term teacher training. It would get the $4,000 then spent annually on the institute conductors' salaries, plus $10,000 a year from the general school fund.

Dr. J. L. M. Curry was scheduled to address the General Assembly in favor of the Training School on January 21, 1891—and a powerful and earnest plea it turned out to be from a man with the promise of substantial Peabody support to bolster his argument. Major Finger wanted McIver and Alderman there to back up the Peabody agent with some words of their own. "I expect you to have the bill for the training school prepared," he wrote McIver.

The institute instructors got to Raleigh ahead of the appointed time, and the three men, McIver and Alderman and Finger, did the preparing. The bill called for a normal school with industrial features—a school with the general purpose of giving "such education as will add to the efficiency of woman's work in whatever walk of life her lot may be cast." Five days before the scheduled Curry address, McIver wrote Mrs. McIver, "Major Finger, Alderman and I will present our question to the Committee Monday night and will invite every one who desires to be present. I am hopeful that our bill will pass."

The day after Dr. Curry's speech, it did pass the Senate. McIver wrote he had a sore throat, adding "Alderman is worn out and his folks are sick at home," but the bill had taken its first hurdle. Tension mounted unbearably for the next few days. As the votes were counted, McIver wired his wife the news, which continued to be good, and then there was a letter, hurried and terse but triumphant, saying "We will win. I can't write. The excitement is too great. The galleries are full. It will still take two days to pass the bill. It will pass second reading tomorrow, the 3rd next day."

On February 18, 1891, the once insubstantial dream was clothed in the substance of legislative approval. The North Carolina General Assembly passed a bill authorizing an institution to be known as the Normal and Industrial School. McIver wanted to call the school simply by the dignified name, Woman's College, but political expediency dictated a different choice. It was necessary to avoid any suggestion of giving women a classical education. McIver's plea for enlightened motherhood as the greatest social need had been enormously effective, but support of the practical politician went to that part of his argument which pointed up the necessity for more teachers. And Charles McIver was on his way to becoming the best politician of the lot.

The State Normal and Industrial School was established, therefore, "(1) To give young women such education as shall fit them for teaching; (2) to give instruction to young women in drawing, telegraphy, typewriting, stenography and other such industrial arts as may be suitable to their sex and conducive to their support and usefulness." Tuition should be free to those who would pledge themselves to teach. Board should be furnished at actual cost, not to exceed eight dollars a month. The institution was to be located at some suitable place where the citizens would furnish the necessary buildings, or money sufficient to erect them.

And what a scramble that final proviso set off. From a project that nobody wanted, this unbuilt school, with a name that made it sound more like a reform school for wayward girls than an institution of higher learning, became a school that everybody wanted. Finally, five towns moved out front in the bidding. Morganton offered a hundred-acre farm and $5,000 in cash and McIver thought at first the institution would go there. Thomasville offered buildings formerly used as a college. Graham offered $20,000. McIver preferred the $20,000, not knowing of any building in the state suited for the school. Durham raised Graham's ante by offering $20,000 plus a site, and Alderman wanted the school to go there. Greensboro became a strong contender in the bizarre state-wide poker game in which the winner would pocket a strange stake—a chance to build a school for females.

As soon as the legislative smoke had cleared North Carolina editors set out to appraise the work of the 1891 "Farmers' Alliance Legislature" (more than half of whose members had been farmers) and expressed themselves as being "Upon the whole, very well pleased with its record." The majority also agreed with the *Mecklenburg Times,* in which Editor Jerome Dowd declared in his lead editorial: "We regard the act to establish a Normal and Industrial School for Women as the most praiseworthy of all things done by the Legislature. . . . The establishment of this school is sufficient to cause this Legislature to be held in grateful remembrance."

Proceeding about the state on his institute duties, McIver depended on letters and newspaper accounts to keep abreast of what was happening. He saw March 4 in a newspaper at New Bern a list of Normal and Industrial School trustees, one from each Congressional district: W. B. Shaw, R. H. Stancill, B. F. Aycock, E. McK. Goodwin, H. G. Chatham, M. C. S. Noble, A. C. McAlister, Dr. J. M. Spainhour, and R. D. Gilmer. State Superintendent Finger was ex-officio chairman. McIver knew all of the trustees except Spainhour, and presently had a note from Winston at Chapel Hill containing reassurance that it was a very good board. Winston also declared "I do not consider that there is any doubt at all of your election to the Presidency of the Woman's College."

While the Normal and Industrial School presidency was unsettled, Winston also declared he believed "it wouldn't take much to make the board elect" McIver president of the University. But that matter was not pursued until some years later, and it was Winston himself who was inaugurated in the autumn as president of the University to succeed Dr. Battle, with the scholarly Walter Hines Page making the inaugural address.

McIver sent Winston's letter to his wife, although in none of his daily letters home that spring did he directly mention the possibility that he would head the new school. There was tacit understanding, however, that discontinuance of the institutes would represent a more stable way of life for them. In a letter from New Bern he expressed regret that he had not been able to provide a home for her and had hardly been able to furnish the money "absolutely necessary to live on," but added: "The fact is when we do get a home and a competency you will have done at least as much to earn it as I have. It will not be mine to give, but ours to share. I think I see more clearly than ever how galling dependence must be to a sensible woman."

A letter from Major Finger substantiated the conclusion that the new school would have a place for McIver. In an off-the-record general discussion, the major wrote, "it was abundantly developed that every member of the Board desires both you and Alderman to be connected with the institution."

While McIver could accept the assurance of a job at the new school, he could not share Winston's—and the public's—certainty of the capacity. Alderman, too, was in the running. He, too, had made a splendid state-wide impression as an institute conductor, and had friends every bit as loyal as did McIver, among them Charles Aycock. Aycock was a friend to both, but he had been chairman of the school board in Goldsboro when Alderman was the town's superintendent of schools and their association had been both recent and close. He told Josephus Daniels who told McIver that he would find it difficult not to support Alderman if Alderman were a candidate for the presidency. Aycock added he was going to try to persuade him not to be a candidate.

Aycock did not have to persuade him. While both McIver and Alderman acknowledged the probability that one of them would be chosen, neither wished to be considered the other's opponent. On June 11, a card from Alderman to McIver stated: "I shall be content with whatever happens in Raleigh as regards headship. If you are to be the man I shall serve you sympathetically as far as I have the power in the field of my word. Institutions are greater than men."

While the issue was unresolved McIver made much the same statement in a letter to Superintendent Finger: "My dear Major: I had a full and free talk with Alderman as to the Presidency of the Normal and Industrial School. He feels as I do about the matter. Neither of us could afford to be candidates. And the selection of either would be no reflection on the other. He would accept a position under my management as I should not hesitate to do under his, if the Board saw fit to elect him, and should offer me an agreeable line of work. What we want is that no personal relations of friendship should affect the choice. That only the highest interests of the Institution should be considered."

But before they got a head for the school the trustees had to find a place to put the school itself. On June 9, Major Finger reported to McIver: "The Board did not make a selection on yesterday but proceeded in a body to visit Durham, Graham, Thomasville, and Greensboro. I say to you confidentially that I think the Board is very much inclined to Greensboro if we can get a sufficiently good proposition."

Greensboro, topping Durham's offer of a site and $20,000, tossed in a bid of a site and $25,000. Durham matched it. Greensboro raised. The final Greensboro offer of $30,000 was accepted unanimously, and the town set its steam whistles to tooting and its bells to ringing in jubilation. Just in case the city should fail to authorize the necessary bonds, a group of enthusiastic citizens signed notes guaranteeing the sum. Nobody had to pay his subscription. The bond vote was unanimous. The location annoyed Alderman, but Durham took its defeat with consummate good grace. "Greensboro was a winner sure enough," Durham's *Weekly Globe* remarked chattily. "She had the boodle and she got the school. Greensboro will please shake."

The eighth annual session of the North Carolina Teachers' Assembly was held in the Assembly's building at Morehead City from June 16 to 30, and McIver as the organization's head was there when he received word of the Board's action in regard to the Normal School presidency. The letter was postmarked Raleigh, dated June 13:

"Dear Sir: At a meeting of the Board of Directors of the Normal and Industrial School, held in Greensboro, you were unanimously elected President of the said Institution, at a salary of 2250 dollars a year. In addition to your duties as President of the Normal and Industrial School, you are required to conduct Normal Institutes during vacation of the School. Salary to begin when school formally opens. Hoping that you will accept the Presidency, I am, dear Sir, Yours truly, E. McK. Goodwin, Sect'y to the Board. By Order of the Board."

Among the congratulatory notes that poured in were two of special significance, offering assistance, as they did, from trustworthy sources. Moreover, both of the writers were in a position to implement their offers: Noble, on the Board, and Alderman, on the faculty.

"My dear Mac": Noble wrote, "I don't know better how to congratulate you than to call attention to the fact that I shall be solid in my support of your administration. I am sure that before long you will be at the head of the leading Educational institution in the State if not in the South. Yours forever, Billy."

"I congratulate you most heartily, my friend," Alderman wrote, "upon your elevation to the headship of the new Institution for which we both have worked quite disinterestedly in the past. You won the place both by your ardent zeal in agitation and by your eminent fitness for the work in hand and I may add by your long experience in the education of women. Your selection will give universal gratification. The Institution is an educational experiment in N. C. It must win its way into popular regard. I want you to know that as I have worked for it in the past so I will work for it in the future and that in all your efforts for its growth and expansion you will find in me, as far as I have power, a helpful, sympathetic and loyal counsellor and friend."

On June 16, using a letterhead of the State Board of Education, Department of Institute Instruction, McIver sent his reply to Mr. Goodwin:

"Dear Sir: Your letter of the 13th instant notifying me of my election to the presidency of the Normal and Industrial School has just reached me. I should like for your Board to know that, in accepting the position tendered me, I am keenly sensible of the honor and the responsibility attaching to it, and that I shall enter upon the discharge of my duties with a determination to do all in my power to promote the success of the Institution. I wish to express my gratification at the action of the Board in selecting Mr. Alderman for the professorship of History and English, for which position he is so eminently qualified. I accept the position with the understanding that it will be my duty to hold Educational Institutes during a part of every vacation."

Success of the Assembly's eight-year effort to obtain a training school gave a jubilant undertone to the teachers' meeting, and President McIver's address, closing with a ringing peroration on ignorance, provided an opportunity to give vent to their satisfaction in thunderous and prolonged applause:

"We are fond of quoting 'Knowledge is power', but I fear we are inclined to forget the tremendous and perilous power of ignorance. I use the word in a broader sense than illiteracy. It is not a power to save or to make alive, but it is a power to damn and to destroy. Ignorance is ignorant even of its own friends. It is the blind Samson that destroys the temple, self and all. It is the wild furor of the multitude crying of its best friend, 'Crucify him! Crucify him! Give us Barabbas.' It is often most dangerous when combined with the highest moral virtues. Give to it sincerity and courage and they only add to the stubborn violence and terrible destructiveness. It has destroyed its best friends and called it self-preservation; persecuted and tortured in the name of the Prince of Peace; enslaved in the name of freedom; killed its best prophets in the name of progress. It makes the Hindoo mother throw her innocent babe to the crocodiles as the very climax of religious virtue. It has sent to the stake many of the purest men this world has ever seen and nailed to the cross its only perfect model. It is a sort of delirium that suspects friends and trusts enemies, that always sees danger where there is none and never sees it where it is. It is blind as night, and thinks itself omniscient. If angels ever weep, it must often be over the works of honest ignorance."

McIver left Morehead City to plunge into the most hectic period of his crowded life. He continued with the institutes, a killing job in itself. At the same time he had to be concerned with all the inner and outer workings of a school in process of being established, with site and architects' plans and equipment, with course of study and textbooks and prospectus. He began at once to engage his teachers. He was in Greensboro as often as institutes permitted, working in quarters in the Benbow Hotel. He was in Raleigh. He was everywhere. Suggestions were in good supply, but final choices, as in the case of textbooks, were largely his own. Noble, as chairman of the textbook committee, gave him "full swing."

In securing teachers he applied the same rule he had drummed into the public: Only the best is good enough to use. He could not always get the ones he wanted. There were teachers in established colleges who declined, with thanks for the honor, his offer to work in an untried school only just wrested from a long reluctant state. In seeking a staff for the industrial arts department he asked Alexander Sprunt & Son, cotton exporters of Wilmington, to release a young woman from their employ to teach at the college. Otherwise, he argued, he would have to leave the state to obtain somebody, or take a man, and he would regret not employing a woman. "She is more necessary to us than to you, and as the success of our enterprise means so much to the women of the state," he was hopeful, he wrote, that the company would release her to fill the chair of Stenography, Typewriting, and Telegraphy. The Sprunts, père et fils, did not take kindly to the idea. They were beginning to discover, with whatever surprise it may have occasioned the early male employers, that a competent woman secretary was an office necessity. They replied tartly that they would leave the matter up to Miss Jenkins. Finally, she declined the teaching post.

The site was not actually chosen until October, when Greensboro's enthusiasm had turned to impatience and its citizens were asking if the Board wanted the earth with a white-washed fence around it, or demanding with unveiled sarcasm if the courthouse square would do. Epps and Hackett, architects, had the plans drawn, and the Board was about to buy a tract held at $5,000 for which they hoped Greensboro would raise the money, when McIver approved a ten-acre site on the edge of town that R. S. Pullen and R. T. Gray, two Raleigh gentlemen, had offered as a gift.

As McIver conducted institutes in various parts of the state, his enthusiasm for the new school proved contagious to parents and young women alike. Mothers resolved, after hearing the plans, that their daughters must somehow go. It was astonishing that they could get so much for so little cost. One girl took quite seriously President-elect McIver's remark, "When the door opens we expect you to be there," and was almost literally on the spot when it did open. (Her name, Mary Vail, was the first on the college register, her check the first recorded in the treasurer's books.) He told the family of Fodie Buie, of Red Springs, that in each county one girl, chosen by competitive examination, would receive a scholarship, and her father promised to sell a small farm, if she won, to raise the eighty-eight dollars Mr. McIver estimated would cover the rest of her expenses. She competed with thirty-five other girls, tied with one of them; whereupon the president assigned her the scholarship from a county that had no applicant.

Her father was as good as his word. He sold the farm, and after setting aside the required amount for school, she used the remainder to outfit herself for attending. She bought, on a shopping spree in Fayetteville, a trunk, goods to make two skirts, three shirtwaists, and a wool petticoat, black cotton stockings, a pair of shoes, and a hat. When the new trunk was packed with all her finery, plus the required two woollen blankets, sheets, pillow cases, and pillow, it was sent to the train in a mulecart.

Fodie, however, did not get away from home without incident. One day as she was going into the postoffice a neighbor, sitting on a box outside, stopped her and said: "'I don't approve of your going to college. I don't see why I should pay taxes to educate Dunk Buie's gal. The state ought not to help. The women's got no call to go to college nohow. All you gals will come back from there a pack of infidels and the whole world will go to the dogs." The statement had the ring of two strident voices, that of the disgruntled taxpayer and that of the supporter of education under church auspices only, which would continue to be heard. And the latter especially would swell to a brassy clamor.

By early April of the year school was to open, 1892, McIver had fairly well determined on a course of study that would consist of Mathematics, Natural Sciences, Ancient Languages, Modern Languages, Vocal Music, Physical Culture, Freehand and Industrial Drawing, Stenography, Typewriting, Telegraphy, Bookkeeping, and Domestic Science, including cooking.

No course of study, and well he knew it, could satisfy all the dissident elements. There were mothers—women whose lives had been circumscribed by just such activities—who did not wish their daughters to study cooking and sewing. Not in college! There were fathers, not altogether persuaded that it made sense to educate girls, who wanted them to study little else. One such parent wrote his daughter: "To prepare yourself to become a good well informed woman, fitted to make a good practacal [*sic*] man a good wife is what I desire. And I do and shall always oppose you preparing yourself to do work only suited to men. Ladies should be housewives pure and simple, and not go to make up the equipment for a lawyer's or merchant's office or counting room."

Pure and simple! How much that said! All of the men wanted their women pure. Many wanted them (or appeared to want them) simple.

Yet the commercial department thus indirectly maligned was precious to McIver, who saw it as one more path leading away from the galling dependence of women. And the Domestic Science stayed, too, although girls who had been sewing since they started on patchwork squares for quilts at the age of five and who already knew how to cook might agree with their mothers that it was a waste of time.

Nevertheless, McIver knew that the politician must be appeased along with the unreconstructed father. And his wisdom in including domestic science was manifest not long after the school opened. A politician, justifying his support of the college, declared (as if two functions only were the end-all and be-all of a woman's existence) that he understood the "ultimate object of the school was to teach a young woman how to stuff a chicken as well as the head of a dull boy."

Noble, who realized that it was "going to be a hard thing to get a first rate prospectus," raised a question about some of the omissions. "How about your instrumental music?" he wrote McIver. "Also your painting? Or maybe you thought best to omit for the present. It might be well to offer instrumental music for the first session if we are to compete with all kinds of schools and offer girls as good instruction with us as they could get else-where."

J. A. McAllister, of Lumberton, was also worried about the absence of instrumental music, but even more so about the impression that the school was for girls who could afford no other: "I have found, among some, the idea that it is a sort of cheap school for poor folks and that probably only those from the lower walks of life will avail themselves of its privileges."

Noble, even as the Lumberton school man, wanted to attract the daughters of wealthy families and went on to say further that it would be a serious blow to give the idea that the school was only for those who contemplated teaching. Advice from Trustee A. C. McAlister, of Asheboro, was concerned chiefly with the girl of good social standing. He wished it said that the "girls will be under the control of the President and will have the immediate oversight of a governess of good administrative ability and *high social* position. We can procure the services of such a lady and should be content with no other." (They could and did get a Lady Principal whose presence was a drawing card for the socially well-placed, but were less successful in combating the notion that the institution was primarily for the training of teachers. The idea persisted for years.)

By July the prospectus was ready to go, and McIver took time out to head a delegation of five hundred North State educators to a meeting of the Southern Educational Association in Atlanta, which he addressed on the subject of Industrial Education for Women. Upon his return an institute session took him to Raleigh. He sent a hurry-up call for Mrs. McIver to come to the capital and help with the selection of tableware and furnishings for the new institution, and he himself began coping with responses to the college circular.

On a hot July day he walked into Major Finger's office with a palm leaf fan (practically a part of his summer costume) in one hand and a sheaf of applications in the other and asked the loan of the state superintendent's shorthand writer. Thus E. J. Forney began an association with the college in its formative stage that would not be broken until his retirement. President McIver happily found in the young secretary someone to whom he could trust the institution's fiscal affairs and the administration of its commercial department.

Events were picking up speed as opening time drew near. In early August the Greensboro *Record* was proclaiming that the Main Building at the college, nearly completed, was the finest in the city. A dormitory was also going forward with dispatch, but it could house far too few of the two hundred girls and more who had already applied for admission. The Board of Trustees had considered it necessary, therefore, to build an additional small dormitory, together with a house for President McIver. Even with the extra accommodations, plus rooms available in private homes, the president had the unpleasant task of turning down more applicants than he could accept.

Major Finger wrote McIver that his house would be ready by September 10, in ample time for a mid-September opening, and that the other buildings were nearing completion as well, but he was too optimistic. Heating equipment did not arrive on schedule and the opening had to be postponed until October 5.

On the eve of opening day, everything was ready, or ready enough. The president's house was unfinished, but habitable, not only for his family but for five of the teachers who could not find other rooms sufficiently near the school. There were carpenter's shavings in some of the dormitory rooms but the girls could sweep them out. The faculty was assembled; that was the main consideration.

It was a faculty of very high caliber indeed. In spite of the low salaries he had to offer, McIver had secured graduates of some of the best colleges extant. The state's own excellent University was represented both by the president, who was professor of the Science, Art, and History of Teaching, and Mr. Alderman.

Other members of the faculty were Miss Gertrude W. Mendenhall, B.S., Wellesley College, who had six years' teaching experience, three at Peace Institute, three at Guilford College (Mathematics and German); Miss Dixie Lee Bryant, B.S., Massachusetts Institute of Technology, who came to the college from the chair of science at the State Normal College of New Hampshire (Natural Sciences); Miss Miriam Bitting, M.D., Woman's Medical College, Philadelphia (Physiology, Hygiene, Physical Culture, also general overseer of the students' health); Miss Melville Fort, a graduate with honors of the Mississippi Industrial Institute and College (Industrial Art); Miss Edith McIntyre, New York College for the Training of Teachers (Domestic Science); Miss Viola Boddie, L.I., Peabody Normal College (Latin and French); Clarence R. Brown (Vocal Culture); E. J. Forney and Mrs. Fannie Bell Cox (Bookkeeping, Stenography, Typewriting, and Telegraphy). Miss Sue May Kirkland was Lady Principal and "referee in matters social and domestic." Mrs. W. P. Carroway was housekeeper. Shortly they would be joined by Ezekiel Robinson, President McIver's faithful Zeke, who would serve as general factotum extraordinary, as janitorial lighter of fires and polisher of lamps, as driver of the college surrey, as mail carrier, as presidential coachman and porter and valet.

There was also a member of that competent staff who was an official without portfolio or pay, an assistant president in countless ways. Mrs. McIver was her husband's good right hand—the reliable aide who could reply to letters, answer questions, interview parents and students, take up the slack when the press of accumulated demands became too much for the president to handle alone. North Carolina had quite a team in the McIvers. And their hour was at hand to launch a momentous enterprise.

The raw new college was not, in all truth, a very prepossessing sight. The chief buildings (Main and Brick Dormitory) were red and squat and surrounded by the uncleared debris of building materials. The campus was ten acres of red mud that had once been a cornfield and not all of the dried and forlorn stalks had been removed. The one tree it boasted was a spindly pine.

But the miracle was that the school should exist at all. Its foundation was laid in the metamorphosis of a Public Opinion that had shaded in the beginning from indifference to hostility. The mortar that held its buildings together was mixed with the figurative dust of illiteracy, inertia, and insolvency. Moreover, each forward step thus represented had been paced by the president himself.

On the day preceding formal opening of the State Normal and Industrial School, Charles McIver, age 32, looked at his work and found it good.

11–

All Things Wise and Wonderful

ALL ROADS led to Greensboro—and the State Normal and Industrial School—for North Carolina's ambitious young women on the morning of October 5, 1892. The girls boarded trains in every part of the state: trains that puffed up the steep slopes in western North Carolina; trains that approached crossings in the rolling Piedmont with a warning whistle; trains that clattered merrily across the flat coastal plains, stopped for a new contingent of college girls, and started off again with a great emission of steam.

A two-coach train from the Sandhills section was typical. Smoke roiled back from its peculiarly shaped smokestack, which bulged in the middle, and cinders sifted into the cars although windows were closed against the nip of autumn. At one end of each car there was a stove. At the other there was a water cooler that periodically toppled from its niche when speed and curve proved too much for its balance, and the young ladies had to lift their high-topped shoes as primly as possible to keep their feet from getting soaked.

The new students sat sedately on the red plush seats and remembered their mothers' warning to seek aid from no man but the conductor. They were clad in the feminine garb of their time, but wore it with a certain seriousness, being on the way to college (even though it was not called college), and with grace, since they were southern girls who had been tutored more or less consciously in a cult that valued and capitalized on charm. Eagerness to reach their destination had a trace of nervousness in it, and the first trainload to approach Greensboro gathered up their belongings and stepped into the aisle as soon as the train began to slow down. A middle-aged drummer halted their progress to the door with a drawled "I wouldn't get off here, girls, if I were you. This is the coal chute."

That first group of arrivals went into the depot at the foot of Elm Street, Greensboro's cobble-paved main street, and waited. Almost immediately they were joined by "A fat friendly-looking man," as one of them recalled, who turned out to be President McIver himself. He shook hands with the girls and surprised them, as he would many times later, by the wealth of personal information he possessed about each one—facts that he had assimilated from applications and subsequent correspondence or deduced from wide acquaintance with families and family names in every part of the state. Concerning a part of that correspondence he kept his own counsel. Some of the mothers, not quite knowing what to expect of a college president, had given him strange commissions. "Will you please take the money," one asked, "and pay her bills yourself, as girls are sometimes careless about business matters? My kindest regards to Mrs. McIver and ask her would she please look after Daughter." "Please put her with a nice roommate," another urged, and still another pleaded "Do *not* let her study to the detriment of her health."

President McIver placed the girls, five to a vehicle, in one-horse carriages, and sent them on their way to school. Their trunks went into a commodious two-horse van. The president waited for the next train.

Finally, when the last train came in, he boarded its one coach and asked if young women for the Normal and Industrial School would remain in their seats until the rest of the passengers had gone. Nobody got up. "Heaven forbid," McIver blurted out. "What am I going to do with you all?" Accepted or not, quite a few of them were determined to go to college. President McIver had 176 girls on his hands instead of the 125 he had expected.

The late comers followed the same procedure as the earlier arrivals, got into hacks, proceeded along the main street, turned left at the courthouse square, and plowed the rest of the way through a mile of sticky mud. They went directly to Brick Dormitory and came face to face with the most formidable personage they had ever seen: Miss Sue May Kirkland, Lady Principal, stately, dignified, correct in every inflection of voice and manner. They would presently conclude that Miss Kirkland "had her favorites" and that the favoritism slanted toward the girl with good social background, but they would value, nevertheless, what she could teach in her exacting fashion of the amenities many of them had not had a chance to learn. Miss Kirkland was the Lady without whom the trustees had judged they could not attract girls from the best families, and she was, indeed, such a social magnet that some of her own young relatives deemed the new school acceptable. "Cousin Sue May," they called her, whereupon the irreverent young promptly dubbed her "consomme." It was a name, one may be sure, that was spoken behind her unbending back. The girls would sit right and walk right and talk right, if Miss Kirkland had her way. They would wear proper dress, hat and gloves included, before they left their rooms for whatever purpose. There would be no pulling on of gloves as they went, since no lady would appear on the street until her toilette was completed. The dining room was in Brick Dormitory. Girls in the small dormitory automatically reached for their hats when the breakfast bell rang. A member of that early faculty has opined that Miss Kirkland, if she can know that the present generation of young women dashes about the campus wearing bobby socks and shorts, must be having a very restless last sleep. Miss Kirkland would have no such indelicacy as females wearing trousers even when girls played men's parts in the drama. Long black skirts were supposed to look enough like pants to give the necessary illusion.

Miss Kirkland lined the girls up around the wall where they stood, silent and awkward and more than a trifle fearful, waiting their turn to be registered.

They managed the overflow of students in their own fashion by arranging that four girls should occupy a room intended for three. They pushed together a double and single bed and the quartet of sleepers lay crosswise. Sixty of the student body, which would grow to 223 before the year was over, would eventually be housed in boarding homes.

The patronage, however, was just the sort of cross section of the state's young womanhood that the school's president and directors had hoped for. It included the daughters of well-to-do doctors and lawyers and merchants and one who was a banker's child and mixed them, on equal terms, with the children of unprosperous sewing machine agents and mechanics, with the daughters of cultured, if impecunious, teachers and preachers, with girls from the farm. A large proportion had already taught. Nearly half were defraying their own expenses. The president's sister Elizabeth, who had attended Peace Institute for two years, was enrolled. Their average age was nineteen, their discipline a matter that would give their president little concern, their conduct based from the beginning on student government of their own devising.

All of them met in the chapel, agreed on their own rules as to time for lights out, rising bell, study hall, and the like, and volunteered for some of the dining room chores, since the money for service was small and threatened to vanish altogether. They kept their rooms, built their fires, and maintained their lights from an oil supply in the basement. A lamp held sufficient fuel for one night only, and woe betide any girl who neglected, even as the foolish virgins of New Testament story, to refill her lamp. One such careless miss, rising betimes to study by the dawn's early light, fell through a skylight into the dining room. Fortunately, she landed on an empty table, and no harm was done except to her dignity—and the skylight.

President McIver was still faced, once he had got the girls housed, with another formidable task—their academic placement. They had attended all manner of schools: the private academy, other boarding schools, public schools that ranged in efficiency from good to fair to impossible. One mountain girl had been to school less than five full days in her life, and turned in a blank page on the examination prepared by the president to determine scholastic levels. Apparently it never occurred to McIver to send her home; it was for girls of limited opportunity that a school was needed. He told her, as he told the rest of them, "Low aim, not failure, is a crime." The girl worked perseveringly at the studies he gave her, passed a few the first semester, made up deficiencies with summer study, and at the end of five years received, at President McIver's suggestion, the Peabody medal that Dr. J. L. M. Curry awarded to "the most deserving girl." The next year she finished the course, wearing for graduation a dress that had been an indirect gift from the president. McIver had given money for its purchase to the home economics teacher with the comment that the girl had come there with little but determination, and he wanted her to have as pretty a dress as any graduate on the platform. Little wonder the students described his attitude as fatherly.

In matters of deportment they found that the president, although never harsh, was firm. In all truth, he had to be strict. Any lack of circumspection, any departure from rectitude, would have collapsed the entire venture around their hopeful heads; already the school's enemies were girding on their armor.

Mr. McIver had the students' unanimous respect. Moreover, a majority of the young women, sensing his acute interest in every individual present, averred they were never in awe of him. Some of the others admitted they were "scared to death" of him, partly, no doubt, because he represented authority, and partly—at least in some cases—because a girl herself had not lived up to his uncompromising standard of behavior. He not only appreciated ability, he valued honesty as well, and perhaps was more intolerant of misrepresentation than anything else. Nor would he tolerate any evasion of responsibility, as one student learned to her discomfort. He had given her permission to visit relatives for a definite length of time, but her uncle, with the airy promise that he would make it right with Mr. McIver, persuaded her to overstay. "You gave *your* word," the president reminded her sternly. "Nobody could take the responsibility for you breaking your word."

On the whole, the Normal girls found him approachable and helpful and unfailingly kind. An early student who served as his secretary for four years, in recalling various episodes of her work with McIver, always came back to the same point, concluded each story with the same sentence: "He was the kindest man I ever knew." He liked in those first weeks sometimes to deliver the mail in person as a means of putting names and faces together. As he handed round the letters, he kept up a stream of comment at which the girls laughed immoderately. They laughed because it seemed politic to appreciate the president's humor. They also laughed because they could not help themselves. President McIver, when he set out to, could be a very funny man.

McIver got on well with his faculty, too. It is true that they found him dogmatic to a degree, but he was always willing to listen to their side of a question, and the fact that he liked to have his own way was somewhat offset by the complete graciousness with which he could capitulate to another's point of view. He was, as one faculty member said, "convincible." Above all, the teachers felt secure in their work. "He had the good sense," still another declared, "to get the best possible people to do the job. Then he had the good sense to let them do it."

The new school became instantly the darling of the North Carolina press—and that would be a help in the storms that were gathering. Indeed, if the papers could be considered reliable, those girls were "the noblest specimens of young womanhood," the loveliest, most talented, and beautiful young ladies of them all. And the speakers were just as effusive. President McIver snared for an appearance at the college every person of consequence who came within hailing distance. He liked to acquaint important people with the school; he liked to acquaint the girls with important people, feeling that it was worth while to know a master in any field. Long ringing of the college bell meant the students were to gather in the chapel, and more often than not, they were being assembled to hear a speaker who was prominent, not to mention chivalrous by his own lights. Finally, the girls got so weary of being called a galaxy of beauty, when they were trying to amount to something, they summoned what courage they could muster and asked speakers to omit the designation. Sometimes press and speakers were not too far off at that! When the president had the college girls dress in white, and paraded them two by two, for special occasions, they did make an attractive appearance.

To be sure the papers could not agree on the school's name. They referred to it variously as the State Female Normal and Industrial School, The White Girls' Normal School, The Female Normal, The N. and I. at Greensboro, or whatever identifying tag popped into the editorial consciousness. Except for the girls, who called it The Normal with great affection, only one person, the Negro head cook, seemed to have the name clear in his mind. "Uncle" Henderson Feribault called it The Enormous and Industrious School.

Examinations required for placing the students continued for three weeks, after which the confusion subsided and the girls began really to get acquainted with their teachers. Mr. Alderman's courses in English were such polished and eloquent lectures that the townspeople crowded in to hear them, making an unexpected rule necessary: Only as many would be admitted as could find seats. Miss Boddie was caustic, but witty. Besides she was so pretty and wore such fashionable clothes her appearance sometimes distracted student attention from the Latin grammar under consideration. She further aroused the girls' curiosity by repulsing the numerous beaus who sought her out, and the students made up their own explanation: She was in love with President McIver. They came to value Miss Mendenhall, a gentle Quaker lady, more for the example she set in excellent character than for her gifts as a teacher.

But it was President McIver who made the most indelible imprint on their minds. James Russell Lowell, of course, had previously stated the premise "Not failure but low aim is crime," but McIver reiterated the idea so constantly that the students accepted it as a part of his philosophy—and theirs. He passed on to them the underlying rule of his own career and, as was the case in many other matters, presented it in a quotation (from Owen Meredith):

> The man who seeks one thing in life and but one
> May hope to achieve it before life is done;
> But he who seeks all things, wherever he goes
> Only reaps from the hopes which around him he sows,
> A harvest of barren regrets.

The entire experience was new and vivid and memorable. The speaker was compelling. The girls listened and memorized and remembered. They remembered so well that every living member of the class could quote accurately, sixty years after, an involved Oriental proverb:

He who knows not, and knows not that he knows not,
Is a fool; shun him.
He who knows not, and knows that he knows not,
Is a child; teach him.
He who knows, and knows not that he knows,
Is asleep; wake him.
He who knows, and knows that he knows,
Is wise; follow him.

Chapel was held each morning on the second floor of the administration (Main) building, and whenever McIver was at the school, he conducted the exercises. On the way up the stairs, walking with a quick springy step, he would glance over headlines in the morning paper he had picked up in his office, and in the course of his later remarks he would give the girls a digest of current happenings. If it were at all warm he would wield a palmleaf fan assiduously while the students assembled. Chapel opened nearly always with the state song, as McIver's dedication to his native commonwealth was something he wished the girls to share. "The State does not consider it has given you anything," he insisted. "State education is not charity." But North Carolina had made an investment in them, had a right to a return from its investment, and desired the return to be "in the form of womanhood, patriotic citizenship, and your best professional service in the field of education."

Day after day he laid much stress on teaching. "Be real teachers," he urged the girls. "Teach children right habits of thought, expression, and feeling and so far as your influence as a citizen may permit teach the men and women of this state a true educational policy. Teach them that we are not too poor to educate our children but that we are too poor not to educate them; that ideas are worth more even in dollars and cents than acres of land;

that education precedes and creates instead of being, as many suppose, the result of wealth. Be of service to the community in which you live. Teach generosity and public service by precept and example."

Service! That was a theme he emphasized repeatedly.

In language that was sometimes epigrammatic, sometimes vigorous President McIver touched in those chapel talks on every facet of the well-rounded personality: On good grooming (Everyone owes it to himself to make the best possible appearance, for that is our passport into public favor when we meet strangers); on courtesy (Thoughtlessness is extreme thoughtfulness of self); on diligence (Idleness is a crime in rich or poor and any healthy person who does not create more than he consumes is a contemptible drone and a moral vagrant). In impressing on the girls that there was a need to conserve heat, he declared "It is a mark of civilization to close a door once you have gone through it." (That comment, refined and restated, was an echo from his farm boyhood: "Hey. Come back here and shut that door. Were you raised in a barn?")

He read the Bible solemnly and well, with First Corinthians, Chapter 13, being his favorite selection.

In the chapel exercises, as time went on, McIver began to do for the Normal students what he had been able to do for the teachers: Endow them with self-respect. He let them know that he expected much of them, and an inherited sense of inferiority, deriving from traditional limitations on members of their sex, began to evaporate under the glow of his confidence. Almost as often as he read St. Paul's eloquent pronouncement on faith, hope, and charity, he read from Christ's incomparable Sermon on the Mount. "Ye are the salt of the earth," he read to the young women from the fifth chapter of Matthew. "Ye are the light of the world."

He believed it; the girls were convinced of that. They began to believe it, too.

Thus they reached a conclusion, tonic to their self-esteem, somewhat at variance with the popular explanation as to why McIver was expending his obviously considerable talents in the unlikely field of female training. Many of his contemporaries had persuaded themselves that McIver's great passion was really Education—which they agreed women could further—and not some erratic notion of equipping ladies to be independent. As they phrased it, to their own satisfaction, McIver believed in education for women because he believed in education.

With the evidence at hand, the girls had a different understanding: McIver believed in education for women because he believed in women.

The placid surface at the new school, reflecting as it did the good feeling between president and students and president and faculty, was nevertheless subjected to frequent ruffling from outside. McIver was harassed continually that first year by biting attacks from a formerly friendly source. Eugene G. Harrell, who had worked alongside McIver for the new institution since it was first proposed, did a complete about-face. He became critical of both the school and its head. He also lined up with denominational groups which considered the state school unfair competition with their own women's colleges.

McIver might have seen the assault coming; perhaps he did. Mr. Harrell's position had been somewhat inconsistent in 1889 when, as secretary of the Teachers' Assembly, he was battling in the Legislature for the training school, and, as secretary of the Raleigh Chamber of Commerce, was supporting that organization's president, the town's wealthiest citizen, in opposing an increased tax levy for the Raleigh schools. (Josephus Daniels in his autobiographical *Tar Heel Editor* expressed a belief that Harrell was really a friend of education but "felt he must follow the lead of the richest men in Raleigh.")

At any rate, as late as August of 1891 Harrell was asking McIver to provide information for an article in the *Teacher* that would set the school "in the very best possible light before our people. I want everybody to honor, respect and *love* the Normal School for Women as we do."

A month after the school opened he had changed his tune. On November 10 he wrote McIver a querulous letter which gave some credence to the Greensboro *Record's* contention that Harrell was a man who had an ax to grind and had failed to get it on the stone.

"I enclose check for first quarter on account of 'North Carolina Teacher's' scholarship. Would have sent it before but really did not know the school was open having no information whatever on the subject except newspaper items. Our house has not received an order for books or stationery from the institution and I learn from friends at Greensboro that all supplies for the State Normal and Industrial School are purchased direct from the north. It this be true the taxpayers may not feel the same interest in future."

His anxiety for the taxpayers sought a wider audience early in 1893 with a communication to the *State Chronicle,* of which Mr. Daniels had disposed the year before, opposing an appropriation for continued existence of the school. Describing himself as "one of the first and now one of the strongest friends of the institution," he charged that the school was not doing the work, "meant to be normal and industrial only," for which it was chartered, hence his opposition. Little attention was paid to the article except by students at the school. Newly come to self-expression, they held an indignation meeting and one of the girls could hardly read the offending article for the hissing. The meeting dissolved in cheers when Miss Kirkland brought in a telegram from McIver which stated "Appropriation twelve thousand five hundred passed senate today vote 20 to 14." When the appropriation bill finally became law, giving the school a new lease on life, the girls seized anything they could find with which to make a joyful noise—tin pans, horns, combs covered with tissue paper—and marched in a torch light parade to meet their conquering hero.

But Mr. Harrell was not through. The April, 1893, issue of the *Teacher* carried a long discussion which he entitled "Report of the State Normal and Industrial School." (The report under fire was prepared in December when the school was less than three months old, hence could not give an accounting of the year's finances.) The *Teacher* charged that the report had failed to account for some $9,000 of cash income, including Peabody grant, scholarships, and various fees, and made strong insinuations that

a "reckless waste of state's money" was enriching President Mc-
Iver. The writer was particularly enraged that "There is no
mention of the amount that it is said President McIver is paying
for rent on one of the handsomest buildings erected by the State,
which he uses as a residence and private boarding-house," and
hinted the president was also making an illegitimate profit on the
students' board.

Furthermore, his editorial comment contained a threat, along
with insistence that the school, being neither normal nor industrial, was a female seminary just like other female institutions
with which it was using state's funds to compete. "It is quite
evident that the Normal and Industrial School must do the work
it was appointed by the State to do—that is, train the young wom-
en for teaching and practical life—or else it will be discontinued
by the next General Assembly. If the president of the institution
cannot realize this perhaps a competent man can be easily found
who will do the work that the State intended should be done for
the North Carolina girls."

One newspaper dismissed Harrell's carping as arising from
a desire to get the job for himself. "The spectacle of Eugene
Harrell continually picking at President McIver" reminded
another "forcibly of a little pup biting and snarling at the heels
of a huge mastiff."

The Board of Directors made a reply to the charges that the
school was not fulfilling its designated function, but President
McIver made none, in spite of insistence from friends and relatives
that he should. "You cannot say," wrote D. E. McIver from
Sanford, "you will not notice Harrell's charges. They must be
noticed or they will sink in and poison the minds of the people
against you."

Only once, however, was McIver stung into taking action of
any sort.

On May 10 there appeared in the *Biblical Recorder* (a Baptist
publication) a statement signed OBSERVER that reviewed and re-
stated in stronger language the *Teacher's* charges of extravagance
and mismanagement. "The *Teacher*," Observer contended, "has
fairly and honestly exposed a vast number of misdoings on the

part of the President which proves him totally unfit to be at the head of such an institution as the State intends the Normal and Industrial School to be."

Editorially, the *Recorder* called attention to the communication: "Observer on the seventh page takes the Normal and Industrial School at Greensboro to task, in our opinion somewhat justly."

It was the editorial paragraph that incensed McIver. He wrote Rev. C. T. Bailey, D.D., editor of the *Recorder,* "As the communication reflects on my integrity, you will doubtless recognize my right to demand the name of the author of said communication.

"I would like also for you to state whether or not you meant by the editorial to endorse the attack on my character. Yours respectfully, Charles D. McIver."

Dr. Bailey gave him the desired information. The communication, he said, had come from the Alfred Williams & Company's bookstore and was in the handwriting of Col. E. G. Harrell. He had not, he went on, meant to attack McIver's integrity nor to endorse any attack on his character, and would say so in the next issue of the *Recorder.* The next week's issue was an interesting document. It not only contained the promised statement, it pointed out that the Normal and Industrial School's funds, handled by Bursar E. J. Forney who was under $10,000 bond, had never been in President McIver's hands, and published a statement from Mr. Harrell besides. "The article signed 'Observer,' " the latter explained "was sent to me by a gentleman through the mails, with the request: 'Please read the enclosed, re-write it, and hand to the *Recorder* for publication if you have no objection.' I had no objection, and therefore complied."

The newspapers had some fun, in their colloquial and sometimes pungent fashion, with the fact that Harrell had sent in the Observer piece. "Rats" captioned one paper over a borrowed item from the Burlington *Herald* which said "Col. Harrell, who is attacking the Greensboro Normal School, not finding an endorser for his course, has taken to writing his own endorsements over assumed names. That is one way." The borrowing journal added a comment of its own: "Harrell wants to sell books. That's another way."

As soon as the Greensboro *Record* revealed Observer's identity, Mr. Harrell declared in the *News and Observer* that McIver was supplying that paper, and others, with editorial matter. The *Record* retorted rather mildly that the article was a total misrepresentation of facts, but the Newton *Enterprise,* which had hitherto stayed aloof from the controversy, came out swinging. The editor, righteously indignant, called the statement a libel on the state press which should be severely resented, an aspersion on the newspaper fraternity which did not print other men's writings as editorials, and altogether "the cheekiest thing we have read in a long time." It asserted, for the people, a belief that an attack on the school before the close of the first year was unfair and picayunish, as well as entire confidence in the superintendent, teachers, and trustees.

Nor could Mr. Harrell have been greatly comforted by the Greensboro *Patriot's* conclusion: "It will take a ten acre field of such men as Col. Harrell to shake the confidence of the people of North Carolina in the integrity of Prof. McIver and the honorable men who constitute the Trustees of this much needed and most excellent school."

In June the matter came to an abrupt halt. "We have closed our discussion of the Normal and Industrial School for the present," the *Teacher* stated.

"I suppose the fight is off now," Joyner wrote McIver. "Harrell seems to have slipped out of the hold he made for himself by lying. It seems to me he has stultified himself. He has no sympathizers here."

Meanwhile, McIver had gone about his adopted course of hewing to the line and letting the chips fall where they might. The first commencement of the Normal was a splendid occasion. The railroads gave special rates. There were large crowds for the graduation in spite of heavy storms. And ten noble and beautiful young ladies received diplomas (not degrees) that were a "life license" to teach in the schools of North Carolina. The president was of a firm mind to confer no degree until it would be worth as much in reality as that of the State University or any other first-rate degree-conferring institution. The Board of Trustees passed resolutions endorsing the president and vindicating his judgment in matters of management, and the papers rejoiced in his complete exoneration of all charges. If the Harrell tempest had proved anything it was that the press was overwhelmingly pro-McIver.

For his part the president congratulated the graduates on being the first class of the first institution supported by the state into which they could gain admission without becoming criminal or crazy, reiterated that the institution expected from them patriotic citizenship and professional service, and promised in turn "Its love and appreciation of your loyalty to its interests; its faith and its hope in your character and purposes; its peculiar pride in whatever success you may achieve in life and that tender sympathy with your cares and discouragements which only a mother can give to her first born."

On their part, the girls turned back to the school a small refund on the amount paid for food—since board had to be furnished at actual cost—for the use of campus beautification. The money went to buy grass seed.

On June 7, the University of North Carolina conferred an honorary doctorate on McIver. It also announced Alderman's appointment to its faculty.

President McIver, in the meantime, had been busy strengthening the school by addition of the best personnel obtainable. Joyner, who had succeeded Alderman at Goldsboro, would succeed him again at Greensboro, and would be assisted by Mrs. Lucy H. Robertson (later president of Greensboro Female College, now Greensboro College). P. P. Claxton, superintendent of schools at Asheville (later United States Commissioner of Education), was joining the faculty to teach pedagogy. The science department had been expanded to include Miss Mary Petty, A.B. Wellesley, who would teach chemistry and physics, leaving to Miss Bryant the professorship of the natural sciences. Miss Maude F. Broadaway, a brand new graduate of the Normal and Industrial School, was remaining to take charge of Physical Culture. Dr.

Anna M. Gove, a graduate of Woman's Medical College, New York, had been secured to take the place of Dr. Bitting. Dr. Gove, upon her arrival, would prove baffling to both men and women, who hardly knew how to account for her or how to refer to her. A medical doctor, that tiny New England lady? Well, then, if a woman writer was an authoress and a woman poet a poetess, a woman doctor was unquestionably a doctress, but even that term hardly seemed specific enough for a slip of a girl in her mid-twenties. So Dr. Gove became "the female lady doctress," and one male physician hitched up his horse and buggy and drove in from the country to see if such a thing could truly be.

The Greensboro *Record,* in commenting on President McIver's honorary degree, declared "the success of this school during its first year has no parallel, and it is already the pride of the State and a great blessing to her young women." The school's success had indeed been phenomenal from its opening day, but it is getting ahead of the story to bring the first year to a close on a totally optimistic note. In the institution's very success lay a threat of its destruction.

When a man is on the right road it is not of great importance whether he be at one point or another. The direction in which he is moving and the rate of his speed are the important questions. —*Charles Duncan McIver*

12—

Battle's Stern Array

IN FEBRUARY of 1893, while taking no apparent notice of Harrell's charge that the Normal and Industrial School was unfair competition to other female schools, President McIver nevertheless was acutely aware of the difficulties foreshadowed in that opinion. He touched upon the matter in a letter to his friend Walter Hines Page: "I am now in the midst of a hard struggle with the Legislature for some money for our institution. If we could only get a few thousand more, I could have five hundred girls here in a very short time. But I fear our very success will hinder us, as private institutions are beginning to pray for protection. There is a sort of creed in North Carolina, you know, that nothing ought to succeed much beyond anything else. She strikes an average on everything and calls it conservatism."

If the private institutions were praying, as well they may have been since they were church-sponsored schools, they were also following the religious dictum that faith without works is void. They would trust in God but they would keep their powder dry. Lines were forming for a battle; that was apparent even beyond the state. About the time McIver was writing Page, the Baltimore *Sun* noted: "The principals of various female private schools in North Carolina are demanding protection against the State Normal and Industrial School at Greensboro."

The story was new only insofar as it concerned women's education. The churches had not been as laggard as the state in providing colleges for girls. The Methodist denomination, one of the protagonists in the Church-State conflict, had been in the field with a junior college (Louisburg) since immediately after the turn of the century (1802). Then it had chartered the first four-year college in the state for women, Greensboro Female College, in 1838—the same year that saw the genesis in Randolph County of a men's school that would later become Trinity College and later still Duke University. The Baptists, whose college for men at Wake Forest dated from 1834, were only ten years behind the Methodists in providing education of college grade for women at Chowan Institute in 1848. The Presbyterians, who chartered Davidson for men in 1848, came along with Peace Institute, a junior college for women, in 1857. Other denominations— Quaker, Moravian, Episcopal, Christian, Reformed—either had girls' schools or co-educational institutions. But until the Normal and Industrial School was opened the state had offered them no competition in educating women, hence no ground for controversy in that particular.

Now the Baptists and Methodists, two strong denominations which had been opposing state support of men's higher education since the University reopened, were consolidating their forces for a new attack on the principle of state responsibility for educating beyond the grade school level.

The University renaissance in 1875 had been the signal for church resistance to higher education by the state. The University had scarcely reopened when Trinity College, through the president of its board of trustees, objected that the state institution, doing the same sort of work as denominational colleges, represented unfair competition. Dr. Columbus Durham, a prominent member of the Baptist Church, concurred in the opinion. Durham wished, he said, to see the University, of which he was an avowed friend, delivered from the necessity of competing with private colleges for patronage, not an institution which could underbid them, cripple them to the point of having no function except the training of ministers, or destroy them altogether. Two years after the University resumed its work he was urging the Baptist State Convention to give support to making the school a "university in reality." The Baptist *Biblical Recorder* went further, asserting if the University remained an ordinary college it could not draw on the state treasury for support.

The statement arose from the fact that the University, for the first time in its history, was calling on the Legislature for an annual appropriation. Since the school's founding, the state had given some support from escheated lands and other non-tax sources, and had assumed responsibility for paying interest ($7,500 annually) on Federal Land Scrip money lost in the postwar crash. But it had made no regular appropriation to the institution, and its action in the Land Scrip Fund stipulated that free tuition and room rent be given one student from each county. The sons of ministers got free tuition, too. Prospective ministers got free tuition. Moreover, the small number of students who were supposed to pay were permitted to sign notes for their expenses when they had no cash on hand. As a result the University could not eke out an existence on the fees actually collected, even with the help of the Land Scrip Fund, and agitation had begun to divert that to a strictly agricultural college. In spite of the inimical views of church leaders, which made the time inopportune to ask for state support, its financial plight was a bull the University had to take by the horns. Thus, under pressure of necessity, President Battle, with the able help of Professor George T. Winston, prepared a brief asking the General Assembly of 1881 to come to the rescue.

The measure the lawmakers were asked to consider called for an annual appropriation of $7,500 and (to make that dose easier for the Legislature to swallow) free tuition to one extra student from each county. The Wake Forest faculty saw in the proposed subsidy not only the bugaboo of state monopoly in higher education, but alarming inroads that additional student grants might make on their own enrollment. The upshot of a meeting they called, attended by Methodists and Presbyterians as well as Baptist friends of Wake Forest, was "A Memorial in Behalf of the Denominational Colleges of the State," signed among others by the presidents of Wake Forest, Trinity, and Davidson. The memorial protested the measure as inexpedient, unfair, and unjust and set forth that the signers meant to oppose it with every legal means in their power.

"The contest is inevitable," sighed the *Biblical Recorder,* "and it may last for years."

The forecast of a battle joined for a long time to come was as accurate a statement as any that emerged from the conflict; in the subsequent tumult—the exchange of epithets, imputations of bad faith, and accusations—truth sometimes came out the little end of the horn. It was to be a vitriolic, name-calling, long-drawn-out campaign; a match with no holds barred; a knock-down-drag-out fight: the last fierce struggle in North Carolina of Church *vs.* State for control of the minds as well as the souls of men.

The initial skirmish in the 1881 Legislature had an outline of things to come. Provision for additional scholarships was dropped early in the debate, but its deletion silenced only one of the denominational batteries. The other was a plea in behalf of lower, not higher, public education, and one McIver would have to deal with again and again. "When only one-third of the children of the State are at school," the churchmen maintained, "when the State is so poor it provides only money enough to keep the public schools in operation 10¼ weeks in the year, when appropriation for the education of each child for a whole year is only 19 cents, it seems unreasonable that the State should pay $80 a year for the tuition of each student it may send to Chapel Hill."

They made quite a fight of it, and succeeded to the extent of a compromise that set the annual appropriation at a lower figure than was requested and left the free tuition situation unchanged. But they were defeated just the same. The state, by making an appropriation out of tax revenues, had admitted an obligation to its University. The principle of state support for higher education had been established.

Four years later, the 1885 Legislature saw a repetition of the forces arrayed against the University, and since there was no proposal to increase county scholarships the issue emerged more clearly as church opposition to any state aid for higher education. Again the clerical groups succeeded only in having the original proposals reduced. Then there was a lull, if not a cessation, in the bitter dispute, until 1893 when Charles McIver appeared to plead with the Legislature for the continued existence of a new school for girls.

In that year the denominational schools had another spur as sharp as competition. The state, as well as the entire country, was swinging into a full-fledged depression, the Cleveland panic. Short crops and poor prices for their economic standby, cotton, had brought profound distress to North Carolina farmers and cut into the normal registration at private schools. There was desperation behind renewal of the old church fight against state aid. The threat of extinction seemed more genuine than ever to church institutions.

While the new State Normal and Industrial School did not escape attention as the natural enemy of private women's colleges, the church leaders concentrated on their old scheme to befriend the University right out of competition. As President Charles E. Taylor of Wake Forest expressed it "The University should be the apex of the pyramid, the crown of the dome of the State's educational system. For such a university, but not for free education, the General Assembly should make such appropriations as may be necessary." A bill introduced into the 1893 Legislature said as much.

The measure was entitled "A Bill to Unify Higher Education in the State and to Elevate the University to the Apex of All Education in the State." It would have "elevated" the university to an institution for graduate and professional work only, leaving a clear field for church colleges in the province of bachelor degrees.

The move brought Winston, whose brief on the University's behalf precipitated the turmoil, back into the thick of the fight as President of the University. It also placed him and Charles McIver under fire from the same attackers, who would find them worthy foemen in their different fashions. Winston was a strategist who could invent methods of his own or turn the opposition's own tactics against them. McIver was, as one contemporary described him, a prince of persuaders. His forte was the great personal charm he brought to bear on individual lawmakers. In haunting the lobbies of state house and hotels he was back on familiar ground.

Moreover, the two presidents got along well together; they always had from McIver's student days in Winston's Latin classes. Quite aside from the bond forged by battling a common adversary, each already knew what to expect from the other. During the crowded days when McIver was conducting institutes and getting a new college under way at the same time, he had managed, nobody knew how, to work along with Winston in an alumni fund-raising campaign. In the course of the effort he got a report from Winston that was touched with some of his old professor's mordant humor. Winston had dunned everybody on the list except five, he stated. Those he dismissed as dead-head, dead-set, dead-beat, dead-broke, and dead.

Winston brought a like discernment to his counterattack on the audacious proposal to lop off the University's undergraduate departments. He took his puckish pen in hand and demolished the plan with mockery. He wrote a letter, anonymously, to the *News and Observer* purporting to misunderstand the bill entirely. He wrote as a citizen of Cary, a small village near Raleigh, who believed the University was about to be moved to Apex, another small village, and he proceeded to set forth Cary's superior advantages as a seat for the school. It was a master stroke. Proponents of the measure could not come to grips with ridicule. (At the time, Winston was widely suspected to be the letter's author. Josephus Daniels, who came into possession of the newspaper early the following year, later confirmed the conjecture.)

The University Magazine also pretended to treat the matter lightly. "Everybody was friendly to the University and anxious to help it," the school publication reported. "The Joint Committee on Education was amazed to see such desire to build up the University. 'Give it $50,000 a year,' said one college president. 'Put it at the Apex of glory and usefulness,' said another. The committee was reminded of the darkey who hugged his sweetheart to death."

The State Normal and Industrial School got its appropriation, as has been seen. The University laughed its opposition right out of the Assembly chambers. But both McIver and Winston went home knowing there would be no truce. The other side was preparing to bring up the heavy artillery.

Confirmation of their fears was not long in coming. Rebuffed in one Legislature the church groups set out deliberately to win to their side the one giant, Public Opinion, that could sway the next one. They poured out words, spoken and written, from platform and pulpit and clerical press. Especially did the *Biblical Recorder* keep up a running fire directed at "State Aid" advocates and all their ilk, and sought support for political candidates favorably disposed to church views on education.

In addition, church bodies swung their official weight behind the propagandists. "It was in December, 1893," the *Biblical Recorder* recalled some years later, "that the Baptists of North Carolina began their organized opposition to the policy of our State in Higher Education." So did the Western North Carolina Conference, M. E. Church, South. The Presbyterians had apparently been too long committed to the benefits of education to put any heart into a fight against its friends, secular or otherwise. They had dropped from the ranks of state college opponents.

In his personal correspondence, as well as his public utterances, Dr. McIver set out to undermine the argument of clerical institutions that the state should not set up a business to destroy private enterprise. The church, he said, was educating only one child in ten; the state was the only agency that could undertake the full task successfully. He drew a comparison between education and light. "Suppose," he invited, "1000 people were in physical darkness and five men had light which they sold to individuals, and each one secured 20 purchasers, making 100 who enjoyed the light, five who made money by it, and 900 who remained in darkness. Suppose then, that someone should suggest by all making a slight effort, each paying a very slight amount, light could be given to the entire community. What would be thought of the five men who said 'Let there be no light except to those who are able to buy it from us, and who are willing to do so; the public should not interfere with our private business'?"

The question, as McIver saw it, was whether the public was interfering with the five men, or whether they were interfering with public progress.

Simultaneously, President Taylor was allowing no grass to grow on the other side of the street. He contributed to the *Biblical Recorder* a series of articles entitled "How Far Should a State Undertake to Educate?" His religious confrères considered his exposition an invincible argument for the "voluntary principle" in higher education as opposed to education supported by involuntary taxation. The Wake Forest College Trustees commended it, the Chowan Baptist Association commended it, and the articles, reprinted in a forty-six-page bulletin, were widely circulated. Dr. Durham surrendered a life insurance policy to pay for the booklets, 25,000 of them, and a grateful Baptist State Convention paid him back.

At the same time—the spring of 1894—the clerical group was obtaining strong reinforcement in the person of John C. Kilgo, who was succeeding John F. Crowell as president of Trinity College, recently moved to Durham. Utterly convinced that higher education must be shaped under religious influence, Kilgo was a zealot who made a dynamic speech, wielded a powerful pen, and wore boldness as his battle dress. He was little concerned with competition as an argument against state education. To him the issue resolved itself more fundamentally into "Christian Education" *vs.* "Godless Education."

Moreover, he found matching aggressiveness alongside him in the Baptist column. Josiah William Bailey, son of Editor C. T. Bailey, was in charge of the *Biblical Recorder,* due to his father's illness, while the Taylor articles were appearing. Young Bailey, twenty at the time, had plans of his own that did not include succeeding his father. But the dust and heat of battle had an appeal of their own, and he did become editor of the paper. He brought to his inherited fight on "State Aid" both the unflagging energy of youth and its certitude. Black was black and white was white. Education must choose between God and Mammon. In a typically intense editorial he would write: "We have got to fight or give over the banner of Christ. It is the battle of the secular against the sacred, of politics against religion, of Satan and the Saviour. Let each man choose his standard, let each follow his captain." No Crusader ever rode off to defend Christianity from the Saracen infidel with greater confidence that he was upholding the cause of Righteousness.

With the second commencement of the Normal and Industrial School behind him, President McIver plunged into a program of summer institutes and heard frequent storm warnings as he went about the state. True, not all laymen in the churches were being stampeded by the prolific arguments in their religious journals. "I am entertained here delightfully," McIver wrote his wife from one small town, "by a prominent Baptist who takes no stock in the Baptist war." There were Baptists as well who made their opinions known in the state schools' behalf. James Joyner was a Baptist who spoke out in meeting to defend North Carolina's educational policy. Charles Aycock was a Baptist, too.

Still, the portents were there for McIver to read. In Nash County "A kind of Methodist educational rally" preceded his institute, whereupon he made a beeline to the courthouse for statistics with which to confound its participants. Only sixty-seven taxpayers in the county were paying as much as twenty-five cents to the Normal and Industrial School. "My figures on the amount each citizen pays on an annual appropriation of $12,500 almost startle people," he wrote Mrs. McIver. It was effective to point out that a property evaluation of $100 paid less than half a cent; of $1,000 less than five cents. One sly insinuation he could refute without research. It was that nobody but a rich girl could go to the Normal!

Warnings came from friends of the school, too. Noble took what comfort he could from the fact that "but one church has tried to shape politics against our higher institutions," but he was so little impressed by church championship of the common school he was sure, if the churches had primary and preparatory schools, they would fight elementary and secondary schools too. "I see Taylor is going for you as well as for us," the University's former president, Kemp Battle, wrote McIver. "The great point is to prevent their committing candidates against us on the stump. You and Winston should try to prevent this." A former student of the woman's college wrote from Rutherford: "I am glad to hear of the 'Normal's' continued success, but I fear we are going to have a hand to hand fight at the next Legislature. The Baptists are working in earnest. Two or three speeches have already been made in this little town against State schools, and some of the best and smartest men in the place are in favor of taking away all appropriations the schools now have."

The whole political scene was disquieting that summer. Dr. McIver encountered growing reaction against a matter he fervently advocated—local taxation in support of schools—due to the prevalent financial stringency. The rural voters were mad. They felt betrayed by the Cleveland Administration. A "sound money" government had saved the gold standard right enough (and little they cared) but had angered the hard-pressed farmers whose disastrous drop in income had turned them into inflationists requiring "easy money" that would mean price increases for their crops and a chance to pay their debts. In rejection of both old-party alignments they were favoring their own agrarian party (Populist) candidates for the General Assembly.

Those candidates, and others, would be primed with arguments in favor of church colleges if the *Biblical Recorder* had anything to say about it. In September that publication declared:

"State aid began hostilities. It began them openly. It is repulsed for the present by the extensive and aggressive resistance to its heretofore unhindered onslaughts. It will play the innocent until the Legislature gives it another appropriation; and then we may well pray for Wake Forest, Trinity, Davidson, Guilford, Elon and the rest; and we may hang our heads in grief or shame—accordingly as we have worked.

"Meanwhile, let everyone know that appeals for higher education may be appeals for State subsidy that will destroy nearly a dozen institutions of higher education in North Carolina.

"Keep 'Christian and Popular Education' prominent in your own and your neighbor's and your candidate's mind. Know that state aid means the crippling of the best institutions of higher learning in the State; know that it now waxes fat while the common schools are suffering; know that it is taking all it can get and crying for more of the taxes you pay; know these things, and let it not be your fault that your neighbor and your candidate don't know them."

Some of the statements were hardly consistent with strict accuracy. State aid had not been "repulsed" by the previous Legislature, surely. Moreover, two of the colleges mentioned, Elon and Guilford, had shown no disposition to worry over their eclipse. They had taken no part in the fight against state appropriations to education and would take none. Dr. Battle noted them among the "conspicuous exceptions" in the denominational struggle. Elon, a college of the Christian Church, and Guilford, a Quaker institution, had in addition demonstrated what McIver called the *wisdom* of giving education to men and women on equal terms.

Nevertheless, both sides were steeled for head-on combat when the General Assembly convened. Equally sure they were fortified by the right, both were prepared for Armageddon.

Representing the Baptist State Convention was a "committee of five brethren appointed to memorialize the Legislature on the friction and competition between the State schools and the denominational schools; and also to secure, if possible, such arrangements as will enable the schools founded and conducted by citizens to do their work without unnecessary competition from State schools." They were instructed to work with similar committees from other religious bodies to secure "concert of action."

The Baptist committee, including both the impassioned Dr. Durham and the articulate Dr. Taylor, stated in their "Memorial and Petition" that "nothing less than a change in the laws which direct the educational policy of the State will relieve the friction." They declared further:

"That the illiteracy of large numbers of the people of North Carolina is a reproach to the state, is unfavorable to its prosperity, and is a menace to its good government; that this illiteracy can be removed only through the agency of the Public schools; and that these will require all the taxes of the people which can be expended for education purposes." The church leaders demanded, in specific reference to the Normal and Industrial School, that no exception from examination for certificates to teach be allowed for any purpose, and that the girls' school and the A. and M. College should provide only the technical training for which they were established and 'not higher literary education.' "

In their demand that all taxes for education go to the lower schools, which were in a pathetic state, church leaders had an argument that was both plausible and popular. It was also insidious in its suggestion that the heads of state colleges, out of selfish concern for their own institutions, would deprive the free schools of their needs.

Their advocacy of the grade school was less effective than the churchmen hoped for two reasons. First of all, their motives became suspect when they required with one breath that the state give support to lower schools and withdraw it from the higher. The threat of competition with their colleges thus appeared commensurate in importance with their anxiety for the public school child.

A second strike against their position was Charles McIver. They found it very difficult indeed to persuade North Carolina that Dr. McIver was hostile to education at any level. His three institute years, when people had seen him in action at close range, rebutted that idea in every part of the state. He had worked, and was still working, for increased taxes for schools, for a better program of administration. Besides, the secular newspapers had shown themselves so solidly behind McIver that any attempt to impugn his motives as he sought to improve his school would bring immediate rejoinder in the lay press.

Nonetheless, the danger to state-supported colleges was both real and formidable. Church leaders were present to add personal lobbying to their written pleas. The Legislature itself was a different aggregation from any McIver had known. Populist representatives sent to the Assembly by distressed farmers had joined with the Republicans to snatch control of the Legislature away from the Democrats. The fusion group had Negro support.

The lawmakers were not friendly to education. Before their session ended they would have abolished the county superintendency of schools and the county boards of education.

Winston especially was wary, and with good reason. According to the *News and Observer,* many of the Populists and Republicans had been elected by denouncing Democratic extravagance in appropriating money to the University. Having gauged the temper of the Assembly, Winston adopted a Fabian policy, while carrying on a persistent campaign to convert the lawmakers into a group to which he could safely entrust a bill for University funds. He fought fire with fire; asserted an interest in common schools as strong as any church's, since "higher education must rest upon the lower," and the University's first concern was the growth of a common school system that could, in turn, nourish it. He could be insidious, too, and was skillful at implying church education was not altogether the godly influence it claimed to be, since Baptist and Methodist colleges had accepted gifts from some very worldly corporations (Standard Oil and American Tobacco Co., respectively).

Odds against the University were lessened by the fact that the institution had consistently educated many of the state's political leaders. As *The University Magazine* pointed out, the presiding officer of the Senate (Democrat), the presiding officer of the House (Republican), and the United States Senator-elect (Populist) were all University alumni. Even so, with all the help available from strategically placed graduates and friends, Winston declared afterward "we came near to destruction." In a letter to his (and the University's) old friend Mrs. Spencer he reported "The Baptist flood roared and surged and threatened. Could they have gotten a vote the first two weeks, we had been abolished root and branch by a 3 to 1 vote." They probably would have been abolished at that. Well over 100 of the Legislature's 170 members were Baptists.

McIver was less uneasy about his own school. He had found, he wrote Mrs. McIver, that "our institution has many strong friends among the plain members of the General Assembly." He supplied them with arguments to buttress their position. If the

Normal and Industrial School and the University were both abolished, the money saved would increase the public school term by only two days. Nor was the girls' school quite the competition it was represented to be. Of the institution's enrollment 81 per cent, by their own statement, could not have attended another college in the state. He challenged the church position that the end of education in its higher form was essentially the training of Christian leadership. He classed the idea as outmoded, along with the original aim of state colleges primarily to produce political leadership. He denied that liberal culture was "not possible or even desirable" for the average person. The opportunity afforded by universal education was the right of every youth.

While the state aid supporters were engaged in a delaying action, ecclesiastical shock troops took the offensive. On March 3, 1895, Dr. McIver wrote Mrs. McIver: "There is no news except that a bill was introduced yesterday to take away all appropriations from the University, Normal and Industrial School, and Geological Survey."

The bill brought to a rolling boil the whole education controversy that had been simmering for months. The *News and Observer* described as a battle royal a hearing on the school question before the educational committee. Durham and Winston led off as the chief debaters, and there was nothing squeamish about the free-for-all exchange of personalities that developed. One of the persons backing up Durham was W. N. Jones, who had helped write the Baptist Memorial. Winston had the two eloquent Charleses, McIver and Aycock, in his corner, as well as a Congressman, a judge, and a Negro preacher—the last a particularly valuable asset in an Assembly in which Negroes held the balance of power. McIver, who thought people listened to him chiefly because he meant what he said and knew what he was talking about, saw no advantage in calling names and called none. The other Charles appeared as a picture of effectual bewilderment. Aycock just did not understand the contest in which church leaders were saying "We love the University, God bless it, therefore we will take away the appropriation."

When the scrap was over, the church leadership found it had been out-maneuvered. The committee voted unfavorably on reduction of appropriations to the two state schools. In fact its members were willing, Dr. McIver wrote home, to make a fight for an additional sum for the Greensboro school, which would have set the appropriation at $13,750 annually. "But I consider it dangerous," he continued, "to monkey with our annual appropriation. A bill for $5,000 extra for two years, making $10,000 for improvements, will be presented and I hope it will pass, though the opposition will be bitter."

The fight against it was both bitter and noisy, according to his running account, but a measure providing for continuance of the old appropriation plus the additional amount for extra class rooms, new dining room, and sanitary improvements passed the House by a vote of 74-18 on the eighth of March.

The following day, when Senate action was also favorable, it was all over but the shouting, which the Normal girls and the state press proceeded to do. The Greensboro *Record* regarded the action not only as highly complimentary to the school, but as showing "that it has so strong a hold upon the public heart that the Legislature could not do otherwise than deal generously with it." Warm speeches made in its favor tended to confirm that conclusion, especially in a Legislature which otherwise set the school system back twenty years by discontinuing county superintendents and county school boards.

McIver, "worn to a frazzle from loss of sleep, watching, standing and maneuvering, to say nothing of the Grippe," and a missing overcoat, dared not leave until the bill was signed and ratified, consequently did not get home for the celebration its enactment occasioned among the college girls. "We were all bitterly disappointed that you did not come home tonight," Mrs. McIver wrote. "The girls had planned to meet you and have a torch light procession and general jollification." A letter from his small daughter, Annie, was evidence that they had not called off their plans entirely: "My dear Papa," she wrote, "We wanted you to come home last night so bad. The girls had a barrel full of pine and set it afire and danced around it. They came over to our house and Mr. Joyner's. The girls yelled for you but you did not hear them. But they heard them down town. Zeke said you telegraphed and said that you heard them in Raleigh and had not slept for a week."

She was a proud and excited girl, but at going-on-nine still a little girl, so she added "Please bring us some candy."

President Winston thought the battle was won for good and all, and the next year left the state to become head of the University of Texas.

But the battle would not stay won. In fact, between that legislative session and the next it developed a frenzied crescendo.

The Baptists, who had borne the brunt of the campaign, were decidedly unwilling to concede defeat. "The Baptists are not quitters," declared the *Biblical Recorder*. "In the same spirit that our fathers bore stripes and imprisonment and infamy and death for religious freedom, the separation of Church and State, the Baptists are called upon to stand for the voluntary principle in higher education."

President Kilgo was not of a mind to retreat either. His attitude toward the education question had been more extreme than the state's Methodism as a whole, and church papers had reflected a moderation not in keeping with his temperament. Therefore, he founded a journal, *The Christian Educator,* which could present his views without restraint. The editors were cooperative. The paper was his organ, and he pulled out all the stops. For three years, in its columns, the clerical position was hammered home: Free schools of lower grade were necessary to training in citizenship and civic duty and were consequently a natural province for the State. It was "a preposterous absurdity" to offer free tuition in higher institutions when free common schools of the lower grades could barely run four months in the year. Hence, every cent of tax money available for education should be spent in the sphere in which the state had a valid interest.

Higher education, on the other hand, could not be truly "higher" unless it was religious in nature. College education thus became inherently a monopoly of church schools; the state was prohibited by the constitution from teaching religion. Manifestly, it was unjust to tax Godly people for Godless education.

The religious periodicals encouraged contributions from churchmen of all ranks who could be relied on for trenchant discourse, and it was a bishop, writing in the *Christian Educator,* who summed up the rights of both the chaff and the wheat: "If they wish Godless and unsectarian colleges and universities, this is a free country; let them build and run them at their own expense. It is asking too much of a Christian people to do this for them."

Each of the major religious camps bolstered its arguments by quoting freely from the other; also if a battler in one camp got into hot water somebody in the other would rush to fish him out. Support was offered privately as well as openly; thus not all of the intemperate language was designed for public consumption. After reading a scathing attack on Methodist Kilgo that had been contributed to a newspaper, Baptist Bailey let fly at the common enemy some choice descriptives that included, in a single letter, fool, knave, blatterskite, skunk, sissy, and three-dollar-pop-guns. (The blatterskite and skunk were said to be "after McIver's own heart.") Indeed, the Church-State conflict was quite picturesque at times in its extravagancies.

In the fall of 1896, the Baptist State Convention reaffirmed its opposition to "State Aid by Taxation" for higher education. The Western Conference of Methodists declined to follow suit, but the North Carolina Conference, in line with *Christian Educator* doctrine, adopted resolutions strikingly akin to those the Baptists had put into the record two years earlier. The Methodists committed themselves uncompromisingly to Christian education; declared for increased appropriations to common schools which they deemed a necessity to the state; denied any disposition to exterminate or do injury to state colleges, but considered it unjust to tax the church to carry on educational work injurious to its own colleges; objected to any free University tuition based upon appropriation of public moneys, believing it "out of harmony with the principles of government, and morally wrong for the State to undertake to furnish higher education to the few at the expense of the many"; and opposed any policy that diverted the Agricultural and Mechanical College and the State Normal and Industrial School from a specifically technical program.

In spite of the intensified onslaught of the churches, President McIver and the other state school heads did not retreat in the 1897 Legislature, even to the point of asking for less money. On the contrary, they asked for more. State support of higher education had again been as much of an issue in the election campaign as the Baptist periodical could make it. The entire state government was Fusionist from top to bottom. Feeling ran high. At one point, McIver wrote home, the church lobbyists got "positively abusive" to a state aid proponent. The man was actually threatened.

Yet, the Joint Education Committee reported "favorably, unanimously, and without discussion" a bill to increase the Normal and Industrial School's appropriation to $25,000 a year, exactly double its previous allotment. Its recommendation passed the Senate with only one dissenting vote.

Dr. McIver regarded the outlook as too good to be true, and could "not help but feel anxious." "The temper of the House was so turbulent last night," he wrote on February 24, "and there was so much political and anti-appropriation lightning in the air that we feared to go in with our bills. At least the University was afraid."

Still, he was having some fun, swapping some good yarns, and getting an occasional laugh out of his favorite waiter Josh who might ask, at the conclusion of a particularly good meal, "Boss, did de viands suit your ingredients?" The viands were not always as good as they might have been, but Josh's conversation was an unfailing tonic.

The worries proved groundless, too. The bill passed by an "overwhelming vote," and the University, with a $5,000 increase, got the same amount as the newer institution. During an ovation the Normal girls gave McIver, he congratulated them that North Carolina had thus early in the school's history "seen fit to place it on a financial level with her time-honored University, and that justice had at last been done by the State to her white women."

The 1897 Legislature also caught up with popular nomenclature. It changed the school's name to the Normal and Industrial College.

Obviously, opposition to "State Aid" was losing ground. There would still be "loud Noes from our ancient enemies, the Baptists," as McIver once phrased it. And acrimonious attacks on him and the Greensboro college would not reach their regrettable nadir until disaster struck from another source. But the outcome was no longer in doubt.

President Kilgo would become a bishop and his Trinity College, enriched by Duke tobacco millions, would become Duke University. Editor Bailey would become a United States Senator. Charles McIver alone would stay on a course that was constant. He would remain exactly what he was described (in retrospect) as being: "The biggest bombshell that ever hit the educational world."

13-

Double Row of Tracks

WHILE PRESIDENT MCIVER, in spite of clerical resistance and political change, was maneuvering each General Assembly one notch higher than its predecessor in financial support of the Normal and Industrial School, the institution itself was not static. Organizations were formed that would continue to flourish. Traditions were born. And the school not only had an increased appropriation from the Legislature its second year, but an increased attendance sufficient to tax classroom capacity. There were 391 girls enrolled in the autumn of 1893, although twice as many had to live in town as the year before. Demand for both living and recitation space would outrun supply throughout McIver's administration.

The second commencement, described in various newspapers as a "magnificent success," focused attention on the institution as the first had done. Railroads again gave reduced rates from all points, and the graduates received a dual present from their alma mater. They got the Bible that was customary on such occasions, but they also got copies of the constitution. The idea, President McIver explained to J. P. Caldwell, of the Charlotte *Observer,* "is simply for the sake of emphasizing the duties of parents and teachers to train for good citizenship. The majority of men today who swear to support the constitution and who wrangle about constitutional rights have never read the constitution and never intend to."

The event reached its climax on a May evening when a young lawyer from Nebraska made a speech that drew the college women away from cloistered thinking toward the main stream of current events. The stream was turbulent. It was two years before the next presidential election, and already the political pot was boiling over with sibilant fury. So many people crowded into the auditorium to hear W. J. Bryan that the Board of Trustees were seized with fear and trembling lest the whole structure collapse beneath the unaccustomed weight. The Normal girls were particularly charmed with the prairie lawyer, who looked strikingly like their own president, and was the same age. Papers elsewhere would in time comment on the resemblance, and a hat checker in New York once refused to take a tip from McIver until convinced that he was not indeed the "silver-tongued orator" whose speeches stirred audiences to a frenzy of enthusiasm.

Times were hard. The girls knew that from personal experience, and since President McIver habitually kept them up to date on news of the day they were also aware that "Coxey's Army" of unemployed men had recently concluded a march on the national capital. Still, bimetalism as the basis of a financial cure had quite possibly remained beyond the scope of their thinking.

Mr. Bryan spoke on money, and left no doubt whatever that he favored free and unlimited coinage of both gold and silver at a ratio of 16 to 1. The Charlotte *Observer*'s correspondent reported that the Normal president had asked for that identical speech, and McIver did not deny it, but the statement was in error. Mr. Bryan agreed to speak only if he could discuss some subject with which he was familiar, and McIver's answering stipulation had been that the address should be non-partisan and one that would not be offensive either to Democrats or Republicans. He admitted to Mr. Caldwell that he somewhat shared the *Observer*'s editorial opinion as to the impropriety of the topic, but he was still glad that Bryan "did speak on a subject in regard to which he had earnest convictions, instead of coming as politicians very often do to talk to educational institutions on education."

To Bryan, McIver expressed a hope that his talk had marked the beginning of a different kind of address for the commencement occasion. "The average commencement address," he wrote the Nebraskan, "has been so much like the old Negro sermon which the preacher said was divided into three parts: The fust p'int is the text itself; the second p'int is the subject matter; and the third p'int is the rousements; but for the sake of convenience and to save time, I will skip over the fust two p'ints and proceed at once to the third.

"I am glad we had an address which did not skip over the 'fust two p'ints.'"

McIver also assured Josephus Daniels that the commencement was an unqualified success. Daniels wrote his hearty congratulations from Washington, where he had gone to serve as head clerk in the Interior Department under Secretary Hoke Smith, and McIver said in answer:

"Our commencement did all that I hoped that it would do. Of course you understand that it was an advertising scheme in the main. But advertising must be done in this day in the most elegant, substantial, and entertaining manner. No other sort of advertising advertises at all. I have had about one hundred applications for next fall since our commencement closed.

"You remember when the Irishman looked at St. Patrick's Cathedral and said, 'Don't it bate the divil?' The other Irishman said, 'Faith, and that is the intention of it.'"

A year later to the day Nicholas Murray Butler, of Columbia University, spoke at the third commencement, and established even more firmly McIver's custom of bringing distinguished speakers to the school. Twenty-eight young women were graduated, and a week after commencement saw ground being broken for additions authorized by the 1895 General Assembly. Wings would be added to the main building, improving its symmetry and affording more classroom space at the same time, and a dining annex would accommodate all students at once, eliminating necessity for dining in two shifts. Within the month college property was also increased by 112 acres of farm land, although there were those who asked rather sharply what a school could want with a farm. Students returning in the autumn of 1895 discovered, too, an addition to the president's family whom they immediately adopted as their own. The McIvers' second daughter, Verlinda Miller, was born August 9, 1895.

Along with visible evidence of growth, a tradition as durable as any physical structure appeared within that same school year. In the spring of 1896 a group of fourteen young women decided to form a sorority. President McIver, who had regarded his student body as a microcosm of democracy, was outraged. Just as he had felt that snobbery was innate in the fraternity system, so now he felt that social division had no place on the campus of a woman's college that was, by its very nature, representative of the state at its democratic best.

The president's adamant stand on the question was reflected in the positiveness of a statement prepared by the girls who had dared to set themselves apart in an exclusive unit:

"We hereby agree to disband our Club, known as the 'Delta Iota Lambda,' and disclaim any intention of having a Greek Letter fraternity.

"The motto on the picture shall be effaced, that no mistaken impression may be given.

"We, moreover, declare it to be our purpose not to join any secret organization in the institution while students of the Normal and Industrial School."

And that, forever after, was that. In time the institution's academic worth would earn it chapters of several honorary fraternities, including Phi Beta Kappa, but the first president's resolve to keep the school thoroughly democratic took such deep root that no sororities would appear.

On the heels of social accord that was *democratic* in essence, Dr. McIver had to be equally emphatic about another development that was *Democratic* (politically) in origin. He had to interrupt a boom to nominate him for governor.

Politics was at fever pitch everywhere in that national election year. Farmers and workers wanted a monetary revision that would strike at privilege and at the Big Business it was believed President Cleveland favored. The administration's tariff act they regarded as little better than the high protective measure it replaced, and the chief executive, far from proving himself an enemy to trusts, had used federal troops two years earlier to break a strike of the American Railway Union against the Pullman Company. He had, in all fairness, secured passage of an income tax law (one demand of the Populist platform in 1892), but the

Supreme Court had promptly declared it unconstitutional. They saw Cleveland, by their lights, as a tool of Wall Street. As campaign lines were drawn, debtor was aligned against creditor, gold against silver, inflation against sound money. Eastern business and financial interests were a badly frightened lot.

North Carolina Democrats were scared too, for a different reason. The Populists, a product of agrarian revolt, and the Republicans were working hard, and it began to look as if the combination would not only retain control of the state's legislative branches, which they had secured in the previous election, but win control of the executive branch as well. (As a matter of record the whole state government was Fusionist for the next biennium.) In looking for a candidate whose popularity transcended party lines, the Democrats wound up at the door of Charles McIver.

It was Democratic editors, hopeful of achieving harmony through the character and ability of the woman's college president, who sent the political balloon soaring. The Sampson *Democrat* introduced the McIver-for-Governor idea. The Fayetteville *Observer* fell in step with the statement that "but few of any political party or race would cast their ballots against him." The Greensboro *Patriot* was sure he would make a good governor, but nearly as sure he was "too engrossed in the great educational work he has undertaken" to accept political honors. Friend Daniels published the editorial endorsements of other papers in his *News and Observer*.

There was no ambiguity in McIver's reaction. He would rather see his educational ideas adopted, he asserted, and feel that he had "been somewhat instrumental in bringing them about'" than to hold any political office within the people's gift.

Free silver could not compete for his interest with free education. The taxation about which he was most concerned was neither protective tariff nor graduated income tax but local taxation for schools. The disparity that existed between expenditures for men's education and women's education disturbed him more than any parity in a gold-silver ratio. His answer to the governorship overture, published in the *News and Observer* and copied by other papers, left no single door open to political preferment:

"I have no political aspirations whatever, and my highest ambition is that I may be able to hasten the day when North Carolina shall open her eyes and see that the question of free silver sinks into insignificance when compared with the question of free education for all the children of the state; that the gold standard of money is as nothing compared with a high and intelligent standard of citizenship, which will permit a discussion of the money problem or any other without intolerance or intemperate abuse; that the tariff tax and internal revenue tax questions are not half so important to this State just now as the question of additional local taxation for public schools, which must be voted upon in about 40 counties next fall; and finally, that solution of no unsolved problem of statesmanship would do more for the present and future prosperity of North Carolina than a recognition of the fact that women's education should be put upon as liberal a financial basis as that of men, and that improvement in our homes and schools—the great conservative institutions of civilization—must be slow, so long as women, who make homes and schools what they are, receive from the State and Federal aid and from endowment funds for denominational colleges only one dollar where their brothers receive ten to help in their struggle for an education.

"Men will continue to talk about maintaining the parity between silver and gold coined at a ratio of 16 to 1, but a blind man can see there is no parity in this 10 to 1 arrangement in appropriations for the education of men and women. . . .

"Holding these views as I do, and desiring above all things, to see them generally adopted, it would be unwise for me to encourage, or seem to encourage, the use of my name in connection with political honors. I appreciate none the less, however, the kind and complimentary expressions that have called forth this statement, which I should not make but for the fact that my silence might be misconstrued."

The year of 1896, if no more a time of decision than any other, was becoming at any rate McIver's year to say "No."

Hardly had the nomination question been dealt with when another emerged full blown—an invitation to become president of the University of North Carolina. Winston was leaving the University presidency. Trustees of sufficient number to assure him the appointment approached McIver about stepping into the vacancy. He wrote one of his friends saying he could not accept the position, stated his reasons, and asked that they be made known. Then with the tempter, if indeed there had been a tempter, shoved squarely behind him, he went serenely off to Buffalo to attend a meeting of the National Educational Association. There his good friend Page set out to persuade him to take the University presidency. Page rather weakened after hearing McIver's reasons for refusing, but the retiring president, Winston himself, took up the persuasion where Page left off. McIver was unmoved. Besides, it was all settled, or so he thought.

The education meeting shared interest that July week in 1896 with the Democratic Convention in Chicago. The platform that evolved at the convention would have had a familiar ring to the girls at the Normal and Industrial School, calling as it did for free and unlimited coinage of both gold and silver at the legal ratio of 16:1. The voice that championed it would have been familiar, too. It was William Jennings Bryan who made the speech that moved 15,000 people to burst into wild acclaim as he finished: "You come to us and tell us that the great cities are in favor of the gold standard; we reply that the great cities rest upon our broad and fertile prairies. Burn down your cities and leave our farms, and your cities will spring up again as if by magic; but destroy our farms and the grass will grow in the streets of every city in the country. . . . We will answer their demand by saying to them: You shall not press down upon the brow of labor this crown of thorns; you shall not crucify mankind upon a cross of gold."

Dr. McIver, back in Buffalo, listened to nearly all of the educational speeches, hobnobbed with the leading educational lights of America, but followed all the proceedings at Chicago with avid interest and "knew of Bryan's nomination as soon as he did himself," he wrote Mrs. McIver. He took a moment out to telegraph congratulations, and a couple of days later resisted with some difficulty the invitation of Dr. Miriam Bitting Kennedy, the

Normal's first physician, and her husband to wait over in their suburban New York home until Bryan was officially informed of the presidential nomination in Madison Square Garden.

As it was, McIver was out of the state for two weeks, and returned to find he was confidently expected to be the next University president. He encountered a statement in the Asheboro *Courier* which fostered the impression: "Dr. Charles D. McIver will be elected president of the University to succeed Dr. Winston unless the present arrangements fall through is the information which comes to the *Courier* from a reliable source. Dr. McIver will make the University hum; a worthy successor of Dr. Winston."

The man to whom he had written his reasons for refusing had withheld the letter, in spite of Dr. McIver's request that it be given the press, in the hope that "upon his return Dr. McIver would change his mind," the *News and Observer* reported.

The Daniels paper at the same time carried McIver's statement to one of its reporters that "his life ambition and his clear duty prevented his willingness" to leave the position he held. Having spent ten years in persuading the people that "the most important work of the State was in the field of the education of women," and believing it still, he could not afford, he told his interviewer, to leave that work for the University presidency.

The resolution was not only pleasing to the alumnae and others interested in the Normal, but Winston's successor was eminently pleasing to the Normal president, due both to McIver's warm interest in University welfare and to the fact that the trustees' choice reinstated, in some theaters, the team of McIver and Alderman.

Edwin A. Alderman was elected to the University presidency on August 1, fifteen days before the Winston resignation took effect. His inauguration, first scheduled for October, was delayed until the first of the year following, due to the disruptive effect political preoccupation was having on state and nation. McIver, on hand for the inaugural, welcomed back to their old Legislative arena an experienced contender against all opponents of state education, and one who was in addition a heavyweight on the side of his own special program. Alderman had imbibed some of the McIver conviction in regard to women's education. He had written forcefully in a report of their joint institute enterprise that "an untaught woman is the most sadly marred of God's creatures." One of his earliest acts as University president was to have women admitted to postgraduate courses.

Before it was time to go to Raleigh for his biennial tussle with the Legislature, McIver added the visual effectiveness of the printed word to his often-spoken conviction that white women of the state—"one third of our population, and in my judgment the most important third"—were getting short shrift in the education scheme. His article, entitled "North Carolina and Education, Our Next Educational Advance," appeared in a special industrial edition of the *Daily Record* Friday evening, January 22, 1897. It reflected a dual purpose—broadening of all educational opportunity and (more specifically) increasing women's opportunity for higher education—which had already gained public recognition as "McIver's double row of tracks." The apt allusion started with a reporter who wrote in a Greensboro paper, after seeing Dr. McIver's hurrying figure on the street: "Something is about to happen. President McIver was making a double row of tracks in the city today."

"The next forward step," as set forth in the McIver article, "would be taken when townships began to supplement State taxes with local levies for schools." But the chief instrument he recommended for use against illiteracy was "Proper provision for the education of women."

"While the State is moving in the right direction now," he wrote, "yet during the past year it spent more on the normal and industrial education of that third of itself composed of Negro men and Negro women than it spent upon the third composed of white women, and it spent about three times as much for the third composed of white men as on the education of white women." If it had spent as much, he declared bluntly, on white women as on white men North Carolina would not have 26 per cent of its white population illiterate. The reasons he advanced were not new; repetition was no hobgoblin to a teacher. He reiterated his constant thesis that "education given women propagates itself, whereas that given to men often dies with those who have received it." He repeated: "Women determine the character of homes and schools. No civilization can go in advance of them."

A month later he had the supreme satisfaction of seeing the state, through its legislature, equalize the sum to be spent on its women's college and its men's university and thus do "justice" to its white women.

Another McIver effort paid off in the same Legislature, which appropriated $50,000 to common schools. He appeared, along with Joyner, before the joint Senate and House Committee on Education to advocate a school measure prepared by the Teachers' Assembly. A newspaper account said "President McIver followed Prof. Joyner with a strong plea for local taxation and efficient supervision. He said many enterprising people were moving from the country to the town where taxation is higher, therefore the people do not object to higher taxes if they get value received in better educational facilities. He thinks no industrial or intellectual prosperity need be expected until an efficient system of schools is established."

The school bill proved gratifying to sectarian interests that had been clamoring for better grade schools, but refuted at the same time what McIver described "as a regular piece of cant that public schools have no one to speak for them, but that higher colleges always have special pleaders." He added, in a letter to Daniels, "I doubt whether all our critics put together have plead more unceasingly or more unselfishly than Alderman and I have done for the public schools of North Carolina."

"Now that the bill has become law," the *News and Observer* pointed out, "the people should know who proved themselves the friends of the common schools. For there were several days when its fate was doubtful in the Senate, and but for the untiring, effective work of President Alderman and President McIver, who came down from Chapel Hill and Greensboro, and staid until this bill was passed . . . this act to appropriate $50,000 to the common schools would have died in the Senate, and never been resurrected."

The Normal girls themselves had lent a hand to incline the Educational Committee toward their betterment. On a February evening they entertained the gentlemen at a County Fair, in which they set up tableaux representing the resources and industries of eighty-seven counties. Some history and considerable imagination went into the "dazzling panorama." Also thirty-five of the girls got the jump on future mores a quarter of a century before a cigarette company had the intrepidity to recommend a smoke as substitute for a sweet. In presenting their tableau of Durham, a town closely identified with the burgeoning tobacco industry, the girls had sewed cigarettes on their costumes. Afterwards they smoked the cigarettes, and the faculty was faced with a wholly unexpected disciplinary question. President McIver followed his usual custom of putting the girls on their honor. He called the offenders into his office and accepted their promise that they would not smoke again.

He still kept his finger on the pulse of everything that was happening on the campus. A girl who rode her horse to school and assumed that, as a day student, she had been unnoticed by the president, learned that such was not the case when Dr. McIver signaled her to halt. He wished her to intercept somebody at the railroad station, and there was little time. "If you ride as fast as you usually do, you'll make it," he told her. She made it.

The genuineness of his interest in the girls was manifest in many ways, as well as its sympathetic quality. The latter was especially apparent to one girl who could hardly have expected executive clemency. She had been caught stealing both clothes and money, but Dr. McIver wanted to spare her as much embarrassment as possible. He wrote her father: "She is so miserable about it she wants to go home immediately. I suggested that it might be better for her to remain until about commencement time so that her coming home would not attract attention or create remarks. I have thought it my duty to make a plain statement to you in order that you may know the worst and be prepared to give her such help and sympathy as only a father can give."

The president might feel obliged, and sometimes did, to report that a student was wasting her time, money, and opportunity, and might as well go home unless something could be done to "bring her to her senses." But he might add, and sometimes did, "in spite of it all, she is one of the most attractive characters we have ever had in the institution."

"We were never in awe of him," one of the early students recalled. "He had a vision and we were following him. No, we weren't following him," she amended thoughtfully. "We were all going along together."

The temper that flashed like summer lightning had not been gentled, however. On one occasion when McIver and Joyner were deep in serious discussion, the farm manager interrupted to report a cow had died and to ask what should be done with her. "What do you usually do with a dead cow?" McIver snapped. "Bury her."

He was instantly contrite. "I shouldn't have spoken to him like that," the president said. "I've got to learn to control my temper."

"It were well," Prof. Joyner murmured. "It were well.'"

The college, designated by newspapers as "the pride of the state," was becoming the state's center of interest, according to the same papers, as the fifth commencement approached. If it had not been a center of interest before the occasion, it undeniably was afterwards.

The commencement was, among other things, a gathering of the faithful. Dr. Curry, who had been instrumental in having the school name changed to college and had helped support the institution with Peabody money, was there to speak on George Peabody. Alderman was there to conduct memorial exercises for the late Major Finger, who had been education's good friend. Josephus Daniels was there to introduce the main speaker. There was even an echo of Chapel Hill days. A play by a young Greensboro attorney, Robert Dick Douglas, was occasion for the surprise unveiling of a portrait W. G. Randall had painted of President McIver, the Mac who had rescued him from hazing. Finally, Walter Hines Page was there to deliver the chief address.

Mr. Page was not oratorical in manner. He spoke in a tone

that was almost conversational. And rocked North Carolina right back on its heels.

The speech lasted an hour. The applause lasted three full minutes. The repercussions lasted for weeks as newspapers discussed the talk pro and con, damned and praised, printed it word for word. It was Page's famous "Forgotten Man" address. In stabbing at the illiteracy of his native commonwealth, the speaker wounded some very sacred cows.

People of the state, in Mr. Page's premise, were an undeveloped resource more valuable than all other resources. Their lack of development was proof that both the aristocratic and the ecclesiastical systems of education had failed.

Under the first, basically a class system, the masses had considered education a special privilege and, believing it unattainable, had come at length to believe that it was not desirable and certainly not necessary. They remained illiterate, neglected, forgotten.

The denominational system was broader in its conception than the first, but universal education, universal free education, was not on the program and schooling was provided less for the sake of the people than for the sake of the church. The forgotten man, one in every four in North Carolina, remained forgotten and was content to remain forgotten.

Blame for his complacency was nailed to the door of politician and preacher. The politician praised him on the stump for virtues he did not have, told him he lived in the best state in the Union, told him that other politicians had some harebrained plan to increase his taxes, told him as a consolation for his ignorance how many of his kinsmen had been killed in the war. The preacher represented his misery as a means to ultimate salvation if he would accept the right creed.

But what he really came to talk about, the speaker went on, was not the forgotten man, but the forgotten woman. She existed by the thousands, not in some country to which they sent missionaries, but right in North Carolina: ill-fed, ill-housed, overworked in a dull round of weary duties that lasted from daylight to bedtime—women without joy or grace, women without hope.

Then he proceeded to discuss their means of hope—"the educational revival that had moved the level of life further upward in ten years than it had moved in any preceding 50." In his judgment there had been no event in North Carolina since the formation of the American Union comparable in importance. "The ability to maintain schools," he asserted, "is in proportion rather to the appreciation of education than to the amount of wealth. We pay for schools not so much out of our purses as out of our state of mind."

His conclusion was the same as McIver's: "A public school system generously supported by public sentiment, and generously maintained by both state and local taxation, is the only effective means to develop the forgotten man, and even more surely the only means to develop the forgotten woman."

He closed by describing the Greensboro institution as one of the first and best fruits of a revolution that was in progress, and the most inspiring sight he had seen in North Carolina.

Dr. McIver devoted his summer, as usual, to furthering the revolution. His speech-making got off to a good start at Lexington where the Junior Order, United American Mechanics, sponsored Fourth of July exercises. A striking procession, with brass band and colorful panoply, gave the place of honor to "The Little Red Schoolhouse," a float full of children. It was the first time Dr. McIver had seen a parade feature the public school, and he decided then and there to join the Order. (And join it he did.) The day was blistering hot, but he entertained the sweltering listeners by talking (in his opinion) "some foolishness as well as some sense," and poked sly fun, to the crowd's delight, at the crazy Yankee notion that the South mistreated its colored population: "In the year 1492 when Abraham Lincoln landed at Plymouth Rock, he saw a Southern white man oppressing a Negro slave. Jumping out of his carriage and flourishing his tomahawk, he exclaimed, in the language of the poet, 'Sic Semper Tyrannis,' which is to say, Take your foot off that Negro's neck. And this was the beginning of the Fourth of July."

McIver discovered in sober truth, however, that the pinching shoe was on the other foot that summer: The white people were feeling put upon. The Negro's place in politics, a question that had been submerged since Reconstruction until Fusion government toppled Democratic party control, was causing race friction again. A solid Negro vote placed the Fusionists in power on their pledge to "restore local self-government." The resultant change of system placed many eastern counties, several large towns, and the state's chief city (Wilmington) under Negro domination. School districts were not exceptions. Dr. McIver learned to his great concern that the issue of local taxes for schools—to be voted on in special elections that autumn—was squarely in the path of the state's erupting wrath against the whole regime. He felt failure to "vote the tax to improve our schools" would be a stupendous blunder, but the situation did not look hopeful. He found the "Democrats of Sampson County against school tax, politics and 'the nigger,'" and their opposition was typical. At Warrenton, where his institute was otherwise a big success, he discovered "white folks generally against the tax."

Josephus Daniels, with newspaper acumen, spelled out the situation for McIver: "The only hope for public education in North Carolina," the editor's letter said, "is in restoring the state into the hands of white people. The tax is going to be voted in very few places, and when it is voted down it is much better for the cause of those who believe in public education to show that the people voted against it because of the character of the public officers than because they do not believe in being taxed for education. The odium of Negro school committeemen for white schools does not rest upon us but it has damned the law and made all our efforts unavailing."

The prognostication of failure was accurate. The local school tax not only failed to make headway, but some towns formerly having such a provision voted it out and celebrated the job with band and bonfire. Every rural district in Guilford County, in which McIver's home town of Greensboro was located, voted it down. "For schools?" Dr. McIver asked the father of seven children on election day. The man was not. He replied "I'm ag'in everything that is holding a poor man down."

Still, even though the local tax principle had sustained a body blow from which it could not recover until another political shuffle restored social tranquillity, 1897 had not been a bad year for the program toward which McIver was making a double row of tracks. Increased legislative support for schools was partly his doing. The Normal School's dollar-for-dollar allotment with that of the University was, on the other hand, a landmark completely his own and represented, besides, his swiftest victory.

In five years he had taken the new school over hurdles the older institution had been more than a hundred in surmounting. No McIver aim, not even his determination to have a training school, had received such rapid acceptance. Nor would any other achievement have more lasting significance. His steps leading to better schooling for every child would, in the course of extended crusading, have a farther reach. But the steps taken for "the express purpose of putting women educationally on a level with men" would be deeper by far.

14—

Horseman of the Apocalypse

"THINGS ARE BEGINNING to look somewhat more serious about the Maine," Mrs. Charles McIver wrote her husband the middle of March, 1898. Dr. McIver was in Washington at the time. As part of a constant effort to enlarge the perspective of his college students, he had accompanied the senior class on an excursion to the national capital. The girls paid their respects to President McKinley, had tea in the home of a Senator, and got some first hand knowledge of government procedure.

The United States Battleship *Maine,* to which Mrs. McIver's letter referred, had been destroyed, while lying at anchor in Havana harbor the evening of February 15, by an explosion that killed 260 officers and men. Two months and a few days later the country was at war with Spain.

The war had, in time, the unifying effect history has shown to be inevitable when countrymen submerge their sectional differences to join against an outside enemy. Yankee came to know that ex-rebel did not breathe fire and brimstone. Southerner learned that northerner did not have cloven hooves and a forked tail.

North Carolina, however, was not immediately able to set aside one troubled outcome of the War between the States—the issue of the Negro's place in politics. The state was tasting anew in 1898 the bitter sediment of its unresolved race question.

The Democratic party, holding undisputed sway from the end of Reconstruction to the fortuity of a Populist-Republican coalition, had barred Negroes from political office and had consequently kept the social peace. Under the Fusion control achieved in 1896 with Negro backing, Negro politicians stepped into positions for which they were not qualified. The inflammable situation, aggravated by Negro magistrates, city attorneys, school committeemen, and other administrative officials who were not far from illiterate, was fast becoming intolerable to the white population. Violence would flare before it was changed, and men would die in a race riot at Wilmington.

The sorry state of affairs had one hopeful aspect. Young men were seeking control of the Democratic party—long under the domination of an over-conservative element—and prominent among them was a forceful lawyer who thought he saw a way out of the state's dilemma. Charles Aycock believed, as he had believed in the days of his Chapel Hill accord with Charles McIver, that universal education was the "imperative and only remedy." An educated electorate, he insisted, was basic to progressive government. True, his argument that the party behind the office holder did the real governing—that no government could be wiser than the average intelligence of the people electing it—was undeniably a party plea for white supremacy, but he lifted it above the ugly level of race prejudice by making it a platform for education. Thus leading educators, who had not welcomed education as a political issue when it was introduced by church factions, now saw it tossed into an election campaign with their blessing. Thus, the stage was set for Aycock's election two years hence as the "educational governor" McIver might well have been.

Meanwhile, during military strife abroad and political discord at home, Dr. McIver packed his days with an extraordinary whirlwind of activities: with consuming interest in every facet of education; with speeches to big crowds and small in northern cities and in southern hamlets that were strung across the whole of North Carolina from seacoast to hidden mountain valley; with visits to schools, Vanderbilt University and Vassar College and Peabody Normal, from which he could learn something to improve his own; with correspondence that accumulated in spite of all he could do; with personal contacts that multiplied as Normal graduates increased and claimed his lively interest in their jobs, their marriages, and their babies.

His unique status was summed up early in the year when McIver addressed the Bingham School at Asheville. Dr. McIver, the school head declared in presenting the speaker, occcupied in his own particular field a position impossible for any other citizen —the position of a man who had within a decade, by the force of his determination and enthusiastic devotion, revolutionized public sentiment. A few years earlier, Major Robert Bingham told the cadets, "agitation of the program McIver advocated had been pronounced, by eminent men, to be unmistakably indicative of approaching lunacy."

McIver was on his way home at the time from a meeting of the superintendent's department, National Educational Association, in Chattanooga. A meeting of the full association would take him later to Washington as one of its chief speakers.

Since education as a qualification for voting was a campaign issue, Dr. McIver naturally had to take a stand on the matter. Agreeing with Aycock, he declared that the state "ought to give notice by law that it would not permit people to become full-fledged citizens, with the right of governing others, who would not educate themselves sufficiently to read the constitutions they swore to support." For that matter, since his opinion had been asked, he thought an educational qualification for matrimony would be worth more in providing enlightened citizenship than an educational qualification for suffrage! Unlike the suffrage qualification, it would apply to women (who could not vote, although he thought they should) as well as men, and "the state could better afford to have five illiterate men than one illiterate mother."

The legislation most needed for improving education, he continued, was provision for local taxation, and in that belief he was abreast of his time. On other questions, as in the case of woman suffrage, he was well ahead of his generation. He envisioned public ownership of books, for instance, and saw compulsory education in the offing, although he realized the state was not ready for the latter. To begin with, there were not enough schools to accommodate all pupils, and parents would "not yield cheerfully to a law which they would consider so radical." Too many of them were already resisting state intrusion into a matter they had entrusted to the church. The ultra-individualist would resist even more emphatically any further abrogation of parental authority.

The 1899 Legislature, Democratic once more, found McIver back in Raleigh for his biennial tug of war with keepers of the state purse. Also Baptist forces were on hand to play out a game in which they held some trump cards. Rev. John E. White appeared before the Joint Committee on Education to speak for the Baptist State Convention, which represented 175,000 people, in opposition to increased aid for state colleges. His theme was not new, but neither was it threadbare: "You can't explain to the taxpayers of North Carolina how in justice to the real interests of the State you can appropriate $60.00 or $70.00 per capita to teach men Latin and Greek and $1.18 per capita to fit the children of the people for the ordinary duties of citizenship. Lay the foundation strong in the minds of the masses, and then you may talk about providing universities and colleges." He disclosed, too, the existence of a deal that the Education Committee, not to mention the state college presidents, considered downright political skulduggery. Some of the politicians had agreed to prevent any increase of appropriations to higher education, McIver wrote home, "if Bailey and the Baptists would not inject the state aid question into the last campaign."

McIver still had hope, however, of obtaining funds for some needed additions at the woman's college. The bill for a dispensary got through without too much trouble, after which he could turn his attention to securing a gymnasium and library. The same senator who had thought a younger McIver clothed in purple and fine linen was still under the delusion that the college president was living sumptuously, but "a mean personal attack," which McIver admitted to his wife would have put him to bed ten years before, benefited him and harmed the maker. And there were light moments to relieve the tension. When somebody rose to ask why the girls could not take enough exercise in the dormitory halls, somebody else drawled audibly "They are full of trunks."

Moreover, a church paper, ranging itself on the side of the educators, administered a neat slap to the *Biblical Recorder*. The *Presbyterian Standard* of March 23 stated: "The *Biblical Recorder* of last week is jubilant over the fact that an appropriation for water works at the University was cut down from $10,000 to $7,500. We can imagine the type of demagogue who can boast on the stump of saving twenty-five hundred dollars by the great State of North Carolina, in sanitary necessities for its University students, but it is a small thing for a religious editor to boast of."

Dr. McIver was back at the college by then, having hurried home to be with his wife when their expected child arrived. Some of the neighbors privately considered Mrs. McIver demented because she was going to let the "female lady doctress" deliver her baby, but Dr. McIver found her in excellent spirits. She had found a nurse for the baby, she told him, and added that the "woman is in fortunate circumstances. She is a widow."

"Now, Lula," Dr. McIver objected. "Isn't that taking feminism a little too far?"

"Oh, Charles!" her answer reproved him. "You know what I mean and you know it's the truth. Since she has to live in, it's fortunate for us she doesn't have a family."

"Now, Lula," he chortled, "Now, Lula."

His working day was long, and he sometimes failed to realize that his assistants were not as tireless as he, nor as able to exclude intrusive matters. On the evening of March 20, he and his secretary were working late at the President's house as Dr. Gove and her nurses did maternity duty. McIver, intent upon his work, paced the floor, swung a set of keys, and dictated rapidly. The secretary, on the other hand, found it hard to concentrate, as she was half listening to the comings and goings in the rest of the house. When the infant had arrived safely, in spite of the unorthodox aid of a lady physician, Dr. McIver stated that was one child he meant to name himself. He gave the baby her mother's maiden name and called her by all of it, Lula Martin.

That spring (1899) the woman's college graduated its largest class so far—"thirty-nine as bright and noble specimens of young womanhood as were ever graduated from any institution," according to the Charlotte *Observer*. Editors were still entranced with the wondrous strange idea that a girl could possess both the womanliness that was expected of her and the mental dexterity that was not. And President McIver, as evidenced by his address at the seventh commencement, was still obsessed by the conviction that women's education was "the strategic point in all culture." Detours into all the educational fields never took him far from that guidepost. Whatever he made the subject of a speech—"Education for Democracy" or "Education for Citizenship" or "The Greatest Problem in Education"—the main theme was the same. He continued to insist that education of women was the surest, shortest, cheapest way to universal education. It was the high road, if indeed it was not the only road, to Parnassus.

After commencement he turned his attention to a couple of hundred letters that had piled up on his desk, many of them requests to speak at Fourth of July exercises and Masonic picnics. He chose to go to Mocksville because part of the proceeds would be used to educate an orphan at the Normal, and the previous time he had spoken there the event took in $800.

Demands for Dr. McIver to appear as a speaker were endless. When an invitation left the date unspecified, he consulted a book of engagements that he always had with him, and named the nearest time he would be available. When there were conflicting requests for the same date, he chose the place, more often than not, which was the smallest and most remote, hence the least likely to have heard his message. The speech itself was no problem. He had a notebook in which there were sixty-six entries, of a few words each, suggesting humorous stories, anecdotes, and the like, from which he could select material most applicable to place and occasion and weave it into his familiar theme. His old nervousness about speaking showed only before he began. Then he was apt to keep moving the water pitcher and glass on the table before him from one point to another. For commencement events he liked to appear at schools in which some of the Normal girls were teaching.

He found time, nevertheless, to keep in good repair his relation with old friends such as Alderman and Page and Aycock and Daniels and Winston, and new friends such as William Jennings Bryan and Nicholas Murray Butler. He visited Page, who had become editor of the *Atlantic Monthly* in 1898. Page visited him and promised to come back and lecture to the college girls. While at Page's Cambridge home, he went for an hour's visit with Mrs. Spencer, who was so glad to see him she said she had a great mind to kiss him, but the dear old lady had grown too deaf to hear his permission. Dr. Butler had written from Columbia University that he wanted to talk over several matters and gave instructions for reaching him: "I am most readily found at my house, 119 East 30th Street, at 9 o'clock in the morning, as I leave shortly after that hour for the university, which is a long distance away from the center of the city." Dr. Butler also stated: "I wish that generous men and women who have poured out so much money in the south for the education of the Negro, could now be induced to see that a mere fraction of that vast fund, if expended along the line that you are developing for the education of white women, would be an almost unequaled service to the cause of an advanced and more effective civilization."

On his way home from Massachusetts, McIver called on Butler as requested, and went besides, among three thousand others, to a dinner for Bryan at the Grand Central Palace, paid a dollar for his meal, and heard a great speech.

The friend, however, who was claiming the most of his time was Winston. McIver was working tirelessly to bring "that stimulating genius" back from Texas to head the North Carolina College of Agriculture and Mechanic Arts. A letter in early June from B. R. Lacy, state commissioner of labor and printing, encouraged him concerning the outcome.

"Dear Charles: You cannot hide your light under a bushel," Mr. Lacy wrote. "Every one is congratulating you on your victory. I heard a prominent judge say a day or two ago 'Winston is obliged to be elected, he has the shrewdest manipulator in the State managing his campaign, one who never gets beaten.' When asked who, he said 'President McIver.'"

The unidentified judge was right. After three years at the University of Texas, Winston returned to head the state college at Raleigh, and the fate of North Carolina's higher education thus came to rest in the hands of an incomparable triumvirate—McIver, Alderman, Winston. They were three congenial men who could frolic together as irrepressibly as boys; each was a person whose sound judgment in questions of education the others could depend upon.

Mr. Daniels, another with whom McIver kept in close touch personally and by letter, was not quite so reliable in his reactions. In his undoubted zeal to further the cause of education, and especially to advance the efforts of his good friend McIver, he occasionally fell in with ill-considered schemes. After he had advocated that a few women be admitted to A. and M. College industrial departments not existing at the woman's college, Mc-Iver urged that he be on his guard when writing about greater opportunities for women lest fewer opportunities result. The plan he recommended might be used as an excuse to lessen the appropriations for the Greensboro school, where the majority of girls would study, and even be interpreted by some to mean that Bailey was telling the truth when he said the woman's college neglected industrial education.

In another letter he expressed pained surprise that the editor had voluntarily copied some comments from *Charity and Children,* a church paper, setting forth the old denominational plaint that McIver and Alderman were hostile to public schools because of selfishness for their own. McIver said he doubted whether all their critics put together had "plead more unceasingly" for public schools than he and Alderman, and thought any effort to prove the contrary should meet with no encouragement from their personal and educational friends. It was bad enough, he believed, that they should suffer for pure political purposes, without being treated as the little boy treated the snake. The boy beat the snake after he killed it in order to teach there was a judgment after death.

The ceaseless round of McIver's activity was beginning to worry Mr. Page, who wrote from his *Atlantic* office to say so: "Let me whisper into your ear in confidence a secret—and a most important and solemn utterance it is. You need to rest this summer. I've come twice within an ace of the last precipice by not taking such advice quite in time, and you are wound up with too active and strong springs to know when the proper time comes. . . . Mrs. Spencer and I had a long talk about you the other night; and we were both glad to discover that we each swear by you."

Rest? How could he? Why, there were innumerable townships in the state that did not have the first sign of a local school tax; in fact, there were only thirty districts in the entire state, all urban, that considered education of sufficient importance to levy a local tax for support of schools. The children of more than 950 public school districts were altogether without schoolhouses, and those in 1,132 more sat on rough pine planks in log houses chinked with clay. Too often the positive command of the constitution that county commissioners keep the schools open four months in the year or risk indictment was a dead letter and nothing more. Moreover, an attitude adverse to schooling still cropped up. A prominent Raleigh man had told Mr. Moses, superintendent of the state capital's schools, that he did not believe in "giving them" more than a seven years' course, and another leading man, and a good man at that, had stated that Latin had no place in the public schools for the reason that inmates of the poorhouse should not be fed on cake.

McIver's answer to Page's plea, then, was to set out in a hack driven by Zeke to conduct an institute at Boone. He carried along his daughter Annie for the pleasure of her company and Mr. Forney for the convenience of his shorthand. The thermometer registered 95 degrees the day they left, and the road stretched a weary 135 miles ahead—a journey of four and a half days. But the very first day confirmed the necessity for such discomfort. Beyond Winston the party crossed Yadkin River on a ferry boat, and Dr. McIver asked the ferryman if he knew anything of the State Normal College at Greensboro. The man could not "allow as how he did," a sufficient answer in itself to any suggestion of slowing down.

A little farther along Dr. McIver saw one of the state's log schoolhouses, a run-down one-room shack on a neglected hilltop. He had Zeke stop and he walked up the slope and looked in the window at crude furnishings of the sort duplicated in numerous other schoolrooms. Before leaving the vicinity, he sought out a committeeman and arranged to make a speech in the school on his return trip.

On the third afternoon at a sultry four o'clock the little company saw a rain cloud hovering over the mountain tops. Only a few rain drops, not enough to bring relief from dust or heat, fell on the travelers, but the drive took them shortly into a valley that had been refreshed and revived by rain—all of which was noted by a silent McIver. A few days later in Boone he likened the coming of education to a community to the coming of rain to a parched countryside, bringing life and growth and enrichment. The strength of his speeches lay to a marked degree in the fact that they were closely related to the experience of his listeners.

Dr. McIver lectured five hours a day and then dictated letters to Mr. Forney for the rest of the afternoon and sometimes into the evening—even as late as midnight. The mountaineers had never in their born days seen a grown man taking down something another man said in funny little squiggles, and they gathered in silent knots by the porch window to watch that phenomenon taking place within the Coffey Hotel. From Boone the McIver party went to Blowing Rock, a beauty stop much admired by McIver and one at which he hoped one day to have a summer school connected with the woman's college.

Back home, Mrs. McIver was seeing countless persons who came seeking the college president, and found just telling them he was not at home consumed a great deal of her time. One day as she was sewing on her front porch a woman came to list rooms for rent to college girls and shook Mrs. McIver's customary composure by her opening remark: "Why, Mrs. McIver, you working! I didn't know you ever did anything."

The idea was widespread among Mrs. McIver's neighbors that she was a poor housekeeper, and in the sense that she troubled herself little with the McGuffey Reader ideal of a place for everything and everything in its place (except her husband's belongings) they were right. She completely respected Dr. McIver's sense of orderliness. One of their daughters has recalled that her father's room had a sort of laboratory neatness; another has said that the socks her mother rolled up and placed in precise arrangement in her father's chest of drawers suggested rows of little soldiers marching.

Most of the neighbors, in all truth, did not consider Mrs. McIver idle, knowing the tremendous help she gave Dr. McIver and the amount of entertaining she had to do, but they found her something of an enigma just the same. It was not surprising that the president's wife, setting out to clean the attic, for instance, was almost sure to be interrupted; the surprising part was that she would not *worry* about the unfinished task. That they considered downright unnatural and, seeking a word to explain it, came up with the conclusion that Mrs. McIver was "impractical."

Dr. McIver could not have agreed with them less. It seemed to him the height of common sense that she should give him help of a sort that could not be hired at any price, and leave household chores to servants who could not only be cheaply hired but had greater physical strength to do them. The top wage for a woman servant was $2.00 per week; more often the help received $1.50 or $1.75. Men in domestic service received a maximum wage of $3.00.

Besides, the colored help liked to run things. Julia Booker, a peerless cook, not only wanted no interference in her dominion but was philosophical about Mrs. McIver's "impracticality" as well, although its most common form was inviting people to eat on the spur of the moment and leaving entirely to Julia the problem of making the food go around. One day when four women callers stayed beyond the limits of a normal visit and were in the McIver parlor at noon, Mrs. McIver impulsively invited them to stay for lunch. She sent Annie to inform Julia, and Annie grumbled: "She must have known an hour ago they were going to stay; why couldn't she have given us a little notice?"

"Now, chile," Julia remonstrated. "You just hush right up. You is old enough to know dat people is de way dey is and we can't do nothing to change 'em. Besides which, your mother was meant for the pulpit, not the kitchen."

Julia brought up her own family in the servant's cottage back of President McIver's house, and at the same time kept watch over the McIver kitchen, not infrequently spicing her service with privileged comment. One night at dinner Mrs. McIver said, "Julia, this must have been an old chicken. It's still a little tough."

"Yes'm," Julia agreed with equanimity. "That chicken was a lady of uncertain years."

Both the household and college help were devoted to Mrs. McIver. On one occasion "Uncle" William, a porter who stuttered badly, was helping her unpack a box of homemade specialties from her mother-in-law. "Mmm, blackberry cordial," she remarked, handing a bottle to William. "That's good. And tomato ketchup," she went on. "That's almost better."

"Y-y-y-yes," stammered Uncle William. "It will l-l-l-last l-l-l-longer."

From Blowing Rock, on a Sunday night in August, Dr. McIver sent home his itinerary. "My plan is to leave here next Saturday and speak in Lenoir Saturday night. Sunday I go down the Yadkin through the Happy Valley and will speak in Wilkes County Monday. Monday night Annie and I will spend in North Wilkesboro and Tuesday Annie will go by rail to Winston and I will stop for one or two days at Elkin. Zeke will make his way home alone from North Wilkesboro."

The stop in Wilkes County took him to the forlorn little schoolhouse where the committeeman, as promised, had assembled an audience, twenty-seven persons, to hear him speak.

Dust was fearful on the first ten miles of the trip from Blowing Rock to Lenoir, then the rain poured. But McIver talked schools, as he could not have done traveling by train, with farm people in whose home he stopped, with the hired man who proudly showed his grain and stock, with the old merchant from whom he bought watermelons, from a potter fashioning on his wheel the same sort of crocks that had filled Sallie McIver's well house, to the distiller who held a government license to make whiskey, and to a couple of Normal girls who prepared supper for him and his party although they arrived after nine o'clock on a Saturday night.

In spite of all the rewarding incidents, it was an uneasy journey for Dr. McIver. He had received at Blowing Rock a letter from Mrs. McIver containing news that the college night watchman had typhoid fever. All diseases seemed particularly virulent that summer; a notion had gained credence that soldiers returning from Cuba (where more had died of disease than battle) had brought with them sicknesses worse than the home variety. Measles had actually been mistaken for smallpox. Malaria was nearly as frightening as typhoid. The State Health Bulletin for September warned that malaria was prevalent in all parts of many counties, including Guilford.

Through much of October, however, the health of the college girls was never better. On the twenty-third, Dr. Gove reported in her daily account to the president that several girls were too indisposed to attend classes, but only one was sick enough to be taken to the infirmary. By the end of the month both President McIver and Dr. Gove were getting alarmed over the incidence of malaria, which had sent thirty students to their beds. Even so, only four girls were in the infirmary, and when the literary societies held their initiation services for new members and had a general reception on November 3, attendance was excellent. A couple of days after that the uncle of one student called to see her on a Sunday afternoon and thought he had never seen her so well. The following day she was too sick to go to class.

By the tenth of November, illness was taking on the proportions of an epidemic. On the eleventh, Dr. McIver wrote the parents of fifteen students who were not improving according to expectations, and promised should the condition of any girl become serious, he would telegraph immediately. In three days the number of students whose parents received such a letter had doubled.

On the fifteenth, a knock on the classroom door interrupted Dr. McIver as he lectured to his civics class. The girls got a glimpse of Miss Kirkland as the door opened, and the sight of her out of her accustomed place was somehow disturbing. They whispered about it, realizing they were a little frightened without quite knowing why. Dr. McIver returned, spoke more breathlessly than he normally did, but otherwise continued the class as usual. The girls learned after the lesson ended that a student— the one whose uncle had rejoiced in her good health—had died.

Within three days the situation had changed from dread to nightmare. Four girls were seriously ill, Dr. Gove reported to the president, but not of malaria. Her diagnosis was typhoid. Within an hour the school had been suspended.

Long ringing of the college bell, signal for a quick assembly in the chapel, brought the girls together to hear they were to go home immediately. In the gray dawn of the following morning, Dr. McIver's secretary was summoned to his office to find two haggard men, the president and Professor Joyner, huddled over a handful of still glowing coals. They were making arrangements to send home the body of a girl who had died of typhoid in the night.

The students behaved well. Many made it plain that they did not intend to "desert"; instead they pitched in to do what they could. They carried trays, cleaned rooms, waited on sick girls, and assisted generally in a situation from which the colored help, superstitious and awed by death, had fled at the first hint of pestilence, leaving doctors and nurses short-handed.

Greensboro women also justified President McIver's conviction that wherever unselfish service was required women would be found performing it. They volunteered by the score to assist trained nurses hastily recruited from cities as far away as Richmond. Sixty-seven girls had malaria, and ten who recovered were stricken with typhoid. Fifty-five had typhoid. There were fourteen student deaths. (A fifteenth victim was the college matron.) Thanksgiving two funerals left the college. To Professor Joyner, as dean of students, fell the task of accompanying the bodies home; many years would pass before the horror of it stopped disrupting his sleep.

The parents behaved well, too. A statement was published, which had been prepared by relatives of girls who were ill or dead, expressing gratitude for the manner in which the sick were cared for and declaring that the college authorities had done everything possible. It was signed, among many others, by Mr. and Mrs. T. B. Bailey, of Mocksville, who lost two daughters, their only children, in the epidemic.

The newspapers took a moderate tone. They required that the truth be known, but at the same time urged that there be no jumping to conclusions. A Charlotte *Observer* editorial said in general what other state papers were saying: "The people of the state have taken a very conservative view of this outbreak; they have deplored it but have arrived at no hasty conclusions about it and the absence of all harsh criticism, either general or specific, has been very notable. A more volatile people would have chosen a victim ere this and demanded his slaughter—not so the North Carolinians. But they do expect to know the exact truth about all the wretched business and will be content with nothing less. Moreover, they will be apt to recognize it when they see it, and it will be a wonder if anything else could be palmed off on them as a substitute." It asked both that the people judge very charitably of any person who might be found to blame, and that there be no effort at whitewashing or concealment.

There were exceptions to both charity and moderation. Church opposition to state education, moribund as it was, had one convulsive outburst left in it, and its death rattle under the circumstances was ugly. The *Biblical Recorder* sought a culprit: "The authorities of the institution, the pupils and their parents deserve unspeakable sympathy. In such a time no one can be hasty in judgment. But on the other hand the public welfare demands a relentless investigation. The epidemic was not necessary. Some one has blundered sadly."

That attack on a stricken institution was more than Professor Joyner could tolerate. Good Baptist that he was, he canceled his subscription.

The Trustees, following tests by a battery of medical experts and sanitary engineers, reported that contamination of a central well, source of the college drinking water, had caused the epidemic, and added their "thorough endorsement" of the course followed by president and faculty throughout. But the *Recorder* considered their exoneration of the management "ineffective," declaring "We do not know what Boards of Trustees and Boards of Health may say, but there is no doubting what fathers and mothers will do."

Ezekiel (Zeke) Robinson, general factotum extraordinary–janitor, mail carrier, coachman, porter, and presidential valet

The office of Dr. McIver during his administration as president of the state college for women

Early Students' Union, the Students' Building which furnished emergency housing for girls of the Normal and Industrial College after the fire of 1904

Present Students' Union (Elliott Hall), Woman's College of the University of North Carolina

The *Presbyterian Standard* had an answer to that. It figured if anybody was to blame it was the editor of the *Recorder* himself.

The publication quoted the *Recorder* as having said "Some one has blundered sadly. The State made lavish provision for the building, equipment and maintenance of the institution." It went on to say it was "sure the people of North Carolina have not forgotten the part which the *Biblical Recorder* took in preventing appropriations to the State institutions during the sessions of the Legislature last winter," recalled its own comment that it was a small thing for a religious editor to boast of, and testified to having thought at the time if a typhoid epidemic broke out "the people of this State would know whom to hold responsible."

In another instance, a doctor whose sister had died sent a communication to the *News and Observer* demanding to know why the press had remained silent. "Why was it these young ladies were huddled in a pest hole? If it be criminal indifference and neglect it is nothing short of murder. If it be incompetence it is surely a scandal." Mr. Daniels, thinking it would be better to publish the letter than to have the doctor send it elsewhere and say he was refused a hearing, sent it to McIver with the suggestion that he or the Chairman of Trustees prepare a reply to appear along with it.

Dr. McIver had no time to reply; no time, indeed, to read the messages of sympathy and support that were arriving by the hundreds—from state officials and important educators and leading citizens, from Protestant and Catholic groups, from Jewish rabbis. Some of the letter writers expressed pathetic gratitude for all that had been done vainly to save the life of one of their own or sent a check to pay for the casket in which a cherished daughter had made her final journey home. It was Mr. Daniels who followed the doctor's statement with an editor's note in defense of his own and other newspapers.

Dr. Alderman, who had explored with Dr. McIver the whole of North Carolina and its thought processes, offered the sanest word of assurance to his friend: "I'm one of the few, I fancy, who can more nearly enter into your mind. You have acted with dignity and that is all one can do at such a time. You have done your duty, too, and this is not the state to be unjust or even unkind to any man, much less a faithful public servant."

He was right, to be sure. The isolated attacks did not reflect public opinion. The esteem in which North Carolina held Dr. McIver was no whit lessened.

The college reopened on the thirtieth of January, 1900, with the Board of Directors assuring both public and students that the institution's physical condition was as near perfect as human skill could make it. Changes included substitution of city water for well water, substitution of single beds and mattresses for the double bedding that had been destroyed, and new plumbing.

The time of trial was not quite over. Shortly after the college resumed Dr. McIver's young son contracted typhoid. Fortunately the case was mild, and there was no further interruption of school work.

The Legislature, when it met again, made appropriations to pay off debts resulting from the epidemic, the suspension, and the necessary permanent improvements, and provide in addition for a practice and observation school building, additional dormitory and recitation room, and better library equipment.

A new century, as well as a new year, was under way, filled with the promise intrinsic in fresh beginnings. The school and its president alike could look forward to wider usefulness.

Educate a man and you educate an individual; educate a woman
and you educate a family.   —*Charles Duncan McIver*

15—

"Free Schools for All the People"

EARLY MONTHS of the twentieth century delineated a wider sphere
of service for Dr. McIver, particularly as the college president's
activity related to the common schools. In the spring of 1900 he
became identified with the significant Conference for Education
in the South.

The Conference had its origin two years earlier in a small
meeting at Capon Springs, West Virginia, at a time when it could
not compete for public interest, even if it had tried, with events
transpiring in Cuba. On June 29, 1898, when half a hundred
congenial guests accepted an invitation from Captain W. H. Sale
to confer on educational matters at his mountain retreat, the
United States Navy was blockading the Spanish fleet at Santiago
harbor. Yet, while the little gathering was neither as dramatic
as Rough Riders storming San Juan Hill nor as symbolic as an
erstwhile Confederate officer ("Fighting Joe" Wheeler) commanding New England Yankees, it too would have far-reaching
consequences and focus attention on new horizons.

The conference was suggested, according to Dr. Charles W.
Dabney, historian of the Southern Education Movement, by Dr.
Edward Abbott, an Episcopal clergyman of Cambridge, Massachusetts (brother of Dr. Lyman Abbott, of New York), in something of a missionary spirit. The main subject was improvement
of education for Negroes and poor mountain whites. A second
gathering at Capon Springs the following year raised its sights
somewhat. The group chose as president Dr. J. L. M. Curry,
whose knowledge encompassed the whole range of southern
education problems, and at the same time it acquired a distinguished group of new members.

Notable among the newcomers was Robert C. Ogden, wealthy New York merchant, who brought to the conference in his private railroad car "some 25 ladies and gentlemen of the North." Mr. Ogden was president of trustees for Hampton Institute, a Negro normal and agricultural school at Hampton, Virginia, maintained under white direction. He had the vision to grasp a principle that both Dr. Curry and Dr. H. B. Frissell, head of Hampton, insisted was fundamental to Negro education: If the southern Negro was to be educated the southern white man would have to undertake the job. Acceptance of that fact removed the conferees' purpose from its narrow frame and gave it new scope and direction. Since southern white people had also to be taught, and since— even before that—they had to be converted to the idea of education for everybody and induced to tax themselves to provide it, the Conference was forced to accept universal education in the South as its mission.

The logic which shaped Conference thinking at the second meeting was already being proclaimed by a strong voice. Dr. Charles McIver often insisted in his addresses "that the Negro's future progress depends upon the progress of the white population where he lives."

Thus when Dr. McIver showed up at Hampton commencement exercises, invited at the suggestion of Dr. Curry, Mr. Ogden regarded him as a "great find." Something of that realization was reflected in Dr. McIver's letters to Mrs. McIver: "I have had a rather remarkable experience for the past few days. I reached Hampton Wednesday at 2:15 and with no notice whatever, after a few talks by Dickerman, Booker Washington, and a few others, Dr. Frissell called on me and spoke very complimentarily of our work at Greensboro. My remarks seemed to 'catch the crowd,' and I have been regarded as something of a new discovery since Wednesday p.m. Thursday afternoon to my astonishment I was called on again at the close of the commencement proper and after three eloquent speeches by Booker Washington, Dr. Curry, and Mr. Ogden (who manages Wanamaker's New York house at a salary of $100,000 a year) I was introduced as a humorist. It was all very embarrassing, but notwithstanding it was

6 o'clock, the exercises having begun at 2:30 p.m., I was obliged to talk. I opened up with the story about Hosea and the major and minor prophets and talked about 20 minutes. It was an immense audience, there being in it 400 or 500 white people, some 50 of whom were wealthy New York, Philadelphia, Boston and Providence people.

"When we closed, a New York banker came to me and said 'I will send you $1000 for your work. I will send it next fall.' Last night at the hotel a rich man and his wife from Brooklyn said they wanted to help my work a little and asked me to send them some literature about the institution.

"I was invited to join the northern party today and so came with them in their special cars to Washington—a delightful party of teachers, millionaires, preachers, old maids, artists, newspaper reporters, etc.—all the guests of Mr. Ogden, who paid everybody's fare and furnished food and refreshment for the party."

The McIver magnetism produced a lasting effect; henceforth he was one of the Conference mainsprings. He captivated Mr. Ogden and other influential members of the Ogden party simply by being himself—a country boy who never got above his raising. He told the same jokes to the high and mighty, used the same homespun anecdotes that had endeared him to simple rural audiences, and "it pleased people more than I had expected it would. The Yankee loves a well applied joke even if he does hem and haw too much to use one successfully himself." Dr. McIver had a quality, deriving both from his enthusiasm and his passionate faith in what he was doing, that attracted important people to him and to his program alike. The banker who promised, and gave, $1,000 to the North Carolina Normal and Industrial College was George Foster Peabody. His friendship for McIver, sparked by the Hampton encounter, was not only a firm and lasting personal relation, it was profitable for the institution as well. In June of the next year, after further acquaintance with president and college, Mr. Peabody gave the school $10,000, one half of which was earmarked for an "educational park." (A former student employed by a Boston firm of landscape architects persuaded her bosses to design the park without charge, and the campus, as a result, was on its way to becoming a thing of real beauty.)

The Hampton commencement was a providential time for Dr. McIver to put in an appearance. The third Capon Springs Conference, held shortly afterward, elected Mr. Ogden president and launched upon a program to transform the group from a council in seclusion to a public forum. Meetings would be held at larger places—Winston-Salem, Athens, Richmond, Birmingham, and the like—readily accessible to larger numbers and better geared to advertise the needs of southern education.

Back home in North Carolina, Dr. McIver's alma mater was reaching out once more to claim him, as one of its own, for the University presidency. Dr. Alderman had resigned the position in May to become president of Tulane. Yet, much as he wished to serve the University—he had been on its Board of Trustees from 1889 to 1895 and on the Board's Executive Committee part of that time—Dr. McIver could not be persuaded to leave "the other side of the house." In announcing his decision, he first expressed to a newspaper reporter the bit of educational philosophy that has been most closely associated with his name: "Educate a man and you educate an individual; educate a woman and you educate a family."

The pace he had declined to slacken in spite of warnings took its toll that spring, and for three weeks after the Normal commencement he was confined to his room with illness. The Trustees gave him a two-month vacation, but his manner of spending it would scarcely have conformed to any accepted idea of leisure. He was off shortly for Charleston to attend a meeting of the National Educational Association, and he helped draft, as a member of its committee on resolutions, a declaration of principles for the organization. The figure that was lengthening its shadow over the regional scene was looming larger on the national horizon, too. Alderman was another who had a voice in that committee, which Nicholas Murray Butler served as chairman.

In August, McIver lectured on history for two weeks in Atlanta to normal classes, gave each talk twice—first to the white teachers, then to the Negro—and thought he could not have found a better way of spending his "vacation." In his method of teaching history, which placed great emphasis on historical firsts, there is quite possibly a key to his own character. He expressed great admiration for Hamilton, first secretary of the treasury, who had, working without precedent, established a sound fiscal policy for a new republic; for John Marshall, who had set up his own guideposts for elevating the Supreme Court to a position of prestige and power; for Thomas Jefferson, who had authored a declaration of independence and pioneered a new faith in democracy. That respect for the innovator, the originator, the blazer of new paths and the lighter of fresh lamps in dark places, suggests a great deal about Charles McIver's motivation in resisting any change of course. There had been good governors of North Carolina and good presidents of the University and good executives of corporations, but no one before had established a college at which young North Carolina women could obtain a practical, useful education at small cost, due to state support. Nor had anyone else been what Page, writing of him in the *Atlantic Monthly*, called "a common-sense, dollar-and-cents knight errant of popular education." He had asked one of the most conservative Anglo-Saxon communities in the world, the article continued, "How can a great man be born of an ignorant mother?" and proceeded to show them "in cotton bales and mules that an educated woman could earn back, with double compound interest, the money spent on her education."

He also maintained with Sibylline foresight that it was less than enough for women to be provided with education; they must have a chance to use it fully. "A new day has dawned for women intellectually," he declared in a speech at Richmond. "You cannot keep a human being with a well trained intellect unemployed. A properly educated man has within him something which makes him go. With the new opportunities of education coming to women, there is a greater demand for an outlet for their activities. It is to the interest of all of us that their great tact, enthusiasm, and power should not exhaust themselves upon chimerical schemes or foolish crusades as has often been the case in the past."

The political campaign in progress in his home state that first year of the new century was in actuality an educational campaign as well. Charles Aycock, as candidate for governor, was proclaiming universal education as a duty of the state. The thesis was not original with him; he admitted that freely. His two good friends, McIver and Alderman, had made exactly that argument the subject of a state-wide crusade a decade earlier.

For his own part, nevertheless, Mr. Aycock was walking a political tightrope with considerable aplomb. The real campaign issue was a constitutional amendment laying down an educational qualification for citizenship. But there were exceptions, contained in a "grandfather's clause," which would have the effect of excluding from the polls only the Negro who could not read and write and leaving the ballot in the hands of equally unlettered white men; the clause provided that persons who could vote in 1867 and their descendants were to be enrolled in a permanent registration. The registration, however, was to be closed in another eight years, and that gave the candidate his cue to pledge education for every child. He promised uneducated white men, fearful that their sons would be disfranchised, that no child would stay ignorant for want of school facilities. Renouncing the expediency of an appeal to race prejudice, he declared at the same time that the Negro must have means to regain his suffrage. And he won quite handily. In fact, he was elected by the biggest majority that had ever been given a North Carolina governor.

The keynote of Aycock's inaugural in January of 1901, as it had been of his campaign, was Education. The governor recalled that he had pledged the wealth of the state to education, education of "the whole people," and reiterated that he meant to redeem that pledge. Apparently he did. When bills were introduced requiring distribution of school taxes to the separate races on a basis of what each paid, he saw the maneuver for what it was —an effort to restrict educational opportunity for Negroes and keep them ineligible to vote. Aycock stated flatly that he would resign before he would be party to any such violation of good faith.

During that session of the Legislature a physician had to take Dr. McIver in hand and put him to bed. The college president had been ill in November, too. The super-charged dynamo that was McIver was running down more frequently. Between times, however, he had lost none of his zestfulness. Early in December he had enjoyed a wonderful visit with Page, who was back in New York with the publishing firm of Doubleday, Page, & Co., and took keen pleasure in a new experience, his first Turkish bath, as well as a familiar one, oysters on the half-shell at Delmonico's. The two men attended together, as guests of Mr. Ogden, the Pennsylvania Society's annual dinner at the Waldorf-Astoria. One of the speakers was Andrew Carnegie, a diminutive Scot with a fabulous fortune, who asserted that rich men were "trustees" of their wealth and should administer it for the public good. "Little Andy" seemed particularly to enjoy giving away libraries. The other speaker was a young English writer who had been captured by the Boers, one Winston Churchill by name.

Frequent newspaper items, moreover, were proof that recurrent illness had not slowed McIver down in the slightest:

"Dr. Charles D. McIver will deliver the commencement address before the graduating class of the University College of Medicine at Richmond."

"Dr. McIver left this afternoon for Woodleaf, Rowan County, where he will deliver an address tonight before a school taught by one of the graduates of the Normal College."

"Dr. Charles McIver will appear on the commencement program of the University of Tennessee at Knoxville." (The institution was headed by Dr. Charles W. Dabney, whom McIver had known since his senior year at Chapel Hill when Dabney joined the University of North Carolina faculty.)

"Dr. Charles D. McIver has made arrangements to have members of the Educational Conference, which meets in Winston on the 18th of April, to spend several hours in the city."

Mr. Ogden hoped, as president of the Conference for Education in the South, to promote mutual understanding between northerners and southerners by having them get to know one another. As a means to that end he inaugurated, in connection with the first enlarged Conference, a custom he followed with its successors. He chartered a whole railroad train and, having loaded it with philanthropists, rich men and women who might become philanthropists, notables in many fields of achievement, and journalists who could interpret what they saw, set out on a tour of inspection. Each excursion was designed to furnish first-hand information on specific institutions and general conditions alike. The company grew at every stop. The initial Special, made up of five Pullmans, had around seventy people aboard when it left New York, but the number had increased to one hundred, among them Daniels and Aycock who joined the party at Raleigh, by the time it reached Greensboro.

Dr. McIver met the train with enough carriages to transport all passengers to his college, where the girls had been given a holiday and several of the visitors made addresses. Later the party visited North Carolina Agricultural and Mechanical College for Negroes, also at Greensboro.

Speakers at the woman's college included Dr. Curry, Dr. Frissell, Mr. Page, Mr. Ogden, and George Foster Peabody, already the institution's friends; Dr. Francis G. Peabody, of Harvard; President James McAlister, of Drexel Institute; Editors Lyman Abbott, of the *Outlook,* and Albert Shaw, of the *Review of Reviews;* Mrs. Potter Wilson; and W. J. Schieffelin.

There was one among the distinguished company who made no speech at all, but the presence of John D. Rockefeller, Jr., with the excursion and at the Conference, was in itself one of those circumstances that deflect the course of history. As a result of that visit, Dr. Dabney reported, Mr. Rockefeller's father formed the General Education Board "to hold and disburse funds for the benefit of education." During the first three decades after its organization in March, 1902, the Board received from John D. Rockefeller, Sr., close to $130,000,000 for the "promotion of education within the United States of America, without distinction of race, sex, or creed." Thus, in Dr. Dabney's view, "events arising out of the movement for Southern education led directly to the inauguration of a series of the greatest philanthropic enterprises the world has ever known."

The fourth Conference, having achieved breadth of representation, attained breadth of policy as well. It determined upon a campaign to secure "free schools for all the people." It authorized an executive committee, the Southern Education Board, to implement the purpose by all methods of popular propaganda, including a Bureau of Information to collect and disseminate facts that would make impressive argument.

Mr. Ogden, directed to serve as chairman of the executive group and select its remaining members, appointed his great find, McIver, at once. Other choices, Alderman, Frissell, Dabney, and George Foster Peabody who was a New Yorker then but Georgiaborn, assured a hearing for the southern viewpoint. Indeed, when Mr. Ogden wrote Dr. McIver in July that he had appointed Reverend Wallace Buttrick, of Albany, to the committee, he expressed the intention of securing still an additional southern man. He had recognized, along with other clear thinkers among his Conference colleagues, that ground for any successful sowing of educational seeds in the South had to be prepared by natives who best understood the difficulties.

And difficulties there were for any movement of northern origin. Countless southerners either remembered the Civil War, ended but thirty-six years before, or had been steeped in the harsh recollections of those who did remember. In their book, since they were acquainted with no other, all Yankees were marauders —either marauding soldiers of the Sherman ilk or marauding civilians of carpetbagger stripe. The older members of that segment were apt to cast all northern benevolence to education in the form of postwar teachers sent into their section by Freedmen's Bureau or missionary society; to recall with undiminished rancor the overzealous ones, intent upon founding universal brotherhood without further ado, who had trampled rough shod over the white population's sensibilities.

Such persons were leery of any interference from the North, even if it were nothing but counsel. As a matter of fact, there were intransigent southerners who resented advice as outspokenly as they did monetary assistance. They simply did not mean to have a bunch of damyankees telling them how to run their business. Mr. Ogden, as conciliatory as possible, countered antagonistic attitudes with insistence that "Northern people interested in the cause came in fraternal spirit, with no pride of opinion or dictation of method, working through men born on the soil and using local machinery," and was sometimes baffled by the manner in which his efforts were misconstrued.

Mr. Ogden, having been convinced that a lifting of white living standards, both in education and economics, must precede any improvement of the Negro's lot, had also accepted Dr. McIver's reasoning that education of white women was the quickest method of achieving over-all general betterment. Yet, when he incorporated into a Philadelphia speech McIver's argument that "the best field for investment in the South" was the training of white women the conclusion was "by perverse and studied misrepresentation," Ogden wrote McIver, interpreted to mean that he considered "white women of lower natural intelligence than Negro women."

"Only prejudice born of ignorance could invent such a construction," he wrote the man whose ideas he had borrowed. It gave him some comfort that Hoke Smith had heard and warmly endorsed the speech, and Mr. Smith, a Georgia lawyer, publisher, and politician, would not have suffered gladly any perversion of McIver doctrine. He had gone on record many times as believing that McIver had done more for the educational awakening of their native state—Mr. Smith was a North Carolinian by birth—than any other man.

Now and then Dr. McIver got a taste of deliberate misrepresentation, too. The Associated Press sent out a straightforward, unemotional summary of an address he made before the Armstrong Association in New York, but somewhere between transmission and the editorial rooms of some southern newspapers, the account got badly garbled. In spite of the fact that a major purpose of the Association was the advancement of Hampton Institute for colored people, Dr. McIver stuck to his guns in assigning the education of white women a primary place among civilizing forces. He was the Negro's friend, he said, and every Negro in North Carolina knew the truth so well that not one had ever voted against an appropriation he advocated, but in his opinion northern philanthropists who had "shown great and commendable zeal in aiding the education of colored men and women in the South" could do a ten-fold greater service to the whole region, including the colored people, by duplicating their gifts for the hitherto neglected white girl.

He told Mrs. McIver that some reports of the speech did not please him, and well they might not have. The Macon, Georgia, *Telegraph,* which identified him correctly as president of North Carolina's "Normal College for Women," nevertheless quoted him as saying that his state, although it had six Normal schools for Negroes, had not a single Normal school where a white woman could go, notwithstanding the fact that the white women of the South set the pace for its civilization. "As the setters of civilization's pace were barred out of school, it was naturally left to be inferred that the South's civilization was at a pretty low ebb," the paper continued, and expressed more than a little ire at a man, so unknown to its editors that they misspelled his name, who had "given currency to further foolish notions about the South."

"Charles D. McIvor," it commented, "announced that the South was 'beginning to get out of the woods,' citing a strike in his town as proof of the assertion. Said he: 'I am thankful for that strike in somewhat the same way as the old man was thankful for the rattlesnake when he prayed; it shows there is something going on.' Possibly some of his hearers were thankful they had a clown to amuse them." (The AP represented the speaker as saying, in regard to the strike, that there had been none before because there was no capital to strike against. "He was glad in a way to see it because it meant industrial development.")

Ogden and McIver accepted spiteful outbursts as inevitable. On such a region-wide stage, in the glare of a spotlight being turned upon the entire school-impoverished South, the central figures unavoidably appeared bigger than life size. They made good targets for the diehards.

Moreover, the unreconstructed editor continued to be no respecter of persons. Before the year was out Albert Shaw, of the *Review of Reviews,* would be perturbed by "the extreme com-

ments of certain Southern newspapers" that were raising a hulla-
baloo because President Theodore Roosevelt had invited Booker
Washington to eat at the White House. In deep-South Alabama,
where Washington headed Tuskegee Institute, nobody raised an
eyebrow when white speakers shared a platform with the great
Negro educator, but an implication in high place of "social
equality" was something else again. "I think so much of the
South," Editor Shaw wrote McIver, "that I hate to see it put in the
wrong by newspapers and men that profess to speak for it."

In July, while attending a meeting of the National Educational
Association at Detroit, Dr. McIver received a telegram from Mr.
Ogden, who was at his summer residence in Kennebunkport,
Maine: WILL YOU COME DOWN HERE FOR CONFERENCE ABOUT SOUTH-
ERN COMMITTEE BEFORE YOU GO SOUTH FOUR TRAINS DAILY FROM
BOSTON I WILL BEAR ALL EXPENSES.

Dr. McIver accepted the invitation and wrote Mrs. McIver
from Kennebunkport on July 18: "I arrived yesterday afternoon
in the midst of a storm. Mr. Ogden met me at the train. This
cottage is on a little projection into the ocean about 100 yards
from the water and 75 feet above the water level. Large rocks
are along the shore but just beyond the river, which empties into
the ocean 300 or 400 yards from here, there is a beautiful beach.
You can understand from this and from what you know of
Mr. Ogden how delightful a place it is. . . . I saw a sign at
Boston Railway station yesterday making it $100 fine to spit on
the floor. What would N. C. folks say if someone proposed to
fine them $100 for spitting anywhere on earth?"

As the two men conferred on creating southern sentiment
favorable to education, methods of public persuasion that had
proved highly effective in a previous campaign, the North Carolina institutes, emerged more and more as a model. And there
was one other man besides McIver who knew those methods
thoroughly. Alderman, therefore, was also summoned by telegram to join his old institute partner. "Mr. Ogden," he later
recalled, "bundled us both into a canoe and carried us with swift
sure strokes up the deep quiet river. Under the pines, on a hill-

side by the river, we spent the day discussing the organization, the purpose, and the personnel of the Southern Education Board."

When formal organization of the Board was effected in November of 1901, McIver and Alderman, along with Dr. Frissell, were chosen district directors and took up again the same campaign tools—press and correspondence and public address—they had used to popularize the public school in North Carolina. Thus by a coincidence they considered benign, since it brought them often together, they were set again to following from the Potomac to the Gulf the same course they had mapped out in their pioneering institute work.

Meanwhile, southern members of the group—McIver, Alderman, Curry, Dabney, and Frissell—agreed during an informal session at Asheville that the work proposed for their Board "divided itself into two great departments: A campaign for education in the South, and work in the North to create interest in Southern education and draw out support for it."

The full Board, convening on November 4 in Mr. Ogden's New York office, organized for business by electing Ogden president, McIver secretary, and George Foster Peabody treasurer. In that and successive meetings they reduced the preponderance of southern members by adding William H. Baldwin, Jr., who was placed in charge of a committee to handle gifts (later merged with the Rockefeller-financed General Education Board), H. H. Hanna, Albert Shaw, and Walter Hines Page, although Page belonged as much to the South by birth as he did to the North by adoption. They lunched with President Daniel Coit Gilman, of Johns Hopkins, who had arranged for them to meet other friends of southern education. They held a dinner session at the Metropolitan Club with Mr. Peabody as host and continued their comprehensive planning.

The organization proposed to raise $80,000 in the next two years with which to maintain a Bureau of Information, hire an executive secretary whom the president was empowered to choose, and finance field work to be done by three district directors: McIver, Alderman, and Frissell. The aim, as Mr. Ogden stated it in a letter offering the position of executive secretary to Rev.

Edgar Gardner Murphy, of Montgomery, Alabama, was "educational evangelization." None of the money, it was stipulated, would go to any institution. Instead it would be spent exclusively to stimulate public interest conducive to "more liberal provision for universal education in the South."

Dr. Dabney was selected to head the Information Bureau, with headquarters in his home city of Knoxville; Dr. Curry became supervisor of a campaign committee, made up of district and Information directors, which was created to conduct the entire enterprise; and Dickerman and Washington were hired as field agents to work under the campaign committee's instruction. McIver was to receive an "honorarium" amounting to $2,000 annually.

With the Board members ready to swing into action, Mr. Ogden invited to dinner at the Waldorf-Astoria a hundred or so outstanding persons who could help their project along. In addition to top ranking educators—among them Gilman of Hopkins, Woodrow Wilson of Princeton, and Butler of Columbia—there were present eminent ministers, such as Lyman Abbott and Charles H. Parkhurst, who could spread the educational gospel from their pulpits; newspaper publishers, such as Adolph S. Ochs and Oswald Garrison Villard, who had potent means to promote the campaign; and business men, such as John D. Rockefeller, Jr., Morris K. Jessup, and William H. Schieffelin, who could dig into their well-lined pockets for the wherewithal.

Except that Dr. McIver got paid for doing what he had been doing all along to promote the public school and had money at his disposal to augment the results, his work with the Southern Education Board changed nothing but the scope of his effectiveness. His influence naturally increased over a greater area as his counsel prevailed among able men engaged in a concerted attack on school deficiency, but his daily schedule, already at saturation point, remained much as it was. College matters continued to take precedence over all others. Indeed, since the major portion of his work as a district director was confined to North Carolina his paid duties, even as his voluntary campaigning had done,

Home of President and Mrs. McIver on the campus of the State Normal and Industrial College

Dr. and Mrs. McIver, with their children, Charles Duncan, Jr., Annie Martin, Verlinda Miller and Lula Martin, on Dr. McIver's fortieth birthday

Mrs. Charles Duncan McIver on her sixtieth birthday

secured a state-wide audience for his aims to expand and strengthen the college program.

He was attempting, for example, to raise an endowment of $100,000, with the interest to serve as a loan fund for the benefit of girls who could not otherwise attend the college. The girl who wanted to go to school and did not have the money was one of his chief concerns. More often than anybody suspected he lent a student money from his own slim purse to stay on at the college, or to return. The *Atlantic Monthly* article which described McIver's knight errantry in behalf of women had declared: "Dr. McIver is not only a man of great enthusiasm and executive ability, but he possesses an immense capital of resource and invention. He is constantly adding new features of self-support for the students at his institution. The letters of hundreds of girls pleading to be admitted and given something to do whereby they can earn their own tuition and board make one of the most pathetic pages in woman's education."

In addition, Dr. McIver wanted an adequate library for the college. In 1899 the Legislature had made a provision of sorts for library expansion, the plan being to move the library into space to be vacated by the physical education department upon erection of a gymnasium building. An appropriation for the building followed the kind of debate that was to be expected.

One senator, favoring the appropriation, said the Greensboro Normal and Industrial College was the fountain head of modern civilization. "Woman is God's given angel to mankind," said he. "She is the home queen and the guiding star of man's existence. She is man's governor at home—however big he may think himself abroad."

Another senator, not favoring the appropriation, said he had enjoyed senator number one's speech to the galleries, whereupon the first senator called the second to order and declared he would have made the same speech if there had not been a woman in forty miles; he carried that sentiment in his heart.

A newspaper that reported the little byplay also reported, as if it were more or less incidental, "The State Normal College gets $5,000 for a library and gymnasium building. It should have been $15,000."

It had to be $15,000 for a library alone if there were to be a building to house the books, and the autumn of 1901 found McIver working toward that goal in his characteristically thorough fashion. He was sedulously enlisting the support of friends who might have some influence on the little Scot who gave away libraries.

Hampton's Dr. Frissell wrote to Mr. Carnegie: "Perhaps you will remember that you very kindly offered to give a library to Hampton and I was obliged to inform you that provision had already been made for it otherwise. I should be very glad if Dr. McIver's school might be the recipient of the library in place of Hampton." Mr. Shaw replied to Dr. McIver's request for help by saying "I do not know that a letter from me would add much to the impressiveness of the facts that you can bring to bear upon Mr. Carnegie's mind, but whatever influence I might have is most heartily at your service. I do not know of any place where Mr. Carnegie could make a better use of $50,000 than to put it in your hands and he ought not to hesitate five minutes about doing it."

Page said he would write a letter, or a dozen letters if they would help, but he knew too much of Mr. Carnegie's methods to think that a letter from him or anybody else would have the slightest effect. He recommended that Dr. McIver prepare a brief and careful statement of the facts and send it to Mr. Carnegie at his New York address. "You may hear nothing from it for a long time, because the probability is he will have the matter thoroughly investigated by his own people in his own way. He will not take your word, nor mine nor anybody's. It is a matter of business with him—just as if he were buying an iron manufacturing plant in Greensboro—but the chances, I should say, are that when you do hear you will hear favorably, always, of course, with the condition that he imposes on every such gift, namely, that the community to which it is given will always give something."

Mr. Page in that instance underestimated his own Scottish friend's power of persuasion. When Mr. Carnegie got around to giving the library no restriction whatever was attached.

The year 1901, then, marked as it was by emergence of the Southern Education Board, wrought no profound change for McIver of North Carolina. He remained a man with the same two strings to his bow: public school opportunity for every child; college opportunity for women whose training would hasten the day of universal education.

16—

High Road to Parnassus

BEFORE THE Southern Education Board adjourned its organization meeting, "a vigorous educational campaign for the public schools of North Carolina" was one of the projects it had agreed upon. Early 1902 found Charles McIver, as the chief instrument of that special purpose, chafing to swing into action.

Governor Charles Aycock, too, was impatient to begin implementing his pledge to educate every child in the state, notwithstanding the obstacles. The idea of universal education was extremely distasteful in some quarters. In several of the eastern counties the colored population equaled, or outnumbered, the white people, and the white citizen considered any scheme to provide schools for the Negro out of his taxes as an intolerable burden. To be sure, Charles the educator was backing up Charles the governor in his unpopular stand on educating the Negro. Speaking before the Southern Educational Association at Columbia, South Carolina, McIver attacked the ingrained notion that to educate a Negro was to spoil a field hand. The right kind of education, he declared, never spoiled anything. Since society recognized that it paid to train a horse, to train a dog, to train a variety of animals for greater usefulness, it could scarcely regard the Negro as the animal kingdom's one exception to the rule. The Asheboro *Argus,* among other papers, voiced the opinion that "President McIver made a masterful and forceful speech with sound logical argument."

The taxpayers could be swayed, the governor was sure, if "sound logical argument" could be laid before them, but any general campaign designed to reach a population that was 80 per

cent rural would require both men and money, and the governor
had no money for such use.

Ah, but Charles McIver had money—Southern Education
Board money—and the general task to which that money had
been assigned "was adoption of the principle of local taxation in
as many rural communities as possible." He could fit a North
Carolina campaign with tongue-and-groove smoothness into the
Board's whole southern effort.

Moreover, he planned to proceed on the premise that the only
way to validate the program in his state would be to secure the
organized help of all educational elements in it. Some of the
most active public school advocates had been working at cross
purposes, and all of them, including the denominational educators, must be brought into harmony. Actually, the heads of
church colleges for women no longer thought of Dr. McIver as
the old troll that would come out from under the bridge to
destroy them. On the contrary, they had been forced to realize
that their schools had been helped, not damaged, by McIver's
insistence that women be educated. The president of the state's
college for women had given such impetus to the idea that private
colleges, too, benefited from an increased patronage. That result
was a matter of immense gratification, McIver told the Watauga
Club, a Raleigh organization of which Page had been a charter
member and which deserved a measure of credit for establishment of the State College of Agriculture and Mechanics.

"None have rejoiced more than friends of the Normal and
Industrial College," he stated, "at the new opportunities opening
daily to women of the state in other institutions. During its
short life the college has had the pleasure of seeing the great
Baptist denomination establish a Baptist Female university, not
only with handsome buildings, but with a handsome endowment;
it has seen the Episcopal Church take charge of St. Mary's and determine to cheapen the cost of education there without lowering
in any respect the standard of instruction; it has seen our noble
and beloved old University—conservative and progressive—open
its graduate courses to women; it has also seen Trinity College
follow the example of Guilford, Elon, and Catawba Colleges by

opening its doors to women and men alike. It has seen other new institutions at Charlotte, Statesville, and Red Springs spring up which give promise of great usefulness in educating women."

Since the governor's prestige could do more than any single factor to unify all the state's forces of education, McIver suggested that Aycock call their delegates into conference. The governor complied, and forty-three men, representing all branches of education, responded. The heads of state colleges were all present. City and county superintendents came, along with representatives from academies, junior colleges, military schools, and denominational colleges. Not only did Elon and Guilford and Catawba, which had not opposed state education at the higher levels, and Davidson, which had opposed it but briefly, send men to the meeting, Wake Forest and Trinity, which had supplied the roaring lions of the opposition, had a representation as peaceable as any lambs. And with the exception of Alderman, the entire bunch of Chapel Hill regulars that once discussed the very matters at hand "up in Ol' Mac's room"—McIver, Aycock, Joyner, and Noble—was reassembled, and Dr. Winston, who came as president of State A. and M., made an acceptable substitute for the missing Alderman.

The group convened in Governor Aycock's office on February 13 and drew up a striking platform against illiteracy. The declaration appealed to North Carolina, first of all, on the ground of patriotism. After 1908 the constitution would require literacy of every new voter; there was "overshadowing necessity of universal education in the solution of problems which a free government must solve in perpetuating its existence." It appealed on the ground of pride. North Carolina was expending the smallest amount of any state on public education and was thus failing to match for its children the opportunities other states provided. The state could not evade responsibility for conditions that had resulted in a multiplicity of small school divisions, inferior school houses, poorly paid teachers with the consequent poor teaching, high rate of illiteracy, and "educational indifference" reflected in the small average attendance of but fifty out of each one hundred students enrolled.

Harmony prevailed throughout the conference. The group set out to launch a systematic campaign to consolidate weak districts, secure better schoolhouses, raise teacher compensation, lengthen school terms, and, as a means to the other ends, supplement state school taxes with local levies. It created a central campaign committee to be comprised of Aycock, McIver, and Superintendent of Public Instruction Thomas F. Toon. Another committee was appointed to furnish newspapers with education news; the campaign fortunately had a supporting press from its inception. Nearly every paper in the state got on the band wagon by publishing the declaration against illiteracy—a platform that McIver called a second declaration of independence. Still another committee was named to make special request that every preacher in North Carolina deliver to his congregation at least one sermon a year on the subject of education.

The movement thus launched under aegis of the state's two Charleses picked up incredible speed when it really started rolling. North Carolina saw education—education, mind you—replace politics as the number one topic of interest. The central committee blandly hinted that a basket picnic might help attract crowds to educational rallies, and the notion caught on. Indeed the "rally" became a sort of cross between a political gathering, accustomed to barbecue and Brunswick stew, and a revival meeting with dinner on the grounds.

Within a week after the conference Superintendent Toon died, and Governor Aycock appointed James Y. Joyner to the state post. The offer cost Mr. Joyner considerable soul-searching before he decided to leave his professorship at the woman's college and take a position at less money. Finally, the potential of wider service influenced him to accept the appointment, and he then took his place with Aycock and McIver on the executive committee of the state campaign. No matter that members of the "inner circle" shuffled their positions now and then. They remained the inner circle!

At the college, five days after the conference, Dr. McIver conducted dedication exercises for the Curry Practice and Observation School Building, which gave prospective teachers a laboratory properly equipped to forestall inadequacy of preparation. The following month he struck a blow against inadequacy of the buildings in which they would teach. He organized an agency, "The Woman's Association for the Betterment of Public School Houses," that proved to be the most practical of all groups for tackling the campaign goal of good school plants. Harping on his old theme that courthouses and school houses, public buildings that had been under men's management, showed visible signs of neglect, he used the college girls as nucleus for a state-wide organization intended to function through small units. Each little group of three or more women would be responsible for beautifying the building and grounds of the school nearest to them. Dr. McIver would use Southern Education Board money to a limited degree to promote the work, but the program would be largely voluntary.

Women of the state, as Greensboro women had done during the typhoid epidemic, justified McIver's faith in them. They set about correcting the uninspiring outlook of little schools without maps, without libraries, without even a picture of George Washington on the wall. They jogged mile upon mile in their buggies. They talked with parents and teachers and committeemen. They took their housekeeping skills right across the school threshold— at which they placed mats to prevent mud from being tracked across the floor. They concerned themselves with getting windows washed, stoves polished, and grounds kept neat, at least to the extent that papers and lunch bags would be burned instead of thrown out of doors. They met requirements for obtaining pictures offered by a magazine, *The Youth's Companion*. They worked tirelessly and effectively.

In mobilizing the whole state, McIver did not overlook one element, the business men, who were not used to being called on to discuss education. He told a group of them in Charlotte he belonged to a class that believed a dollar should be converted into an idea. Others, probably some of those present, believed that an idea should be converted into a dollar. Both classes, he conceded, were in a measure wrong, and he thought it would be wholesome to have them come together and temper each other's judgment.

He gave the same evaluation of ideas to county superintendents of public instruction whose traveling expenses he paid, as district director of the southern campaign, to sectional conferences: "The only real estate, I say, is brains." It was difficult, he admitted, for a rural people to discard the primitive notion that land is the only real estate and realize "that brain is better property than land and that ideas and inventions multiply a thousand fold the natural products of the earth." The conferences were called "to discuss the best methods by which the rural public schools can be strengthened and to organize a systematic movement for their improvement."

The general Conference for Education in the South met at Athens, Georgia, in April, and continued to widen and deepen the flow of public opinion for education. It was attracting by then, in addition to the philanthropic-minded, state officers, trustees and professors of colleges, teachers and public school officials, and representatives of women's clubs. Governor Aycock was one of the speakers.

Dr. McIver, having been in New York to attend installation exercises for Nicholas Murray Butler, who had been chosen president of Columbia University to succeed Seth Low, traveled by way of the Ogden Special to Athens. As a result, he came under the accurately observing eye of a correspondent for the New York *Mail* who supplied his paper with a thumbnail profile of the southern educator:

"The most successful and irresistible anecdotist in the Ogden party was Dr. Charles D. McIver, head of a college at Greensboro, member of the Southern Education Board and chief pleader of the cause of higher wages for teachers in the South. He is a smooth-faced, white-necktied man with a perennial and engaging smile."

Dr. McIver was chief pleader, too, for better professional training that could command better pay—an order of events that put the cart before the horse for a majority of persons already in the field whose pay would not cover more education. Certainly the rural teacher in North Carolina, the only teacher three-fourths of the state's children would ever know, could neither go far afield nor spend much for summer school. Dr. McIver's answer for the women among them was the state college conceived to meet teacher needs. In May he innovated there an intensive course of instruction to benefit country teachers whose short school terms were already ended. The May session placed at their disposal all facilities of the practice school in which regular education students observed and taught under skilled supervision.

In June the college celebrated its decennial. The observance was part of a commencement that appropriately glanced backward over the long way a fledgling school had come in ten years, but only briefly. In the main the exercises had a forward look. The cornerstone was laid with impressive ceremonies for a new students' building; thirty-four young women received their diplomas, Bibles, and constitutions; but most significantly President McIver announced that henceforth baccalaureate degrees would be conferred upon completion of a five-year course. Diplomas would continue to be awarded at the end of four years, but an extra year was required to make a degree from the institution correspond in value, as he was determined it should, with that from the best private colleges. His state college must, to achieve its widest usefulness, have entrance requirements low enough to admit the product of public schools. As a consequence, it did not offer until the sophomore year a course equivalent to the highest prevailing freshman standards. As soon as the public high schools were efficient enough to graduate students ready for work of college grade, the fifth year would be dropped.

After commencement the president wrote alumnae that he had four scholarships, and hoped to secure two more, that would pay all expenses for a half-dozen graduates who wished to earn the bachelor's degree. The scholarship was a gift, not a loan. Six former students did return as degree candidates, and a member of the newest graduating class increased the number to seven.

Then Dr. McIver set off for Knoxville—the second trip in a month, since he had spoken at the University of Tennessee commencement—to teach civil government in the first Summer School of the South. The school represented a concrete aim of the Conference for Education in the South to establish in the heart of the region "a summer school of highest grade" so that southern teach-

ers would not have to go to other sections for summer training
of "solid academic worth." The General Education Board, the
Peabody Board, George Foster Peabody, Albert Shaw, Robert
Ogden, and others put up the money, and the University of
Tennessee was selected for its location. The summer school had
no organic connection with the university but the institution, at
the request of President Dabney, offered all its facilities—classrooms, laboratories, dormitories—free of charge and threw in gas
and electricity and janitor service for good measure. The accommodations were still insufficient for seventeen hundred teachers.
Shelters under the trees made up extra lecture halls, and a large
pavilion, seating three thousand persons, was erected.

Dr. Dabney early solicited McIver's help for the school. He
had written in February: "We find that the maximum salary we
can pay for a professor for the full six weeks in the summer school
will be $200. Now, we believe that men like you and Alderman
will do for us in three weeks more than the ordinary man will do
for us in the whole six." It was on the basis of a three-week
tenure at maximum pay that Dr. McIver went to Knoxville. His
arrival touched off a reception in his honor that the Knoxville
Journal and Tribune considered the most important happening
of the day, although it noted that the opening was "replete with
important events." Over a thousand teachers from twenty-five
states gathered in the pavilion to welcome him and hear him
speak.

He managed a day off to attend in Chattanooga a meeting of
the Southern Educational Association, and went immediately
from his Knoxville classes to Minneapolis for a convention of the
National Educational body. He had a busy time in Minnesota.
Between speeches and attendance at meetings of state directors,
of which he was one, committee appointments involved him with
resolutions, nominations, memorials, appropriations, and a "com-
mission for investigation of taxation and education."

The Minneapolis papers listed him among "Interesting Folk
Attending the N.E.A.," commented on his resemblance to William Jennings Bryan, photographed him "in characteristic pose"
among leading members of the educational convention, and de-

scribed him as "a leader in the battle for a better public school system in the South." He himself represented his "battle," in one address, as being for the education of the southern woman. It was not a pretty piece of theory that her influence would work miracles, he maintained. It was being proved in North Carolina.

He rushed back to Greensboro to meet with the college's Executive Committee and plunge into the North Carolina education canvass.

The preceding June the central committee had opened headquarters for the state campaign in Joyner's office, and secured Eugene C. Brooks, of the Monroe schools, as executive secretary to conduct the intensive Aycock-McIver-Joyner program.

The campaign fired its opening gun, and a double-barreled one at that, with a rally at Wentworth in Rockingham County. Former Governor Jarvis spoke in the morning, President McIver in the afternoon. Liking praise himself, Dr. McIver bestowed it freely. He told the papers Jarvis's speech was one of the greatest he had ever heard. The newspaper boys said the same of his. Every teacher in the county and over one hundred committeemen were among the fifteen hundred people in attendance—a crowd of the size previously assembled for political gatherings and nothing less. In fact, the Greensboro *Telegram* remarked editorially that the rally had the appearance "of a combination political meeting and religious gathering."

Subsequent meetings had the same appearance. North Carolina had never seen the like. The rallies were held in courthouses, schoolhouses, churches, in any building available, and when crowds exceeded seating capacity and overflowed outdoors, the meetings were held in the open air. Politicians drew bigger audiences than they had in the hottest political debates. Clergymen, lawyers, business men, and farmers took to speech-making for the cause of education. Whenever it was possible an educator was teamed with lay speakers, but everybody was trying to get into the act, and various prominent persons got so enthusiastic they would not even accept traveling expenses.

A meeting of the Southern Education Board in early August took McIver to Abenia, George Foster Peabody's estate on Lake

George. From there he returned for further participation in the North Carolina campaign, and from speaking engagements in the western counties went on to Georgia to conduct normal classes for a week in Atlanta. Indeed, so habitually was he asked to return to towns in which he had lectured before, his schedule somewhat resembled that of a circuit rider making his rounds.

Just to mention the places at which Dr. McIver appeared during the first three-quarters of 1902 (or any other year, for that matter) would be to chronicle an amazing expenditure of energy for travel alone. The triple magnet that drew him from one point to another—the untaught child, the unprofessional teacher, the unbuilt school—did not lose its force with distance. It pulled him from New York, where he could tap financial resources, to Hickory and Granite Falls, North Carolina villages the very names of which suggested another kind of strength. It constantly deposited him among the assembled friends of education whether in Georgia or Tennessee or Minnesota.

His chief regret, as he wrote Mrs. McIver from Shelby, was that the endless treadmill left so little time for his own family: "Give my love to the children," his letter said. "I'm glad Charlie is at work. It will do more than anything else can to make a man of him. I am so anxious that the children should grow into useful workers in the world. I have not given them the time and attention I wish I could have given them. It is hard to work for everybody else's children all the time and do what ought to be done for one's own."

When he was in Greensboro, therefore, he tried to make up for repeated absences by spending every possible moment with the children. For years the townspeople had been accustomed to seeing one or more of the McIver youngsters riding between their father and Zeke on a buggy seat. Annie, slipping into young womanhood, traveled with him frequently during her vacations from school. Verlinda spent hours with him in his office, and if he was writing semi-informally to one of the women teachers she knew, she would add rows of little zeros that stood for kisses. Lula Martin, the youngest, went faithfully to the administration building to walk home with her father at lunch time when he was at the college, and so striking was the resemblance between the laughing-eyed fair man and the merry-eyed dark child, so imitatively did she lengthen her small step to match his stride, that Miss Boddie stopped dead in her tracks one day to watch, shook her head pensively, and said: "Even your shoes turn up in the same places!"

Nor did he shirk his share of the discipline. Lula Martin's curiosity was her undoing. The little girl would run away, in spite of all, to go exploring—to investigate college laundry or barn or any place at all that was out of bounds. Mrs. McIver took the matter up with Dr. McIver:

"Charles, you'll simply have to do something about Lula Martin. She ran away again today. I've got to know where the child is."

Dutifully he did something about Lula Martin.

"Honey," said he, "you don't want to worry your mother, do you?"

"No, Sir."

"You don't want to hurt her feelings, do you? Or get her upset?"

"No, Sir."

"Well, you do, you know, when you run away. Why do you do it?"

"I don't know."

"You'll promise me not to do it again, won't you?"

"No, Sir."

That being that, he dealt with the uncompromising attitude in accepted fashion. He switched her legs.

She howled far louder than the small punishment called for, and, having fulfilled requirements of the situation, he took the heartbroken miscreant onto his lap to dry her tears and wound up crying with her.

The little girl came by her curiosity honestly, from that same affectionate father. Dr. McIver had always wondered what a "first rate wreck" would be like, and on his way to Atlanta he found out. The "fast mail" on which he was traveling was derailed near Toccoa, Georgia, and his sleeper was telescoped with the day coach ahead. As quickly as he could he wired Mrs. Mc-Iver that he was not hurt, and since nobody else was either, his graphic account of the accident was almost a merry one—including reference to an engine that lay flat on its side and whistled mournfully for twenty minutes, a colored woman who interspersed her prayers with yells of murder, and a bonfire of shattered woodwork that lighted up the pre-dawn darkness. Nevertheless, that wreck was "sufficient."

On the eighth of September he was back at the college for the best of its openings so far. Then he turned right around and went to Georgia again, to Athens that time, for a meeting he and Dr. Wallace Buttrick and Hoke Smith were holding for county superintendents of Georgia.

All of his appearances, moreover, constituted something of a triumphal tour that year. The word "inspiring" had been added to newspaper accounts of his speeches, but the word "ovation" appeared even more frequently. He had ovations in Knoxville at commencement exercises, the summer school reception, and a public address in July; he got an ovation in Minneapolis during the N.E.A. meeting. In Atlanta the teachers passed resolutions of thanks for his help and added congratulations to the State of North Carolina upon his services as "president of the magnificent woman's college." They asserted in addition that "the cause of education regards him with pride and pleasure."

Assuredly his popularity was widespread and genuine. In the sense that any public figure is "loved" he was greatly loved. Among his associates, of course, he enjoyed a devotion that was personal and deep and lasting.

It would be futile, to be sure, to maintain that everybody loved President McIver. Indeed, it was to be expected that so positive an individual, who quite liked to have his own way, would sometimes antagonize the people with whom he worked. That, however, was not the case. It is true that he "was wilful in a good sense," as Alderman put it; that he frequently seemed to be telling committee equals what to do instead of consulting with them, but their resentment, as one man recalled, faded before "a smile that was almost a grin." Sometimes his confrères agreed with him, sometimes they did not, and working harmony was not disrupted in either event, because he won without triumph and he lost without rancor. Some of the denominational leaders, openly his enemies for a long time, were grateful, now that opposing sides had buried the hatchet, that he was too "magnanimous" to hold grudges.

Local criticism of McIver appears to have been largely carping: "Why can't he leave a water pitcher alone?" "Why does he have to straighten a crooked window shade on a platform before he can make a speech?" During the fever epidemic the Greensboro *Record* scolded people for "belittling their betters" and commented pointedly that there was no open criticism, but a sly circulating of rumors by people who protested rather too much that they personally liked Dr. McIver.

A young teacher upon whom the McIver mantle as head of the college would one day fall knew the president in those days. And Dr. Walter C. Jackson, himself one of the best loved of administrators, felt that Greensboro with practical unanimity "appreciated" Dr. McIver. Just the same, some of the population did fall into the category of the old man who had admired all his wife did and still did not like her. Some others were occasionally exasperated, but still admiring.

One of the latter was a young printer, Joseph J. Stone, who thought it lacking in dignity for a college president to have "a conniption fit" because somebody abbreviated his first name "Chas." (Dignity, if he had but known it, was precisely the crux of the matter. Charles McIver abbreviated his own name, and addressed all letters to his wife as "Mrs. Chas. D. McIver" until he was elected president of a college.) The two men, both trigger-tempered, had "one hell of a row," Mr. Stone recalled a half-century later, when Dr. McIver heatedly objected that the printer had included the objectionable abbreviation in a telephone directory, although the copy was set as the telephone company supplied it. No permanent discord resulted. Mr. Stone did the college printing as long as McIver lived, and it was he who declared firmly: "McIver was a real genius. He did more to sell the idea of women's worth than any man who ever lived. He was the biggest bombshell that ever hit the educational world."

Probably Chub Dick illustrated as well as anybody could the attitude of an average McIver detractor: a person who had not approved of Dr. McIver's program, who had been sure it would fail, and who had to acknowledge, in spite of himself, the success he had made of it. Chub was a big, black, very ugly Negro who was a superb harness-maker. The much-traveled Dr. McIver commissioned Chub to make a leather contraption for fastening small pieces of luggage together and told him, with irritating detail, exactly how the job was to be done. Chub set about doing it exactly, too, knowing full well the contrivance would never work. But, lo and behold, it worked just fine. Chub's comment —a nimble mixture of apology and surprise and grudging admiration—summed up fairly well the thinking of those with kindred experience: "Well, Doctor," said Chub, "You is got some kind of sense."

The McIvers' home was still the best place in town to have a good time. The house was full of guests every evening when Dr. McIver was there—the Ogdens, the Peabodys, the Pages from out of state, important people, official and otherwise, from every part of North Carolina. It was the custom at eleven o'clock in the evening of summer days for all comers to assemble on the back porch for a feast of watermelon or homemade ice cream. Dr. McIver had a large metal container in the basement in which melons, bought by the wagon load, were iced. Mrs. McIver carried on the traditions of hospitality when he was away; especially did she treat members of the college faculty not living at home as members of the family at all festive meals: Thanksgiving, Christmas, Sunday dinner. True, hers was a quieter manner. It was only when Dr. McIver was at home that the place seemed the center of a tornado. Even teen-age Annie, who revered her father and cherished above all other compliments his saying that she was a very satisfactory daughter, sometimes regarded his departure as welcome calm after storm.

During all the comings and goings, moreover, college welfare had primary claim on all his endeavors, whether far or near.

His report to the college Board in December showed, for instance, that he had collected $37,000 for his loan fund; of that total, $27,000 came from friends he had made for the school out of the state. Also, he had an offer from the General Education Board, comprised in large part of similar friends, to give the college $15,000 on condition that an additional sum of half that amount be raised locally. The money would maintain a manual training department and expand scholarship and loan funds. The trustees accepted the gift.

Within the state, Dr. McIver's efforts, whether for increased local school tax or increased dormitory space at his institution, dovetailed in a design for bettering the whole North Carolina school structure, with the woman's college for capstone. When the public schools improved they could send the college more and better prepared students. As the college prepared more and better teachers the public schools would improve. It was a beneficent cycle. He reported that the college, no longer an experiment, was recognized in North Carolina and beyond its borders as a great educational force, pleaded that young women not be turned away for want of living space, and pointed out the state's gain in having teachers trained in an atmosphere of equality which did not base its recognition of worth on class distinctions of any kind. "The distinguishing characteristic of Americanism is its theory, and, I am glad to say, its usual practice, of giving to every man, woman, and child a fair chance in life," he further commented.

In many respects the year just ending was a forecast of the one, 1903, to follow. The first week of the new year found Dr. McIver in New York to attend meetings of the Southern Education Board with the eleven other members—the twelve apostles, Mr. Ogden called them—and he noted sadly that Dr. Curry was very feeble. (The following month Dr. Curry, who truly deserved the title of an "apostle" of education, died at Asheville, and McIver attended his funeral in Richmond.)

The year continued true to pattern when the North Carolina Legislature met, and he was in Raleigh battling, with Aycock's warm support, for money with which to expand the Normal and

Industrial College. He did not secure funds for additional dormitory space, but he did carry the Legislature in the general direction of his desires with appropriations for some other improvements.

He continued to work through district educational conferences for better rural schools.

In March a large number of southern newspapers, and that was no deviation from the norm either, were off on another tear about the race question. Press reports out of New York gave the impression that Negroes attended a Unitarian Club banquet at which two members of the Southern Education Board, Page and Baldwin, were present. "Dined with Two Negroes," headlined the Charlotte *Observer*.

Dr. McIver, secretary of the Southern Board and right in the midst of the outraged editors to boot, got the full force of their blasts. He would make no public statement, he informed a sympathetic South Carolinian—editor of the Columbia *State,* who sent a clipping from his own paper—but he did reply that the Southern Education Board had no more to do with the Unitarian banquet than the Columbia *State* had, and should not be held responsible for the personal conduct of its members.

Alabama's member of the Board, Rev. Edgar Gardner Murphy, was relieved to learn that his colleagues were "not at dinner with Negroes, but that the Negroes came in after the dinner was over to hear the speeches," but wishing to avoid "even the appearance of evil," suggested that McIver remonstrate with his friend. He himself had attempted to and got from Page the stinging retort that if anybody other than the reverend gentleman had tried it he would have been thrown out.

Although he acknowledged, by means of a quotation apropos the wisdom of going according to one's conscience, that the matter was strictly Page's own business, Dr. McIver did "remonstrate" after a fashion :

"I regret particularly that this incident should have occurred just at this time, and I regret especially that it should have occurred at a meeting where the topic seems to have been Southern Educational conditions.

"Of course, every man has a right to his opinion about this or any other question. In the words of our local phrase maker, a Greensboro colored man who is more or less familiar with the scriptures but who is now unfortunately on the chain gang, 'As de Possum Paul say to Peter and John in a writing of the Corinthians, let every man be fully persuaded in his own mind and guided according to his deviator.' I should like, however, to have the full facts in regard to the meeting, and if there is any better method of counteracting the effect than silence, I should like to know it."

He was not unmindful that the precarious balance of southern race relations could be easily undermined, and accordingly wrote to Mr. Ogden prior to the next Conference for Education in the South: "For the benefit of the work of education in the South it is important that the Richmond conference should, without apparent effort to do so, correct impressions, based upon the New York *Times* report of the Unitarian Banquet, by which an effort is being made to place the Southern Education Board in the attitude of scheming for social equality and mixed schools for the races."

The North Carolina campaign proceeded a second summer, only more intensively, along the same lines sketched out for the first, and by autumn when many of the participating school men had to return to work, more than 350 rallies had been held, local tax districts had increased from 36 to 181, and 676 new schoolhouses had been built.

For a time the campaign had to get along without McIver's aid. He was ill toward the end of June, and it was not until August, when he came home with his daughter Annie from resorts on the Maine coast, that papers began to note that he had "sufficiently recovered from his recent bad health to resume again his active strenuous work."

His reckless expenditure of energy that autumn included one great sentimental enterprise, a reunion of non-resident North Carolinians. The idea was original with him, and he was chairman of the homecoming's board of governors. Alderman, who had felt sure in the beginning that he could not attend the celebration, came up from Tulane to make the chief address.

Page had taken no offense at McIver's remarks on the Unitarian affair, and his letters in regard to the reunion afford a running commentary on the event, which was held the twelfth and thirteenth of October:

September 28—"Let me give you a word of warning about Senator Ransom. They had him up here at the New York Carolina Society a year and a half ago, and he spoke four mortal hours and a half. If you have him on deck, you'll have to give him a solid week."

September 29—"You are doing one of the most loyal and public spirited things in the whole history of the state, and you are taxing your strength and time and pocket in the noblest way. I'm bound to show you that I'm with you in every such effort. You're the best fellow and the most useful citizen in the state, and this move to get the scattered-abroad back is characteristic of you. But they'll be slow to start; and, really, you can't blame 'em. Almost every one of 'em was driven away from home by the necessity to make more money. Many of them for many years have been abused by the state press. Think of Buck Duke going to a love feast! There's really no reason except loyalty to you and fondness of you and admiration for you why any one should go— as they look at it."

October 5—"Don't trouble to meet me. I'll have my grip sent to your house—that the idea? Mrs. Page says I may speak at any time or place or on any subject you wish! But I think I oughtn't. Don't have too much speaking. Let's all get drunk some other way."

October 20—"Reunion a great success. You did the thing with great distinction and without a hitch. I'm going to contribute to a monument to you before you die. (The Normal College is your monument already.) I think it would be well if stress could somehow, somewhere, by somebody be laid on your genuine but well-balanced interest in Negro education."

The reunion kept McIver from attending a meeting of the Peabody Board to which he had a special invitation from Dr.

Gilman, who said McIver had convinced him that rural education should get some of the help that had been going to towns and cities. McIver sent a paper which pointed out that rural communities had received no aid at all from the Peabody Fund, except such as had come to them indirectly from normal schools and institutes supported by the trust. And 75 per cent of the southern population lived in those communities. On October 13 Dr. Gilman wrote him:

"When your jubilee is over you will be interested, I know, in hearing about our Peabody meeting last Thursday. It was decided to begin the policy of aiding rural schools and $10,000 was set apart for that purpose. Your paper was distributed to all members of the Board and awakened a great deal of interest. I think it must have influenced the action of the Board in deciding to begin at once the bestowal of aid upon rural schools."

Dr. Curry's death, leaving the position of supervisory agent for the Peabody Fund open, resulted in both an old and a new experience for Dr. McIver. The opening gave him a chance to move into a different field of educational administration; that was not new. The place did tempt him to leave the college, and no other had done that. Pressure to make the change was being brought toward the end of 1903 by persons whose opinion he valued. He was Hoke Smith's choice for the job. Alderman thought he should take the more influential position. Dr. Dabney wrote him: "I very much hope, both for patriotic and for selfish reasons, that you will decide to take this Peabody work. I should be very doubtful whether the College could spare you, but I am sure the whole South needs you."

In New York, when the new year 1904 found him still debating the choice, George Foster Peabody added his plea to that of other friends, and Dr. McIver wrote Mrs. McIver: "I am not sure about what I ought to do." When he boarded a train on the evening of January 20, he was still an undecided and troubled man.

Then, as if he were indeed a child of destiny, the decision, or so he indicated to Smith, was taken out of his hands.

His train got into Greensboro at seven o'clock, but the hack driver did not make his usual reply in kind to the McIver banter. He was strangely silent until his fare was seated and the trip under way, then he blurted out: "Dr. McIver, did you know your college burned down last night?"

The teacher should not be merely an instructor of youth, but the
most influential adviser on all matters of legislation pertaining
to schools and the training of children for useful citizenship.
Aggressive educational statesmanship among teachers and public
officials is the need of our time.   —*Charles Duncan McIver*

17−

Widening Horizons

AFTER THE DRIVER had asked his question, it was Dr. McIver's turn
to be silent and finally to ask a question of his own: "Was anybody
hurt?"

"No, Suh. Not as I knows of, Suh."

Nobody was hurt. The main dormitory, housing 305 girls,
was completely destroyed, as were the laundry, kitchen, dining
room annex, new cold storage plant, and the powerhouse.

The fire was discovered at 3:45 in the morning by the night
watchman, who saw the kitchen roof in flames. He attended first
to emptying the building where the students, having finished mid-
term examinations the day before, were having a deep and well-
earned sleep. Fifty girls escaped with the clothing they could
snatch hastily to put on and nothing more. Others set up a wild
clamor of the college bell, and still others, until firemen relieved
them, played water from a hose along the halls while the building
was being evacuated.

Meanwhile, the engineer of a shifting engine on the nearby
Southern Railway tracks saw the flames when they broke through
the kitchen roof and started blowing his whistle. Other whistles
took up the warning as customarily happened in event of fire.
An alarm was turned in to the city fire department just at four
o'clock, fifteen minutes after the fire was first spotted.

If there had been any doubt concerning the affection, local
and statewide, in which the college was held, it was dispelled by
the fire. The city took swift action. The street car company gave

students free transportation to town, and the Clegg and Benbow hotels gave them meals. Banks and business houses offered to assist girls who had lost their belongings, and individuals started a cash collection for their benefit. Private homes offered rooms and board.

At 9:30 the long bell called the students to chapel. The young women were naturally in a state of acute excitement, but they filed in silently; silent chapel assembly had become a tradition. The usually neat girls presented a motley picture, attired as they were in such mismated garments as they could share among themselves. But the president was in his accustomed place. At length the bell stopped ringing, and in the ordinary course of events Dr. McIver would have started the exercises with the state song. On that morning, however, the program did not include the lively strains of "Carolina, Carolina, heaven's blessings attend her." Instead, the president lifted his hands and announced as the opening music "Praise God from Whom All Blessings Flow." Many of the students later recalled that they felt their blessings were on the meager side, but Governor Aycock, arriving somewhat later, attempted to inject a light note by saying he was glad to see them all clothed and in their right minds.

They would go on, Dr. McIver told the girls. He did not at the moment know how, but school would continue. He asked how many would remain and leave the rest to him, and 400 of the 535 girls enrolled put up their hands. (There were 230 students residing in boarding homes and rented wooden buildings. Approximately 100 of the total number dropped out after the main dormitory was destroyed.) The displaced students slept that night in the administration building on cots or pallets supplied by Belk's, a local department store. The next day Greensboro presented a cash donation that it had hastily collected for the burned out students. Alumnae in Winston sent two large trunks filled with clothing. The president's co-workers elsewhere were generous, too. Mr. and Mrs. V. E. Macy, of New York, who had already contributed $1,000 to the loan fund, sent $100 each, as did Mr. Peabody and Mr. Ogden. Cash gifts totaled nearly $2,000.

On the third day after the fire the Board of Directors, seconded by the governor and a majority of his Council, voted a three-week suspension so that arrangements could be made for temporary accommodations. The Southern Railway immediately offered free trips for the students to their homes and back.

A temporary structure would be built, it was decided, to provide kitchen and dining facilities, but the unfinished Students' building figured chiefly in the reopening plan. It was heated, and its floor space divided into cubicles curtained by sheets strung along a frame on little rings. Each alcove was just large enough to hold a single iron bed, an improvised wash stand, a table, a chair, one drop light, and a trunk, in case the occupant still had a trunk. It was home during the spring term for 175 girls. One young woman who had lost her clothing reappeared wearing a topcoat given her by Charlie McIver, and thought it unreasonable of the president to object that such garb was lacking in decorum for a campus leader.

At any rate, with the makeshift arrangements underway, President McIver, feeling it "his duty to say at the first opportunity" that he could not accept the position as General Agent of the Peabody Board, wrote Hoke Smith to that effect: "I have as you know given my life to the establishment of a great institution for the liberal education of women and the training of teachers. I cannot leave it, or appear to desert it, in the hours of its adversity, and it is due that I should say as much to you, who have indicated your purpose to advocate my election by the Peabody Board. Appreciating fully the immense opportunity for useful service open to the representative of the Peabody Board, and appreciating thoroughly the compliment of being your choice for that responsible and difficult position, I am, very truly yours, Charles D. McIver."

College reopened on February 23, and the students were greeted with the encouraging news that they were to have an adequate library at last, and with it the development of real training for librarians. James Bertram, Mr. Carnegie's secretary, had written that Mr. Carnegie, having considered the facts Dr. McIver had set forth about the State Normal and Industrial College and the evidence that the library would be liberally supported, would "be very glad to pay for the erection of a Library Building to cost $15,000."

Dr. McIver got the letter, re-mailed from his office, while in New York. His letters to Mrs. McIver—one on the twelfth of February and two on the thirteenth—recount his procedure on receiving the news.

February 12: "I understand that Carnegie has planned to give us $15,000 for a library. I want more than that if I can get it in the right way."

February 13: "I have spent a pleasant morning with Mr. Schurz [Carl Schurz, editor, author, liberal political leader, and reformer], and he has written me a letter to Mr. Carnegie and I am to call on the latter at five this p.m. Don't know whether it will do any good or not. May do harm but will risk it."

He was taking a chance. Mr. Carnegie said at first, apparently not knowing he was committed to give the college a library, that of course if he had already given one to Greensboro "there would be no use" in giving another to the institution. When his caller spoke of other needs for the college library, he appeared resentful that a beneficiary of his generosity was asking for more than had been promised and indicated he thought an additional request was "greedy."

"About that time," Dr. McIver stated in his letter, "after I had hammered away at his queer mind, sometimes making a good, and sometimes an unfavorable, and sometimes no impression at all, I was about to give him up as a bad case, when Mr. Schurz came in and guided the conversation by asking questions. I told Mr. C. that I wanted to show him a larger amount that $15,000 could be profitably invested in our library. I did not press the point, however, and branched off on the education of the white country girl which evidently impressed him as it had impressed Mr. Schurz this a.m.

"After an hour and a half of such hurly-burly talk as he and I and that open-minded German had we arose to go.

"As I got up to leave he said of course if your library costs a

few thousand more it will be all right. So I made at least $3000
by my visit.

"As I was leaving he said you will be able to get money from
your state, the way you talk. He said, 'I've got a lot of faith in
you,' and then made some reference to my being a Scotchman.

"He then insisted on my accepting a seat in his box at Carnegie
Hall to hear a great Philharmonic Musical concert tonight. He
gave me the ticket and as I was leaving the house I met Mrs.
Carnegie, who was just coming in from a drive. They were both
at the concert tonight and I enjoyed being with them. Mrs. C.
is an exceedingly cordial and agreeable woman and the concert
was magnificent and more than 100 men in the orchestra. Mr. C.
said in his most smiling way, 'Go on and build that library. I
am very glad I met you and I want you to come to see me again.' "

Apparently the steel magnate had learned in an afternoon
what North Carolina already knew, according to Dr. Walter C.
Jackson: "Nobody could sell an idea as effectively as McIver. He
was a prince of promoters." (The amount Dr. McIver made by
his visit was actually nearer $4,000 than $3,000. In the Biennial
Report of the college Board of Directors for the two-year period
ending September 15, 1906, it is noted: "Since our last report,
Mr. Andrew Carnegie has added $3,868 to his previous gift of
$15,000 for erecting and equipping a library building, and the
building has been completed and admirably equipped at a total
cost of $18,868.")

Not only were the girls, cramped and uncomfortable in their
tent-like quarters, cheered by news of the library, but by the even
happier prospect that their college, like the legendary phoenix,
would rise from its ashes stronger than ever. The Council of
State met the first of March, and acting under a law authorizing
it to pledge the credit of the state "in cases of extreme emergency
or dire necessity" authorized the college directors to borrow
$80,000 to build a new dormitory.

The cornerstone was laid at commencement. The building
would be named in honor of Mrs. Cornelia Phillips Spencer.

An advertisement in the program of the Teachers' Assembly,
which met at Morehead City in June, revealed that the college

had by that year expanded in every direction from its modest beginning: its faculty, as one case in point, had more than tripled the original fifteen members. Facts about curriculum and costs were included, while the courses, five of which led to diplomas, were described as literary, classical, scientific, pedagogical, commercial, domestic science, manual training, and music. The remainder of the notice read: "Advanced courses leading to degrees. Faculty numbers 49. Board, laundry, tuition and fees for use of textbooks, etc., $160 a year. Annual expense of free tuition students, $115. For non-residents of State, $180."

At intervals during the spring, Dr. McIver worked assiduously in behalf of Alderman, who was under consideration for the presidency of the University of Virginia. He knew—his friend had told him—that a decision to leave Tulane would be difficult, and Alderman would not make it until, and unless, he had to. But McIver wanted him to have the chance, believing that the man and the position were made for each other. He talked with Prof. Charles W. Kent about the matter and at Kent's request wrote a long letter stating the qualifications of a person about whom he was better informed than anybody else. He knew first hand, and set down, Alderman's experience as a teacher and a trainer of teachers, his personal and public felicity of expression, his growing acquaintance with educational leaders, his reverence, although a progressive man and a modern scholar, for tradition. He dismissed, too, any rumor to the effect that Alderman was an invalid or a phrase-maker or a man disinclined to constant industry by pointing out that "no such man could have established and maintained for 20 years a permanent and growing reputation for power and usefulness."

Dr. Alderman was chosen president of the University of Virginia, and accepted, assuming his duties in mid-September of 1904. Dr. McIver attended his formal installation on Thomas Jefferson's birthday, April 13, the following spring.

The seventh Conference for Education in the South took Dr. McIver to Birmingham toward the end of April, 1904, and the accounts sent by an astute reporter to the New York *Daily Tribune* indicate that the Conference program for public schools was essentially the McIver program, and that Mr. Ogden's propitiative attitude was bearing fruit:

"Most of the speakers at the conference have been Southern men. The Northerners are here as learners and their remarks have been incidental. The chief matter of practical concern was local taxation, and the Southern state superintendents and college presidents were a unit for better schoolhouses, longer terms and better teaching for both races.

"The Southern educators are working in perfect harmony with the Northern philanthropists who take an interest in their problem. And the Northerners are perhaps more interested in white than in Negro education, for the training of the great body of white people isolated in the rural districts to intellectual freedom and an understanding of their economic opportunities is at the foundation of all southern progress. A few Southern politicians and newspapers are filled with alarm at what they call 'the Ogden movement,' but predominant public opinion at the South is undoubtedly progressive, and the tact of Mr. Ogden and the sanity of those who are cooperating with him, both North and South, have given the reactionaries no excuse for a demagogic campaign against the conference." The only danger to the "education of all the people," the reporter believed, was some ill-timed radical exploit, North or South, by which unreasoning prejudice could undo the work of governors like Aycock and Montague (of Virginia), and teachers like "McIver, Dabney, Alderman, and Hill." (Hill was chancellor of the University of Georgia.)

The National Educational Association held its forty-third annual convention in St. Louis from June 27 to July 1, while the World's Fair was in progress in that city. Dr. McIver believed he had pleased people by his short response to addresses of welcome that had consumed a couple of hours, and the St. Louis *Chronicle* was sure of it: "Charles McIver of North Carolina won the heartiest applausive award of the day by his witty address, and he was encored for several blushing bows."

Dr. McIver worked hard at the conventions he attended. He also received honors in recognition of the growing influence he exerted. He was chairman at that session of the committee on resolutions and had to keep in check some "educational anarchists" who were inclined to fight for resolutions for woman suffrage and against receiving gifts from robber barons. He was elected a vice president of N.E.A.

A different sort of recognition, contained in a letter from Knoxville, took him by surprise, and as he was about to answer he received a follow-up telegram which read: "Would you accept presidency of University of Tennessee if offered? Please wire immediate reply. Trustees in session. Edward T. Sanford." His good friend Dabney had resigned, and shortly afterward would take over another presidency at the University of Cincinnati.

The covering letter said that the salary would probably be fixed at $4,000 without a residence, or $2,600 with a residence. McIver wired as requested, saying that the delayed letter had just been received, that he could not accept, that he appreciated the consideration.

He answered in person a note of dissimilar character, but it too came from a man with a bag full of offers from which he extracted one every now and then to tempt McIver away from his attachment to public education. B. Frank Mebane, a North Carolina industrialist, sent around a missive which read "I am here and fixing to split the whole thing in twain and want you to take one of the pieces. Let's get together." They got together and made a pleasant day of it, but President McIver was homesick. And he still had other commitments to fill before he could return to Greensboro. He could not stay in St. Louis, as he wished to do, for the Democratic Convention, but had to be on his way to Tuscaloosa for a week of lectures at the University of Alabama, and after that, stop in Knoxville to assist with the Summer School of the South. He had a good week in Alabama, working with a summer school enrollment of 350, and was later assured by the university president that "No speaker has been so honored by large and increasing audiences as you were."

The University of North Carolina conferred fresh distinction on him that year, too, with a second honorary degree, Doctor of Laws.

The Southern Education Board, scheduled to meet in August, promised a pleasant interlude; Dr. McIver felt it was "rare that such a group of men can meet in a semi-social way year after year." Mr. Ogden's letter apprising him of the date expressed something of the same sentiment: "I take the liberty to remind you concerning the meeting of the Southern Education Board that is called for Wednesday, Aug. 10, at 10 a.m., at the residence of George Foster Peabody, Esq., Caldwell, Lake George. The sympathy, fellowship and perfect confidence that enter into the character of the Board and the mutual relations of its members have created associations of peculiar beauty that are an inspiration to all of the practical work undertaken by the Board. The delightful social experience at the home of our hospitable host added to this creates a combination of reasons why we should regard attendance as a sacred duty."

The trip to Lake George afforded opportunity as well for an overnight visit with Page at his suburban New Jersey home, as recounted to Mrs. McIver: "Ralph, Frank and Katherine [Page's children] met us at the river yesterday with a big new automobile and took us home over a delightful road ten or fifteen miles in less than an hour. It beats the train and street car for comfort. The view of New York City from the heights beyond the river was very fine as the boulevard runs up the river for several miles. I just wanted you to know that I had got ahead of you in this automobile business. Page apologizes for having this $2500 automobile saying his boys and the magazine and the manufacturer had made some sort of advertising contract by which he gets it at about 1/3 cost." To that Mrs. McIver replied, "I do not see any cause for Mr. Page to apologize for having an automobile—as good as he can get. I should like to have one myself—though I would rather have a house and a farm. The applications continue to pour in. How I wish we had another dormitory, more class rooms—*more everything.*"

The men meeting at Lake George recognized that education could not be divorced from other considerations. They talked politics, for one thing. McIver was of the opinion that Mr. Peabody's becoming treasurer of the National Democratic Committee would strengthen the Southern Education Board in the South, although he did comment to Mrs. McIver that "the great trouble about the Democrats is that there are too many varieties." Also while he was there, B. Frank Mebane inserted himself into the picture again. He stated from Spray in a letter of rather imperious tone: "I will give you $5000 a year for a period of five years to come here and take charge of the Educational Department located at Spray, near Spray, or in Rockingham County, as I may elect, but my election would be governed by your judgment. This proposition to be accepted or rejected by the first day of September."

The "educational department" he had in mind was a foundation to provide industrial and normal training, but McIver's own Normal and Industrial College was already providing both. Mr. Mebane would have to do much better than that before President McIver would need any two weeks to make up his mind.

As in its infancy, the college in 1904 had to postpone the opening for a time in order to have the new dormitory ready for occupancy. History steadfastly repeated itself in another area, too, when the fall semester began on October 6. The enrollment, as in every autumn, was larger than it had been the autumn before. Also the president, rejoicing in the splendid beginning, had to cope with homesick girls without the aid of Mrs. McIver as he had done initially when the illness of their children had required her attention; she was at a health resort taking treatment for rheumatism and he missed her. She was poise to his restlessness, tact to his impatience, calm to his storm. It was his plan to join her for a few days, but his departure had to wait until after a meeting of the Guilford County Association of University of North Carolina Alumni, of which he was president. Nor was it educational organizations alone to which he gave his energizing touch. Young Men's Business Association, public library, historical society, chamber of commerce, every civic enterprise could count on him.

In announcing his brief trip one paper noted "Dr. McIver has been urged by his physician to take a rest, as he has not fully recovered from his sickness last summer, when he began the Herculean task of making the reunion a success."

He "rested" by going to Yale University to address the Connecticut State Teachers' Association on "The Teacher as a Citizen"; by going to Raleigh to speak before a state-wide organization of county superintendents; by going to Chicago for a committee meeting; by going to Jacksonville to appear as a speaker before the Southern Educational Association, which chose him president.

Dr. McIver considered his work with county superintendents as particularly vital since the rural districts were "just beginning to come alive to the necessity for better public schools." He contended that aggressive educational statesmanship among teachers and public officials was the need of the time, and the county superintendent, to exert the influence he should, must become more than "a mere examiner of teachers or gatherer of statistics." He should be more than a match for the best of professional and commercial men in all discussions involving the school.

At Raleigh, Dr. McIver was presented by Dr. Joyner, who said, not mentioning a name, they were to hear "one who, before he closed, would speak of the need for public education, and demand that young women be given an equal chance in the world—a man who had recently been introduced by a new title, the 'Alma Mater of North Carolina.'" Dr. McIver "blushed mightily," the *News and Observer* reported. He was scheduled to speak on the cooperative work of the Southern Education Board, but in line with Joyner's expectations he did get in some telling remarks on the poor pay of teachers, which was "less in some cases than that of state convicts working on the roads."

As for his stand on woman's merit, nobody any longer impugned Dr. McIver's sincerity when he declared women to be the most important segment of the population. But sometimes women did try his patience. He told on occasion of attempting "to influence a Southern woman, a widow, who wished to bequeath a few thousand dollars to education, to give it to an institution for the education of women. She took the matter under careful and conscientious consideration and in a few days told me she had decided to use her money to aid the education of boys and men; that her husband was a man."

"Between us," he sighed in a letter to his wife, "I wish that women loved one another as they do dead men or criminal boys."

In his Florida address, "The Forward Movement in North Carolina," he had occasion to sum up the education campaign that had combined for his own state the excitement of politics and the seriousness of religion and produced, among other conspicuous results, well over a thousand new school houses. The summary was particularly gratifying to another Carolinian in attendance at the Southern Educational Association's convention. McIver's friend Aycock was one of the speakers.

Early in the year 1905 Dr. McIver reported from New York, where he had gone to confer with Mr. Ogden about Southern Education Board questions: "I have just had a satisfactory interview with Bertram and I think we will get what I asked for. Mr. Bertram says that Mr. Carnegie has just subscribed $10,000 this year to the Southern Education Board."

Dr. McIver was in Raleigh a week later when he heard definitely that Mr. Carnegie would give the additional money requested for a college library. Moving in his accustomed groove, he felt he "was doing some good in the scramble before the appropriations committee" of the state Legislature, and was trying to do no harm.

In March he delivered his speech, "The Teacher as a Citizen," before the Central Illinois Teachers Association in Peoria. He told the Illinois teachers that both their state and his own were laboring under the delusion that they could save money by employing low-priced teachers. And it was the teachers' own fault! The citizenship of the country was being trained by persons whose average salary was less than a dollar a day for the working days of the year because the teacher was "not the citizen he ought to be." He should not be merely an instructor of youth, content to deal exclusively with the generation that was to follow and wait until he was dead before his opinions on civic matters would carry any weight. The teacher should be "the influential adviser on all matters pertaining to school legislation and the training of youth." Compensation for teachers was small because "we have never had a large enough company of bold teachers who were determined to make the people see the truth in regard to taxes and in regard to teachers' salaries." If they would go to the tax books and get the facts they could make many a man ashamed of himself who complained bitterly because he thought he was paying the entire school tax of his community. "Let us teach honestly and boldly," he urged them as he had urged North Carolinians, "that education is not only the best thing in our civilization but also the most expensive."

The eighth session of the Conference for Education in the South met at Columbia, South Carolina, April 26-28, and he was there a day in advance of the Ogden Special for a meeting of the Campaign Committee and a discussion with state superintendents. He concluded the latter with a feeling that it had been "most valuable," but reported to Mrs. McIver "I am very tired."

George Foster Peabody noticed the fatigue with some concern and asked that he be allowed the "privilege" of providing Dr. McIver with a European vacation, the overworked educator to "go over and have a good time with a letter of credit and come home, not as my guest, but as of the Lord's family, I being a steward to make it restful in a measure for you. Do not say me nay please."

President McIver did not say him nay. Before sailing time at summer's end the need of a restful interval was apparent even to him. At Albany, where he addressed a convocation of the University of the State of New York, he was so ill that he had to consult a physician and had a feeling that his speech was not up to standard. Cordial audience reception, however, indicated that he had done better than he imagined, and his subject, "The Teacher and the Business Man," was not one that could make undue demands on him. It was a plea, voiced many times before, that teachers throw off "the life of a recluse, mingle with business interests, and exercise the same practical influence for good as do members of the clerical profession."

From Albany, Dr. McIver went to Asbury Park, New Jersey, for the National Educational Association's forty-fourth convention, at which he suffered the only major defeat of his life. He was a candidate for president, and by the time he arrived New York papers were headlining "Boom for McIver." They gave much space to him as a prominent southern educator, a leader in all movements for industrial education, a forceful speaker, and an active participant in the agitation going on for higher salaries.

His bid for the presidency kept him busy every minute until one or two o'clock in the morning, people were in his room constantly and conferences were necessary at all times, he recounted to Mrs. McIver, but he foresaw before the election had taken place that he would not secure the president's post: "My friends defeated Thompson of Ohio but Thompson's friends combined with Schaeffer of Penn. and took away enough support to defeat me, I feel sure, though I have not yet heard definitely." Among the friends for whom he had a special appreciation were Dr. Joyner, who "handled the situation beautifully," and Julius I. Foust, of the Normal and Industrial College faculty, who was described as "a trump."

The New York *Herald* told the full story in a special dispatch from the convention point:

"Politics had been sizzling for three days. Cut and dried arrangements went awry. The electioneering of the New York clique to seat Professor Charles D. McIver, of North Carolina, in the presidential chair went for naught. Although McIver won in the first caucus of the Election Committee, beating out Professor Thompson, of the University of Chicago, by a sixteen majority in a total vote of forty-four, the battle re-opened last night, and until far into the morning the fight raged. Before breakfast it was resumed, and at nine o'clock, when the committee went into executive session, Professor Maxwell and other adherents of Mr. McIver declared that he would win.

"But the West brought forth the argument that Nathan C. Schaeffer, of Pennsylvania, who became the residuary legatee of Dr. Thompson's support, had been beaten by Professor Maxwell by a single vote last year and was entitled to his portion of salve this year. It was 'anything to beat the South,' as represented by Professor McIver. The Ohio men boldly announced that if Ohio couldn't get the plum the South should not have it, and, by hook or crook, they won over enough McIver men from the West to elect the Pennsylvania compromise candidate. The vote stood 14 to 17."

Dr. McIver placed the decisive vote at eighteen to twenty-seven in a telegram to Mrs. McIver, but lost by three votes or nine, the election was close. It was so close, indeed, that opinion was freely expressed that Dr. McIver could have the place virtually unopposed the following year.

He said nothing of that consensus to Mrs. McIver, but did state "My race for President has not hurt me, but rather helped me and helped N. C. and the South."

His publicity during the convention and after appeared to substantiate that opinion. The Herald ran his picture as a "chief figure" at the N.E.A. session, and *The Outlook,* Dr. Lyman Abbott's publication, described him within the month as "the soul of the forward movement in his region." The magazine further declared: "In the Southern States there is no man better entitled to be called a champion of the public schools, and of the whole idea of popular education, than Charles Duncan McIver, of North Carolina. . . . He is a man of intense earnestness, energy, insight and common sense. For the past 20 years his voice has been raised in behalf of popular education, not only in every county of his own State, but throughout the South and in great National assemblies. There is no abler speaker on the subject than Dr. McIver."

Dr. McIver's anticipation of a two-month European junket was keen. Nevertheless, loving company as he had since his youth, he was unhappy about going alone. His first choice of companions was unable to make the trip, both for lack of money and reasons of health; Mrs. McIver that summer lost a premature infant and was not well enough to travel even if Mr. Peabody's offer had covered her expenses.

Dr. McIver, with a nagging anxiousness, worked out a code with which she was to cable him every Friday how matters were at home. He also regretted not being on hand to see Charlie off to the University. Then he tried to persuade his friend Jim Joyner to accompany him and became deeply depressed when Dr. Joyner declined, not wishing, as he said, to leave Mrs. Joyner for so long a time.

Mrs. Joyner, however, saw the subject in a different light, and on the evening before the steamship company had to be notified, her insistence, plus the effect refusal had produced on his dearest friend, moved Dr. Joyner to change his mind. He telephoned to say so, and in his ninetieth year he was still recalling the "ring in McIver's voice" when the decision was made known.

The president's absence from the college could well have become permanent. On his way to New York, Dr. McIver had to turn aside another effort to tempt him from ivy halls into the market place. An official of the American Tobacco Company tried to convince him that he should go into business; or to be specific about it, that he should consider becoming the tobacco corporation's representative in Mexico. And there was still an additional and more definite offer before sailing time. In New York, Mr. Mebane, who was nothing if not tenacious, improved on his previous proposal.

"I took breakfast this a.m. with Mebane," Dr. McIver wrote home, "and this afternoon dined with him and Mrs. Mebane at the Claremont Restaurant near Grant's tomb, after going with them on a two hour automobile ride. Mebane offers me a position for five years at $6000 and $6000 of stock a year. $1000 a month sounds tempting. He says he will give me $500 and all expenses to stay here and take my vacation with him instead of going to Europe, which of course I am not foolish enough to consider; but the other proposition is worthy of our consideration." Mr. Mebane, reputedly a millionaire many times over, was not through. He would be heard from again.

McIver and Joyner sailed early in September, and on the way to the wharf they agreed upon travel terms. "Let me sleep," McIver asked of his friend; "I've lost so much sleep." Joyner replied, "I'll make a bargain with you. We'll not talk shop, we'll not visit any educational institutions, the violator to pay $50." Neither had to pay the forfeit. They did drive through the University of Edinburgh grounds, but that was touring, not an official visit, and did not come under the agreement.

From the outset, the sea voyage gave Dr. McIver "the first day of perfect rest and freedom from care that I've had in a long time." He slept eight to ten hours a night. He took time, even so, to write Mrs. McIver and his host, Mr. Peabody, a running account of his trip. He was a tourist in every sense of the word, missing nothing, but his comments were sometimes trenchant, often entertaining: "I enjoyed the Folies Bergere Thursday night more than any spectacular show I ever saw. After one peculiarly beautiful scene Joyner said to me in all seriousness and in his most characteristic way, 'All too short,' which remark might have had two meanings as I told him. We know nothing about staging as compared with the skill of the French, but the French are not in it with America in railroads, mails, express, etc." Crossing from France into Germany was "a change from an airy tiddle-de-winks civilization to sturdy dray horse conditions, and I like the latter much better." In Scotland he found the "people are more like our folks than any we have struck." There he visited relatives, the MacIvers (as they spelled the family name) who had founded the Cunard Steamship Line, but retired in an enviable state of prosperity from its management in 1883. David, the M.P., was away, but his brother Charles welcomed the American Charles and gave him a small volume of McIver history. Dr. McIver also bought a book of reminiscences by Evander McIver, cousin to that other Evander, Scotch Iver, who had emigrated to America.

Nor was all the entertaining correspondence one-sided. Mrs. McIver occasionally included an amusing bit, as she did with an incident Mrs. J. R. Weatherspoon, his sister Elizabeth, encountered in her Sunday School class. Mrs. Weatherspoon drilled the children in one particular question and answer until she was sure they had both letter perfect. The next Sunday when she asked in review, "Where do we learn to love and obey God?" she confidently expected the right answer, "In the Bible alone." The answer she got was "In a bottle of cologne."

Moreover, Zeke felt called upon to inform his employer that all was well back home: "Dear Sir: Mrs. McIver has kindly read to me a very Interesting Account of your trip across the waters, and I cannot tell you how much I injoyed it or how glad I am to know you are having a grand time. Now for business. The school opened up all right and we had the building in fine shape in spite of the mess it was in when you left. everything is going nicely. and all seems satisfied and happy. it may interest you to know that a load of watermellons passed today and that I am behaveing myself alright. it is useless for me to try to tell you how much I have missed you, for you know that already. try to take good care of yourself and when you tyer with the scenes of the Old Country, we will all, welcome you home again. With the very best wishes for your helth and happiness, I am your humble servant Zeke. Please remember me kindly to Mr. Joyner."

In London, seeing a "loud-checked vest" in a window, Dr. McIver went in to buy it, and an astonished Dr. Joyner asked "What on earth is that for?" "It's for Zeke," he was told. "I can't think of anything that would please him more."

Dr. McIver's trip relieved but did not entirely overcome his fatigue. He was more irritable upon his return than anyone remembered his having been before. And the exhausting schedule he had temporarily put aside was there waiting to be taken up again. Almost at once his position as president of the Southern Educational Association required his presence in Nashville, Tennessee, where that organization and the Association of Colleges and Preparatory Schools in the Southern States held a joint session in November.

At the college, where his return made the greatest difference, the comfortable feeling prevailed that a sure hand was at the helm again. One improvement was immediate. The dining room had been serving dessert only once a week; the students and resident teachers were starved for sweets. One faculty member admitted to such a craving for desserts that she would often eat a candy bar in private although it made her feel guilty, since the girls had none. Dr. McIver, with his penchant for keeping up with every college activity, saw the situation in a single inspection visit, and the food was better from then on.

Everybody could rejoice in what Alderman called the "spacious single-mindedness" that had enabled the president to resist large financial rewards and remain in charge of the institution. Under his guidance the college, notwithstanding the early hostility of powerful opponents, had grown secure in both political support and popular favor. In addition, it had weathered pestilence and conflagration. Nothing could stop it now.

18—

And Lo! McIver's Name Led All the Rest

ABENIA, George Foster Peabody's home on Lake George, was a
place of tranquil beauty. The former owner had reputedly spent
a half-million dollars on it, and Mr. Peabody had made improvements of his own, including new verandas that furnished excellent open-air meeting places when the Southern Education
Board convened there in August, 1906. Board sessions, in con-
trast to the serene setting, were strenuous. The members had to
allocate large sums of money; they had to give attention to large
expenses, all privately defrayed. They had to determine policy.

Sometimes the "twelve apostles" would have a cruise on Mr.
Peabody's yacht along the placid mountain-rimmed lake to its
farther end. Then they would lunch at the club house, occasionally in company with other influential persons Mr. Peabody had invited. It was at such a luncheon that Dr. McIver had met Carl
Schurz. Indeed, Abenia afforded to a dozen congenial men a
rare blend of work and relaxation and social relationship.

For Dr. McIver, it also afforded a reunion with his dear friend
Edwin Alderman. "After I left North Carolina," Alderman
stated, "by a strange coincidence to which he often alluded, we
drew closer to each other in actual intimacy than ever before. We
met often each year, sleeping in the same rooms and talking in
the night. I saved my stories for him, and he saved his for me,
and his were always better than mine."

Quite possibly the difference lay, as it did in other instances involving McIver, in the story teller, not the stories. During the intensive North Carolina education campaign that superb teller of tales was accompanying two other speakers to a rally in a village a few miles from Greensboro. The others were scheduled to speak ahead of him, and that was good programming. He could quite easily become so carried away with his subject that he would forget about time. At any rate, one of the men had a pre-appearance case of stage fright. "Don't worry about it, Clem," said Dr. McIver. "Just tell them this story." The companion did as he was advised; he told the story and nothing happened. There was not a titter. When Dr. McIver's turn came, he told the same story, and the audience roared.

No matter who had the better stories, McIver and Alderman enjoyed their meetings, and the 1906 house party at Abenia was no exception. As they sat at Lake George that summer "in the home of a dear common friend," as Alderman related afterward, "Charles McIver and I were talking of life and its meaning and the flight of time that had carried us so swiftly past boyhood to middle life. Our moods alternated between the kind of boyish, unrestrained merriment possible only to men who have grown up together and a certain strain of premonition and sadness." Dr. Alderman did not indicate whether even then the shape of an illness that would confine him for dreary months to a sanatorium was casting a foreboding shadow, but he did recall saying, "Charles, you will outlive me and you will probably have to write some resolutions or say something about me when I am gone. Make it short. Just say that we had a good time together pounding away at real things." McIver, the "robust" one of the pair answered quickly, "Though I look stronger than you, you may outlive me after all, and I give you the same counsel."

McIver's year up until that time had been full, as all his years were full, and had followed something of a set pattern. In January he had gone to New York for a meeting of the Southern Education Board. He had met also with the General Education Board, which had made grants that were, like the personal gifts of Southern Board members, beneficial to the woman's college. "This college," he stated in a report, "has given some prestige to North

Carolina's name beyond its borders and has had the good fortune to interest influential people in the educational development of the State which it serves." The college head, of course, was the instrument through which both purposes had been achieved.

In February he received a telegram from Mebane which read MR R M OGDEN IS HERE AND YOU HAD BETTER COME OVER. At that time, Dr. McIver encountered once more a hardy perennial that knew no season, an enticement from Mebane that had been renewed and enlarged. He discovered that the home and farm about which Mrs. McIver had been wistful were included in the offer, and the proposed cash stipend had gone up by $1,500 to $7,500 a year—a luxury income in that day when a dollar was worth a hundred cents. And whether or not Mr. Mebane was proceeding on the theory that every man has his price, he had scaled his offer upward to the point at which Dr. McIver could not turn it down flatly without consideration. He went to Raleigh in some anguish of spirit to seek counsel from two of his friends, Joyner and Daniels. Daniels was of the opinion that his mind was made up all along; that nothing was sufficient to deflect him from the course he had projected for himself a score of years before. Dr. Joyner believed he was having a struggle and was trying to get assurance that the choice, whichever it turned out to be, was the right one.

The two men could do no less, however, than state their considered belief that the work he was doing was the most useful in the state and nothing should induce him to give it up, but they were aware that their argument did imply an inescapable personal sacrifice for their friend and his family. They knew he was in debt; he had at times borrowed money from both of them, and as he pointed out, it was all very well for Daniels to advise unselfish service when every blow the editor struck for his paper was strengthening a property that would belong to him and his children; that it was all very well for Joyner, who had property as well as salary to make him independent, to argue that McIver would be happy in no other work, but at the peak of his earning years he himself was not laying by a penny for his wife and children to use in the event of his death.

Yet, in spite of the self-denial involved, the conclusion was what the men, knowing McIver well, had expected. It had been foregone from the day in Winston when he had selected fair dealing in education for women as a fixed star to steer by. He would stay right where he was.

Dr. McIver's educational appearances were also in an established pattern that spring and summer. New names of towns appeared along with those of cities he was revisiting, but the addresses reflected an unchanging emphasis. At Baton Rouge, he argued for expert school supervision before the Louisiana Public School Teachers' Association. At Lexington, Kentucky, he met with state superintendents prior to the annual meeting of the Conference for Education in the South. He was a leading Conference speaker as usual, making an address that Joyner said produced a profound impression. Dr. Joyner agreed with Alderman that "The personality of Charles McIver interested and attracted men more than any sum of his attainments." Incidentally, McIver and Alderman addressed the same session of the convention— two men who were, in the battles they aided jointly as well as in brotherly affection, twin stars who remained a sort of Castor and Pollux of the educational firmament as they had been in their institute days.

At the woman's college commencement President McIver announced that the year 1905-06 had been memorable for an important change in the college course. He had achieved the supreme satisfaction of seeing his college come of age. "When the present class graduates," he stated, "its members will have earned the degree of Bachelor of Arts, Bachelor of Science or Bachelor of Pedagogy; heretofore it has been necessary for those who received the college's diploma to remain a year longer to secure a degree." The change meant, he pointed out, that standards for admission and graduation had been raised until they were equivalent, although not identical with, those for students at the University and other leading colleges of the state.

"The urgent need of the college," another story often told, was additional dormitory space and additional income with which to strengthen the faculty.

In little personal matters, too, Dr. McIver's summer was at times a new variation on a familiar theme. Julia Booker's son Henry came before a Greensboro court for stealing, and Dr. Mc-Iver, admitting that he knew nothing of the merits of the case, inquired of court officials if he might get an attorney for the youth. He wanted to do what he could, he said; Julia had been a faithful and honest servant for years. He had a similarly helpful attitude toward Giles, a Negro from the McIver home place he had given employment at the college. Giles wrote from another town to say he was in trouble and needed money to get out of jail. Dr. McIver sent the necessary amount by telegraph, not letter, and a day or so later Giles showed up at his job as naturally as if he had never been away. No questions were asked, even when the colored man paid the money back.

From Tuscaloosa, Dr. McIver wrote of a repeat performance at the University of Alabama: "I have been very successful with my work here and feel that I have helped the cause and en-couraged its friends." The chance of doing additional good took him on a side trip to Tifton, Georgia, where a vote on local tax-ation was imminent, and institutes in western North Carolina gave him occasion for a fatherly sort of pride in students from the college. "Our girls are not numerous in this section," he told Mrs. McIver, "but they tower above the average."

By then it was August and time for a trip to Abenia and a stopover with Page en route, not to mention another brush with a man who was unwilling to accept "No" for an answer. "Mr. Mebane and Mr. Tracy have just about completed the organiza-tion of a million dollar financial concern here intended to finance largely Southern industries, especially the textile products of the South," he wrote home from New York.

"Mebane says he is anxious for me to go in with him living here or at Spray, but. . . ." The comment was left unfinished. Mrs. McIver was quite capable of finishing it for herself.

An account of his return stop in New York, as set down on a hot and humid twelfth of August, indicated some of the other demands being made upon him: "St. Clair and Logan Howell want me to help them in their magazine scheme, but I'm not sure I can do it. I must give them a little time however. St. Clair has asked me for a $50 article on teachers' salaries, 2000 words, but I don't know that I can prepare it before I go home. Page is dead bent on my writing the story of my work and that is his special object in getting me out at his house Tuesday night. Dr. Dickerman needs my Lexington speech and I must get it to him before Wednesday. I have about half finished it."

The next day he started a search for "a music man" for the college, and a week later, August 30, his letter told of having interviewed two candidates for the place. It said in addition "I have a good seat tonight and am looking forward to hearing Bryan where I heard Patti and read the *Progressive Farmer* with you 15 years ago. I expect to see Mr. Bryan this p.m. about going to North Carolina." On the following day he was able to report that the Bryan meeting was great and that Bryan would go to North Carolina, probably in September.

Mr. Bryan, who had inaugurated whistle-stop campaigning during his first candidacy for President of the United States, did make a political swing through North Carolina in September by special train. Very early on Monday morning, September 17, Dr. McIver set out to join the Special at Raleigh, leaving before breakfast. At two o'clock lunch in the capital he engaged in the banter that Josh the waiter expected of him, saying when the meal was set before him, "Now you can go and bring me another just like it." Actually, in spite of the jest, he ate little.

By the time the Special reached Durham, he was feeling ill, and when Bryan left the train with his retinue to make a speech, Dr. McIver said he would stay behind and get some medicine from a drug store. He reckoned without the Great Commoner's drawing power; the drug store was closed. He returned to the car, in which a reporter, H. E. C. Bryant, had stayed to prepare a story for his paper, and remarked to the newsman that he was in acute distress. The reporter suggested that he "stretch out" on the long lounge seat at the end of the car, and tried to help make him comfortable.

When the rest of the party returned from the speaking, Dr. McIver appeared his buoyant and jovial self, but shortly afterward he spoke of a sharp pain in the chest and remarked that his indigestion had returned. Somebody suggested brandy and he took a little. It failed to help. Suddenly he collapsed. There were doctors on the Special, but their efforts to revive him were futile. Charles Duncan McIver was dead.

Apoplexy was assigned as the cause, as it almost invariably was during early years of the century in any case of sudden death from natural causes.

At Hillsboro, a message was dispatched to J. I. Foust, dean of the woman's college faculty: "As train left Durham Dr. McIver had stroke of apoplexy and never recovered consciousness. Break the news to his family. Notify undertaker to meet Bryan Special."

Mr. Foust entrusted the task to the family's good friend, Dr. Gove.

The remainder of the Special's journey to Greensboro was a funeral procession. Aboard the train, political excitement had given way to mourning. At every stop the train left the same sense of stunned grief, silencing cheering throngs with the news it carried, and spreading deep gloom at every little town in which the populace had regarded the educator as an intimate acquaintance. Charles Duncan McIver was dead.

In Greensboro, the news traveled fast, but it was heard with disbelief. There had been no confirmation, people told one another. At the station where an enormous crowd was gathering to meet Mr. Bryan, the people seemed incapable of believing it; Dr. McIver had been so vital and alive and tireless it was not immediately possible to associate him with death. One person, realizing the dynamo that had been McIver had in truth overtaxed itself, murmured sadly, "He burned the boiler out." It was not until the undertaker backed a hearse up to the platform that the truth penetrated. Charles Duncan McIver was dead.

The scene at the station was eerie as the Special came in. The silence was complete. And Mr. Bryan, who had been led away from the car in which Dr. McIver died sobbing like a child, declared he could not keep his speaking engagement that evening.

The local politicians, needing his help urgently in a tense political situation and arguing that he could not disappoint an immense audience already assembled to hear him, did at length persuade him to appear, but Bryan agreed only on condition that he be permitted to eschew politics altogether and deliver a McIver eulogy. For an hour and a half, speaking without notes, the matchless orator commanded utmost attention from his audience with an appreciation of his "dear dead friend who measured life by what he put into the world and not by what he took out of the world."

All of North Carolina's newspapers, as the Richmond *Times-Dispatch noted,* "vied with one another in praising his character and work," but the statement was true of many others outside the state, including the New York *Times.* Moreover, magazines edited by his friends—*World's Work* (Page), *Review of Reviews* (Shaw), *Outlook* (Abbott)—echoed the superlatives in their next issues, and in addition the *South Atlantic Quarterly* published Page's appraisal of McIver "as the most influential leader of the people for popular education that this generation of men has known." All of the articles reviewed his contribution to education, especially the education of women, as "a high clear record of achievement," finding "essential grandeur in the unbroken unity of this upward-striving story." Yet it was possibly the *Biblical Recorder* that had the highest word of tribute, since its opinion represented McIver's winning of a battle in which the editor had been an arch foe: "No man in his generation has surpassed McIver in serving North Carolina." Dr. Kilgo, another powerful antagonist in the church-state fight, joined as well in speaking of the state's great loss, and his Trinity College flew the national flag at half-mast to denote the passing of a leader. At McIver's own cherished University the college bell tolled, counting his forty-five years. He would have been forty-six on the twenty-seventh of September.

On September 19, Greensboro stood still for the funeral of its foremost citizen. Every plant and business house was closed, and elsewhere coincident to the hour little schoolhouses to which he had been a benefactor held simple memorial services, along with the more impressive ones held at colleges over the state.

Among the throng that attended the funeral, the largest ever assembled for a funeral service in Greensboro, there was a group of the country's leading educators who had gathered from Virginia and Georgia, from North and South Carolina, from New York. Some were men who had known and loved and worked with McIver from his youth. Others, representing the great educational philanthropies, had come to know him more recently. Unfortunately, the little group that had been education's "inner circle" in North Carolina from their Chapel Hill days was not quite intact; Dr. Joyner was immobilized by floods in western North Carolina. As for the others, they fell to recounting some of his humorous anecdotes and laughing through their tears— proof, in Page's opinion, that he had touched the fundamental emotions.

Charles McIver had been equal in distinction to any of the North Carolina men in his close circle of friends who stood apart and wept and laughed in remembrance. But there was a difference. Winston had gone out of North Carolina for a time and returned. Alderman and Page had gone to stay. McIver had remained at home. His service to his fellow man had encompassed a wide area, it is true, but his influence elsewhere could not match in depth and breadth and warmth the devotion he had lavished on his native state, and in that hour and place the people knew it. Distinguished names in that gathering were abundant, but the name of McIver, who had kindled both light for a better today and hope for a brighter tomorrow, led all the rest. His name had the luster of visions. His name had the magic of dreams.

Epilogue

THE North Carolina Normal and Industrial College re-opened on the twentieth of September, 1906, the day following its founder's burial. The student body, larger than any previous enrollment, shared with the rest of the state a keen realization of loss, but they had as well a sense of inheritance. A man had died, but he had left them a legacy. It was Opportunity. To Charles Duncan McIver—and he would be increasingly remembered by his full name—more than any other man they, and other women after them, owed the fact that North Carolina parents had come to think in terms of college education for their children, girls and boys, and not exclusively for their sons.

Nor were the college objectives greatly altered, then or later. Dr. McIver had built firmly and enduringly; the institution would remain committed to the McIver principle that the real worth of a college is "the mental and spiritual atmosphere of the place." Moreover, his idea that both liberal and practical education should be combined in a single individual as well as in a single institution persists to this day. The original "purpose of the institution to give such education as will add to the efficiency of the average woman in whatever walk of life her lot may be cast" proved adaptable to the changes, and they have been many, that would take place in the position of women. The former chancellor, Edward Kidder Graham, gave the aim a new expression, but did not alter its essential meaning, when he stated the premise "that the daughters of our State must be educated for citizenship in *their* time."

Actually, Dr. McIver had done more than state his philosophy in regard to a strong college. He had drawn up a blueprint of its ideals:

"The love of truth for truth's sake; the belief in equality before the law; the belief in fair play and the willingness to applaud an honest victor in every contest, whether on the athletic field or in the class room or in social life; the feeling of common responsibility; the habit of tolerance towards those with whom one does not entirely agree; the giving up of small rights for the sake of greater rights that are essential; the recognition of authority and the dignified voluntary submission to it even when the reason for the policy adopted by the authority is not apparent; the spirit of overlooking the blunders of others and of helping those who are weak; the contempt for idlers and shirkers; the love of one's fellow-workers even though they be one's rivals; patience in toil; self-reliance; faith in human progress; confidence in right; and belief in God—these are the characteristics of the atmosphere of a great and useful college."

Growth was intrinsic in the close relationship established in the beginning between the college and the state it was designed to serve. The state's expansion in population and economy was reflected in the college; the college's progressive thinking was reflected in the state. The process of growth had been reported year after year in Dr. McIver's reports. It would continue until the original ten acres had expanded to 166, until the faculty of a dozen members and three assistants had increased to well over two hundred, until the meager housing and equipment had been exchanged for every modern attribute, physical and scholastic, of an institution with the high standards of excellence and full accreditation toward which the founder aspired. Even the name by which it is popularly known, Woman's College, is the name Dr. McIver had wished for it at the start. The official name became Woman's College of the University of North Carolina in 1932 when the institution which had been known since 1919 as the North Carolina College for Women became part of a consolidated University, together with the State College of Agriculture and Engineering at Raleigh and the University at Chapel Hill.

That the old Normal and Industrial School has evolved into a distinguished liberal arts college, while still emphasizing preparation for earning a living, is certainly in line with the McIver thesis that women equipping themselves for "independence" should not neglect the cultural aspects of education. In fact, he thought extensive training in the liberal arts was more important for women than for men. He often said in his addresses: "If equality in culture be desirable, and if congeniality between husbands and wives after middle life be important, then a woman should have more educational opportunities in youth than a man, because a man with fair native intelligence will continue to grow intellectually during the active period of his business and professional life whereas his wife has little such opportunity due to the confinements of home and the duties of motherhood."

The opponents of his college told the truth when they contended during its infancy that it was not exclusively a school for technical training, but "an institution of higher literary education." In all truth, even as a college for teachers, it could not have been less. One could not prepare young women to teach Latin or Literature without first teaching them the subjects. The chief point was that then, as now, the school combined the academic and applied arts. The institution that equipped girls, from its first day, to become self-supporting with normal and commercial courses also assumed that they would fill women's traditional role in the wider community life—a role already made more vital and complicated by their enlightened status. Resultantly it set a pattern, adjustable to fresh horizons, of educating the college woman to meet all demands of an increasingly variable social order.

In endorsing that dynamic concept the present institution seeks to include among the powerful imponderables of its atmosphere the same elements which activated the founder and his early associates: "permeating values" which former Chancellor Graham has re-stated as "truth and the love of truth, justice, tolerance, the discipline of free men and women, self-reliance, independence of spirit, the habit and pride of responsibility, faith in human dignity and progress, and belief in God."

So it is that Woman's College of the University of North Carolina undertakes to fit its graduates, whether engaged in home or career or a combination of the two, for the complex requirements of times that are constantly changing, often confusing, and always challenging. In the very real sense that its program is identical in intent and purpose with that inaugurated by President Charles Duncan McIver, the College is living proof of Emerson's observation that "An institution is the lengthened shadow of one man."

Notes

Quotations from Charles Duncan McIver which serve as chapter heads were taken from his addresses. A quotation cannot be assigned to a particular speech since he repeated his main arguments and theories under a variety of titles.

CHAPTER ONE

Manuscript genealogies of the McIver and Dalrymple families by Mrs. Minnie McIver Brown, a privately published (1922) McIver genealogy by Helen H. McIver, tombstones in private burying grounds and the Buffalo Church cemetery furnished the facts of Charles Duncan McIver's ancestry. Dr. McIver's unfinished autobiography was authority for information about his mother's Irish antecedents. Records in the Pittsboro courthouse were the source of material concerning the extent and cost of Scotch Iver's lands. All family lore, such as the remark Evander made to the doctor who came too often, together with matters of social custom, was encountered in the reports of various persons. Mrs. John Dickinson, younger daughter of Dr. McIver, provided the legend that her great-grandfather would not look at a new baby until he had paid the doctor who officiated at the birth.

CHAPTER TWO

Charles McIver's autobiographical writing contains a full account of his Civil War boyhood, including the school his father taught. The autobiography had two beginnings, one made when Dr. McIver was thirty, the second two years later. Both stated the intention of bringing an account of his life up to date, and then adding a chapter annually, for the interest and information of his children, and in the hope that it would "show something of the customs of my generation."

Additional information, with descriptions of both the Wealthy Miller Duncan and Harrington homes, came from notes in the handwriting of his mother and wife found among his papers. Visits to the old Scotch Iver home and to Dr. McIver's boyhood home established essential information about them. Items of historical fact were checked in a number of North Carolina histories, including those of Samuel A. Ashe, William K. Boyd,

R. D. W. Connor, and J. D. deR. Hamilton, and *Life in America* (two volumes) by Marshall B. Davidson.

The Melinda Chauncey mentioned in this chapter was my great-grandmother.

CHAPTER THREE

Mr. J. H. McIver, of Lumberton, Dr. Charles McIver's youngest brother, supplied details of their boyhood home and farm in interviews and numerous letters.

The public school background sketched in this chapter was gathered principally from *Public School Education in North Carolina*, by Edgar W. Knight (1916); *A History of the Public Schools of North Carolina*, by M. C. S. Noble, dean of the school of education, University of North Carolina (1930); and *Universal Education in the South*, Vol. I, by Charles William Dabney (1936). All of the volumes of history mentioned above were also consulted. Berkeley was the Virginia governor who thanked God there were no free schools in his state. The quotation is given in Volume II, page 353, *Life in America,* and on page 315 of *Behold Virginia: The Fifth Crown,* by George F. Willison. Among the revenues, none from taxes, accruing to the Literary Fund were dividends from stock North Carolina owned in certain banks and navigation companies, license fees paid by liquor dealers and auctioneers, a balance in the Agricultural Fund established in 1822, and income from vacant swamp lands and lands vacated by the Cherokee Indians. The Fund got $300,000 in 1836 from the State of North Carolina's share ($1,435,757.40) of a surplus in the federal treasury which was distributed among the states.

A chapter on "Schooldays" in the McIver autobiography assesses Charles McIver's teachers. In addition, something of his early schooling is learned from his school compositions and from a brochure, *Charles Duncan McIver,* by Frances Gibson Satterfield, an alumna of Woman's College, University of North Carolina. Mrs. Satterfield obtained some of the information firsthand from one of the teachers mentioned, Mrs. Bertha Buie Cole. The brochure was prepared for the fiftieth anniversary celebration of the Woman's College. Another commemorative volume, *Old Favorites from the McGuffey Readers,* edited by Harvey C. Minnich to celebrate the hundredth anniversary of the appearance of the first McGuffey Readers, provided the McGuffey material.

CHAPTER FOUR

Mrs. J. A. Brown (Minnie McIver), who told the story of the judge and his commencement speech, was an intimate friend as well as relative of Charles McIver's only sister, Elizabeth, and as such was thoroughly familiar with the Henry McIver household. During talks I had with her at her Chadbourn, North Carolina, home, and in a voluminous correspondence, she supplied, as did Mr. J. H. McIver, much detail and anecdote of life on the McIver farm. Moreover, her memory has proved amazingly accurate in all particulars. Whenever she did not trust her recollection, and insisted that a statement—usually a date—be verified, the ultimate account has invariably emerged as she remembered it. It was Mrs. Brown who gave the recipe for syllabub, which she still uses; it was her parents, Archie and Augusta Chandler McIver, who were embarrassed by their man servant.

With the exception of the quotation about the piety and moral courage of the Buffalo Church people, which was contained in a letter to Miss Lula Martin during their courtship, all quotations from Dr. McIver in this chapter came from a questionnaire he answered to furnish information for a projected volume on important North Carolinians (*Men of Mark in North Carolina*). Dr. Lacy's opinions came from a volume of his sermons and addresses collected and issued by the Presbyterian Committee of Publication, Richmond, Virginia, 1900. His address at the centenary celebration of Buffalo Church, 1897, gave various facts of church history, too, including the item of information that Dr. John McIver, as precentor, led singing with a flute.

Dr. Kemp P. Battle's *History of the University of North Carolina* is authority for entrance requirements at the University when Charles McIver entered (Vol. II, pp. 86-87), plus information on outstanding alumni prior to 1868 (Vol. I, p. 783) and the commencement of 1877 (Vol. II, p. 120).

CHAPTER FIVE

If one wonders how a boy's feelings about leaving home could be anything but literary license on the part of his biographer, the answer is that it probably could not unless the young man himself had somewhere set down his experience. That Charles McIver did in one of his letters (August 17, 1884) to Miss Martin. Again, Dr. Battle's second volume of the University's history, in the pages from 54 to 234, supplied pertinent information about buildings, attendance, proscription against hazing, awards, commencement addresses, and the like. Two other books drawn on for incidental information were Dumas S. Malone's biography of Edwin A. Alderman (Doubleday, Doran & Co., Inc., 1940) and *Impressions of Men and Movements at the University of North Carolina* by Henry McGilbert Wagstaff, Professor of History, 1907-1945, edited with a prefatory note by Louis R. Wilson (University of North Carolina Press, 1950). *Selected Papers of Cornelia Phillips Spencer* (University of North Carolina Press, 1953), another volume edited by Mr. Wilson, with introductory comment, affords a sampling of Mrs. Spencer's opinion on many subjects and includes the quotations given here.

McIver's grades, and notations accompanying them, were copied from reports preserved among his other papers. Quotations from Alderman, as are all other statements of his throughout this volume not otherwise accounted for, came from a memorial address he delivered shortly after Dr. McIver's death. The statement that the "note of life was simple, rugged, even primitive" was also his. Chapter One, pages 3 to 20, *The Life and Speeches of Charles B. Aycock,* by Connor and Poe (Doubleday, Page, & Co., 1912) was the source of personal information about Aycock, together with a description of his voice and manner of speaking. It was Dr. Dabney who described McIver's activity at a baseball game.

Dr. James Y. Joyner, Dr. McIver's classmate and lifelong friend, recalled much of their college experience during an interview in his ninetieth year. Reminiscing through much of a leisurely day at his LaGrange home, he remembered where "Mac" roomed and got his meals and spoke of his popularity, his gift of mimicry, his "sprightly and charming" conversation, and the gatherings he dominated around the Old Well and in his room. The story of William George Randall was pieced together from various sources, chief of which was a letter in which Dr. McIver mentioned the artist's attitude toward him. Mrs. James R. Young, Dr. McIver's daughter, recalled the hazing incident as heard from her father. I heard from my father, the late J. Spencer Howell, that the young man walked barefoot to the edge of the campus, and am under the impression that he got the story directly from Dr. McIver, but the impression is unverifiable as my father died before research on this account began. Mr. Harry McIver (J. H. McIver) recalled that his brother got a gold watch from their father as a graduation present.

CHAPTER SIX

The amount of McIver's debt for education as well as the statement that he took a job teaching at $45 a month as the best means to pay it off were included in the *Men of Mark* questionnaire, along with the comment "I remained in the profession in order to fight for the causes to which I have thus far devoted my energies." Information about the teacher's certificate came from the certificate itself, and quotations from "As We See It" came from the handbill so entitled. Dr. Malone's book (page 26) is authority for the statement that Dr. Curry persuaded Edward P. Moses to go to Goldsboro, and reports of the North Carolina superintendent of public instruction furnished dates and facts about the growth of the public school idea. Dr. McIver made various references to having cast his first vote for public education, Mrs. McIver's notes tell of his stand on the subject, and the "I sympathize with Dr. Deans" story was repeated by many persons, including Dr. Joyner, Mrs. Brown, Mrs. Satterfield in her brochure, and others. J. Burton Hendrick, in the first volume of *Life and Letters of Walter H. Page* (Doubleday, Page & Co., 1932), gave a full account of Walter H. Page's editorial position, and Josephus Daniels' *Tar*

Heel Editor (University of North Carolina Press, 1939) recalled (pp. 94-95) something of Page's outlook as reflected in *The State Chronicle*. Mrs. Dickinson gave the account of her mother's change of church affiliation and that of her parents' wedding, which she too makes an altogether hilarious chronicle. Mrs. McIver quietly joined her husband's Presbyterian church after the marriage, according to the McIver brochure by Satterfield, page 27. Mrs. McIver also left notes telling something of the wedding and her appreciation of the visit from Charles's Grandfather Harrington.

CHAPTER SEVEN

Dr. McIver's first speech on behalf of women was not, of course, in written form, having been completely impromptu. He did, however, set down later in pencil, on an ordinary tablet, the beginning, as best he could remember it, of his efforts to obtain "Just and liberal treatment for women in the matter of higher education." Quotations from the maiden speech, as given in this chapter, are from those penciled recollections. The arguments he marshalled for educating women are taken from newspaper accounts, notes for his speeches, and prepared manuscripts of his addresses, which his secretaries complained he rarely referred to at all. The latter fact appears in an article by Miss Emily Semple Austin, who was his secretary for four years and nine months, included in *Leaves from the Stenographers' Note Books,* a booklet containing sidelights on Dr. McIver at work as recalled by three of his secretaries: Miss Austin, Mrs. Fodie Buie Kenyon, and Mr. E. J. Forney. Mrs. Kenyon also noted in a letter written in August, 1952: "He never read a speech; he just got up and talked."

Quotations from Dr. McIver's letters and writings are exact with one exception. The word Negro is capitalized in conformity with current usage, as it was not in his lifetime.

CHAPTER EIGHT

It was Mr. Daniels (*Tar Heel Editor*, pp. 458-59) who described McIver as a "thorough-going Scotchman" and recorded his activities in Raleigh.

Mr. Caldwell's letter giving McIver credit for his change of attitude toward education was written March 19, 1893, on a letterhead of the "*Charlotte Observer*, Daily and Weekly, Caldwell and Tompkins, Publishers": "I am quite in earnest in my desire to do something for the cause of public education, and for my interest in it I am more indebted to you than to all other men combined." A copy of the "Memorial" to the Legislature afforded a digest of that paper's contents. Mrs. McIver left among her papers notes telling of the supper which the House speaker and his wife had at the McIver home. She did not mention the man's name, but Augustus Leazer, of Iredell (*Tar Heel Editor*, page 338) was

Speaker of the House in 1889. The amount of objection to public education and grounds for the objection were discussed by Major Sidney M.
Finger in his biennial report as state superintendent of public instruction,
1889-90.

Chapter Nine

The sources of much of the material in this chapter, as in the majority of them, are obvious: Reports McIver and Alderman made as Institute
conductors, Mr. Finger's reports as state superintendent of public instruction, and the letters and newspapers quoted. Dr. Dabney and Mr. Daniels,
among persons who knew both men, described in their writings the different platform manner of the two orators, as did Dr. Joyner in an interview. Also Page's biographer, Hendrick, and Alderman's biographer,
Malone, noted the dissimilarities, with Dr. Malone concluding (page 37)
"Alderman may have charmed more audiences but McIver won more
hearts."

As for Dr. McIver's letters to Mrs. McIver being love letters all his life,
the statement can be readily verified once his papers are available. (They
are now in the library of Woman's College, University of North Carolina,
restricted to my use.) Meanwhile, not liking to make a statement un-
supported by any proof, I offer the following quotation from one of them,
written June 2, 1891, in substantiation: "I love you better than I did seven
years ago, and I hope you love me better, though, I confess, that we had
a quite pleasant arrangement even then."

Chapter Ten

A graphic account of Mrs. McIver's broom-and-pail sprees, based on an
interview with Mrs. McIver, was contributed by Virginia Terrell Lathrop,
an alumna who was then head of the Woman's College News Bureau, to
North Carolina newspapers (Greensboro *Daily News,* Raleigh *News and
Observer*) Oct. 6, 1940.

Dr. Spainhour, the one trustee unknown to Dr. McIver on the original
board, did the college what President McIver described in a biennial report
(1901-02) as a unique service. For a period of ten years he clipped from
newspapers all references, complimentary or otherwise, to the college, and
preserved them in scrapbooks (Woman's College Library) that furnish
excellent reference material on early days of the institution.

The speech President McIver made at the Teachers' Assembly on the
tremendous and perilous power of ignorance was printed in *The North
Carolina Teacher* of June, 1891, and again the following year by the
North Carolina Alumni Magazine when he repeated the peroration as part
of an alumni address at Chapel Hill in 1892. Fodie Buie (Mrs. James
Talmadge Kenyon) told the story of her competitive examination and
preparation for college, together with the remarks of her neighbor, in

"Little Pictures of Old Times" in the *Alumnae News* of November, 1941, and February, 1942. She elaborated on her early experiences and impressions in letters to me. Miss Ruth Fitzgerald, connected with Woman's College for forty-nine years, stressed in an interview that the "commercial department was very precious to Dr. McIver." Mr. Forney contributed an account of the meeting between him and Dr. McIver to *Leaves from the Stenographers' Note Books.*

CHAPTER ELEVEN

Educate a Woman (University of North Carolina Press, 1942), a volume compiled by Virginia Terrell Lathrop in connection with the fiftieth anniversary celebration of Woman's College, captured in words and pictures much atmosphere of the college's early years; it also provided some of the information used here. Other highlights of the opening and first days of the institution are found in the "College Collection" of the Woman's College Library. The two-coach train from the Sandhills was the one Fodie Buie (Kenyon) took to Greensboro, as described in the *Alumnae News;* Mrs. Kenyon's articles gave other details of the first days, including identification of Pattie Carter as the girl who fell through the skylight. The composition of the student body was described in Dr. McIver's report to the General Assembly. Mrs. Joseph Gant (Mamie Banner) was the secretary who reiterated of Dr. McIver "He was the kindest man I ever knew" during an interview in her Burlington home. Mrs. R. Murphy Williams (Lillie Boney) and Mrs. R. D. Douglas (Virginia Brown) were among the alumnae who spoke of the unanimous respect in which their school president was held. Miss Mary Petty, whose influence has touched thousands of North Carolina girls and continues as she remains near the college in retirement, was the faculty member who described President McIver as "convincible." Miss Annie Petty, who joined the faculty in 1895 and served as librarian for twenty-five years, carried to the president each morning the newspaper he scanned so effectively on his way upstairs to chapel. Both she and Miss Cornelia Strong, of a later faculty, recalled the statement "It is a mark of civilization to close a door once you have gone through it."

The statement from *Tar Heel Editor* concerning Mr. Harrell's activity in the 1889 Legislature appears on page 374. Miss Anne Page was the student whose reading of the *Teacher* article was often interrupted by hissing. "College Collection" notes supply the information that the surplus board money contributed by students to beautify the campus went to buy grass seed for the slope in front of the main buildings which the girls called "the switch patch."

CHAPTER TWELVE

I acknowledge a big debt to Dr. Luther Gobbel, whose *Church-State Relationships in North Carolina Since 1776* (Duke University Press, 1938) not only gives a full account of the church-state battle but is so thoroughly annotated it made research into the original sources easy. Dr. Battle's history of the University also gives an account of the beginnings of the fight. The state press consistently reported on the controversy, including resolutions and memorials of the religious bodies, and thus the record is readily available in the Spainhour scrapbooks. It was the *Biblical Recorder* of February 16, 1881, that forecast a long struggle.

Wagstaff's chapter (*Impressions of Men and Movements at the University of North Carolina*) on President Winston afforded an estimate of his methods and effectiveness; the author commented, too, on Dr. Kilgo and his trenchancy. The direct quotation from Winston, and his opinions on the place of a state university, came from an address on "Higher Education in the South" made while he was president of the University of Texas, as reported by the Milwaukee *Sentinel,* July 10, 1897. The speech also sketched the position of denominational colleges.

The letter in which McIver compared education to light was written to Maxcy L. John of Laurinburg, February 4, 1894. The *Biblical Recorder* of August 4, 1897, stated, of the time when Taylor's articles were running serially in that periodical, "We were just 20 years of age; and on account of our father's sickness, had charge of the Recorder, but had no idea of ever becoming editor of the paper, having made other plans." Mr. Bailey became editor of the *Recorder* in 1895. The same publication, in its issue of July 6, 1898, recalled: "It was in December, 1893, that the Baptists of North Carolina began their organized opposition to the policy of our State in Higher Education . . . President Taylor's invincible arguments and exposures of the wrong of the State's policy appeared in the spring of 1894. That summer and fall and the following months, until he fell in November, 1895, in the thick of the conflict, the zealous, devoted and powerful Durham carried forward this cause until the whole state was stirred." The "intense editorial" quoted in this chapter appeared August 31, 1898.

The following are Dr. McIver's handwritten notes for a refutation of the Taylor position:

Dr. Taylor objects to *any appropriation* by the state for aiding in higher education on the following grounds:

1. Because state appropriations, as he claims, injure Wake Forest and other denominational colleges.

2. Because the state ought to give the amount given to higher education to its lower public schools.

3. Because the principle is wrong. The intimation is that the money appropriated to higher education is not for the general good.

4. Because, as he claims, no state institution can teach religion.

The student who wrote from Rutherford about the Baptists working in earnest was Miss Birdie Bell.

Dr. Malone (Alderman biography, page 84) and Dr. Gobbel in his book on church-state relation (pp. 146-7) are agreed that Dr. Kilgo's stand on religious education was less moderate than that of the Methodist Church as a whole. The Bailey letter to Dr. Kilgo, written November 9, 1897, is quoted on page 179 of Dr. Gobbel's book.

CHAPTER THIRTEEN

The young women who disclaimed all intention of forming a Greek Letter Fraternity, and thus helped to establish the no-sorority tradition were, in the order of signing the agreement: Sadie Hanes, Elizabeth C. Gibson, Emily I. Evans, Mary Shepard, Lilla M. Young, Emily M. Gibson, Carrie Lawrence, Nan M. Wood, Frances L. Hill, Ophelia D. Howell, Margaret MacRobert McCaull, M. Douglas, Annie L. Steele, and Annie R. Hawkins.

In *America's History,* by Todd and Curti (Harcourt, Brace and Co., 1950), pp. 525-532, may be found a concise and clear discussion of the monetary situation leading to conditions that prevailed during the Cleveland administration.

The complete text of Page's "Forgotten Man" is included, pages 1-47 inclusive, in his book, *The Rebuilding of Old Commonwealths* (Doubleday, Page & Co., 1902).

Dr. McIver's close bond with the students was not confined to this period alone. For instance, it was Miss Miriam McFadyen, of the last graduating class under President McIver's tenure, who amended her statement to say that students were going along with Dr. McIver in search of a vision, not following him. Miss Virginia Brown (Mrs. R. D. Douglas), quoted in the next chapter concerning events when she was a student, was the young horsewoman who carried a message to the station. Mr. Forney told the story of the man with seven children who was ag'in everything that was keeping the poor man down (*Leaves from the Stenographers' Note Books*).

CHAPTER FOURTEEN

Incidental data about the Spanish-American War came from *Encyclopedia of American History,* by Richard B. Norris (Harper & Brothers, 1953), pp. 288-290. Mr. Aycock's opinions, directly and indirectly quoted, are taken from his speeches included in the Connor and Poe volume: *Life and Speeches of Charles B. Aycock.* The figures on school districts without local taxation and without schoolhouses, as well as those having only log buildings chinked with clay, are found on pages 114-15 of that same volume.

Miss Emily Austin, in a letter from Tarboro written April 25, 1952, told of events in President McIver's home the night Lula Martin McIver (Mrs. Dickinson) was born.

Dr. McIver's description of George T. Winston as "a stimulating genius" appeared in the Charlotte *Observer,* April 5, 1903. "A Mountain Trip," contributed by Mr. Forney to *Leaves from the Stenographers' Note Books,* contains a part of the information concerning the western swing in the summer of 1899, and Dr. McIver's letters home give additional details. Anecdotes about Julia Booker and "Uncle" William were furnished by Mrs. Dickinson. Mrs. Douglas recalled, in an interview, the interruption that brought Dr. McIver news of the first fever death and gave extra details in a letter (April 28, 1952). She further noted in the letter: "I believe I forgot to tell you of the personal interest Dr. McIver felt in any student who had peculiar needs. His quick kindness solved many problems. His was an active sort of sympathy. He neither asked nor wished thanks."

Miss Austin was the secretary summoned to Dr. McIver's office in the dawn hours; she wrote of it in *Leaves from the Stenographers' Note Books.* "College Collection" notes, newspapers, records of Board meetings, and Dr. McIver's report to the General Assembly give full accounts of the epidemic. Numerous letters of encouragement to the president are preserved among the McIver papers.

Chapter Fifteen

The Southern Education Movement, volume two of *Universal Education in the South,* gives Dr. Dabney's account of the origin, development, and outcome of the Conference for Education in the South. An additional item of information concerning the first session is taken from an announcement of the ninth annual meeting of the Conference at Lexington, Kentucky, May 2-4, 1906: "A number of years have passed since Captain W. H. Sale, of Capon Springs, West Virginia, sent out his first hospitable invitation to a Conference of this kind and gathered to his mountain retreat, in the summer of 1898, some 50 congenial guests from different parts of the country for the untrammeled discussion of educational subjects."

Miss Kittie Dees was the student who persuaded her employers, Manning Brothers, Landscape Architects, to design the college campus without charge.

Chapter Sixteen

Dr. McIver's report as a district director gave "a vigorous educational campaign for the public schools of North Carolina" as an aim of the Southern Education Board. *The Life and Speeches of Charles B. Aycock* is again authority for information on Aycock and his views. Reprints of the platform against illiteracy furnished the contents of that document as well as the names of all those in attendance and the institutions represented. Dr. Dabney's book (second volume of *Universal Education in the South*) gives full information on the Summer School of the South (page 106).

Mrs. Dickinson recalled Miss Boddie's remark about the resemblance between her and her father, and also the whipping, vividly remembered, that he gave her for running away. She tells another story of herself, too, that illustrates the type of visitors familiar to the McIver household. On her first day as a student in the Curry Observation and Training School the boy seated behind her pulled her hair, and she retaliated. The teacher, seeing only her act and not the offense that provoked it, sent her to the office of some one called a principal, a being of which she had never heard and could only fear the worst. But when she got to the office she saw nobody but a good friend, Julius I. Foust, seen often in her home. She got a running start and landed in his lap intent upon seeking protection from that fearsome creature the "principal." The principal transacted business for the rest of the afternoon over her dark curls.

Dr. Jackson told of reaction to Dr. McIver's nervous moving of water pitcher and his straightening of crooked window shade. Mr. Stone supplied the story of Chub Dick. That salty old gentleman, in his eighty-fifth year at the time, reminisced away an afternoon at his country home, Kellwood, near Greensboro. He was one of the signers of the notes that guaranteed the new college for Greensboro.

The Reunion was, as Page said, a success. It drew back home to see the transformation being wrought there, through enlightenment, native Tar Heels from thirty states and the District of Columbia. Its board of governors included in addition to Dr. McIver as chairman: Robert R. King, Caesar Cone, J. A. Odell, J. W. Fry, G. S. Bradshaw, Lee H. Battle, treasurer, R. D. Douglas, corresponding secretary, and Andrew Joyner, chairman of the press committee.

Mrs. Gant, a student at the college when the dormitory burned, told of the hack driver's remark to Dr. McIver, and described living arrangements in Students' Building (next chapter), as did Mrs. Ernest Pitcher (Catherine Nash) and notes in the "College Collection."

CHAPTER SEVENTEEN

Dr. Malone, in the Alderman biography, tells of Dr. McIver's efforts in behalf of Alderman on pages 169-70.

The New York *Sun* gave the account of McIver's Albany speech that is quoted. Miss Cornelia Strong was the teacher who recalled her sense of guilt from eating candy bars not available to the students. She joined the faculty that year and was somewhat aghast upon arriving to learn that she had no contract. She learned that nobody else had one either and nevertheless felt secure, and she soon came to share the general complacency about it, as well she might have. She stayed at the college over forty years.

CHAPTER EIGHTEEN

The Clem referred to in the fourth paragraph—a story told by Mrs. Dickinson—was Mr. Clem Wright of Greensboro. In recounting the incident to Mrs. Dickinson he drawled good-naturedly, "Now, Lula Martin, you know that was a dirty trick."

The effect of a McIver story when encountered without the teller's magic is much the same now, whether the stories are found in print, where they are not particularly funny, or whether they are told by persons who recall them exactly in spite of the lapse of time. The latter laugh merrily, remembering how *he* told them.

The interview in which McIver sought the help of his friends Daniels and Joyner in regard to the Mebane proposal was recalled by Mr. Daniels both in a *News and Observer* McIver Memorial Number and in his own autobiography. Dr. Joyner spoke of it personally.

Charles Duncan McIver, Memorial Volume, prepared in accordance with a resolution of the Board of Directors of the North Carolina State Normal and Industrial College, contains the full address by Edwin A. Alderman, along with speeches by several other persons, made at memorial exercises for Dr. McIver held at the college November 20, 1906, resolutions passed by many organizations, and excerpts from seventy-six newspapers and periodicals. It was Mr. Page, writing in the *South Atlantic Quarterly,* who told of how "men prominent in educational work from Georgia, North Carolina, South Carolina, Virginia and New York, through their tears fell to telling humorous anecdotes that illustrated his unbounded cheerfulness and kindness." Newspaper accounts of Dr. McIver's death were prepared by reporters on the Bryan train, including Mr. Bryant and Mr. Andrew Joyner.

EPILOGUE

Dr. McIver's statement to the effect that the real worth of a college is the mental and spiritual atmosphere of the place and his summary of characteristics that make a great and useful college appeared in his centennial report on the Normal and Industrial College.

All statements from former Chancellor Graham, including the quoted phrase "permeating values," were made during a Founder's Day address at the Woman's College, October 5, 1950.

Index

Academies, Scotch Presbyterians establish, 26; students of excel at University, 49; Special Act a threat to, 58. *See also* names of individual institutions

Agricultural and Mechanical College, 112, 154, 184-85, 213, 261

Alderman, Edwin A., and McIver become friends, 51; quoted, 51-52, 71, 73, 81 118, 193, 223, 251; member of education's "inner circle," 53; wins oratory medal, 55; adopts McIver's attitude on women's education, 74; credits McIver with training school idea, 75; school superintendent at Goldsboro, 86; receives appointment as institute conductor, 90; platform manner of, 95; helps prepare training school bill, 113; considered for presidency of Normal and Industrial School, 116; on faculty of Normal and Industrial School, 118; appointed to University of North Carolina faculty, 141; becomes University of North Carolina president, 169; becomes president of Tulane, 198; chosen president of University of Virginia, 237; mentioned, 58, 83-84, 91, 93, 96-97, 100, 103, 105, 108-9, 112, 117, 124, 133, 170-71, 183-85, 203, 206-7, 214, 228, 230, 238, 250, 252, 254, 259, 275

Alexander, Dr. Annie Laurie, 111

Alumnae News, 270

Angelet, 33, 35, 43

Appomattox, 21

Asheboro *Argus, The,* 212

Asheboro *Courier, The,* 169

Atlantic Monthly, 29, 183, 185, 199, 209

Austin, Emily Semple, 268, 273

Autobiography, Dr. McIver's unfinished, 264-65

Aycock, Charles Brantley, enters University of North Carolina, 48; member of education's "inner circle," 53; wins oratory medal, 55; elected Governor of North Carolina, 200; mentioned, 49, 86, 116, 151, 156, 179-80, 183, 202, 212, 214-15, 217, 220, 226, 233, 238, 243

Bailey, Rev. C. T., 139, 150

Bailey, Josiah William, 150, 159, 161, 181, 271

Baltimore *Sun,* quoted, 143

Baptist Female University, 213

Battle, Kemp Plummer, 54-55, 83, 115, 145, 152-53, 266

Bible, The, guide and stay of Scots, 6

Biblical Recorder, quoted, 146, 152, 158, 192, 258, 271; mentioned, 138-39, 144-45, 149-50, 181, 193

Bingham, Major Robert, 180

Bingham School, 179

Bitting, Miriam, M.D., 125, 142, 168

Boddie, Viola, 125, 133, 222, 274

Broadaway, Maude F., 141

Brown, Mrs. Minnie McIver, 265-67

Bryan, William Jennings, quoted, 168; mentioned, 163, 183-84, 256-58

Bryant, Dixie Lee, 124-25

Bryant, H. E. C., 256, 275

Buffalo Church, 6, 36, 39-40, 266

Buffalo Creek, 22, 24, 36

Buffalo Lyceum, 40

Buie, Bertha, 33, 265, 270

Buie, Fodie, 121, 268-69

Burlington *Herald,* 139

Burwell, John B., 73-74, 78, 83

Butler, Nicholas Murray, 164, 183-84, 198, 208, 217

Caldwell, J. P., 87, 162-63, 268

Cape Fear River Region, 4, 20

Carnegie, Andrew, 201, 210-11, 217, 234-36, 243

Carroway, Mrs. W. P., 125

Catawba College, 213-14

Central Express (Sanford, N. C.), 97

Charity and Children, 185

Charlotte Female Institute, 111

Charlotte *Observer,* quoted, 72, 182, 192; mentioned, 87, 162-63, 227, 273
Chatham County, 5, 7, 22
Chauncey, Melinda, 21, 265
Chauncey family, 21
Chowan Baptist Association, 150
Chowan Institute, 112, 143
Christian Educator, The, 158-59
Churchill, Winston, 201
Church-state conflict. *See* State Aid
Civilization, chief factors of, 77
Civil rights bill, agitation for, 27
Claxton, P. P., 141
Cleveland panic, 147
College Collection, Library, Woman's College, 270
Colleges. *See* names of individual institutions
Columbia (S.C.) *State,* 227
Conference for Education in the South, origin of, 195; mission of, 196; elects Ogden president, 198; General Education Board an outcome of, 202; authorizes executive committee, 203; establishes Summer School of the South, 218; mentioned, 201, 237, 244, 254
Courtesy, valued by Scots, 43
Cox, Mrs. Fannie Bell, 125
Curry, Dr. J. L. M., General Agent of Peabody Board, 58; makes plea for training school, 113; president, Conference for Education in the South, 195; mentioned, 94, 107, 131, 173, 196, 202, 208, 226, 267

Dabney, Charles W., historian of Southern Education movement, 195; heads Information Bureau, 208; quoted, 230; mentioned, 201, 203, 219, 238-39, 269
Dalton, David Nicholas (Dicky), 60, 83
Daniels, Josephus, goes to Raleigh as lawyer and editor, 81-82; quoted, 82, 136, 176; mentioned, 83, 116, 137, 148, 164, 171, 173, 183, 185, 193, 202, 253, 269, 275
Davidson College, 43, 144-45, 152, 214
Dialectic Literary Society, 49
Dickinson, Mrs. John. *See* McIver, Lula Martin
Douglas, Robert Dick, 173
Douglas, Mrs. R. D., 270, 272-73
Dowd, Jerome, 115
Duke University, 144, 161
Durham, Dr. Columbus, 144, 150, 153, 271

Education, in 17th century England, 25; aristocratic concept of in southern colonies, 25; denominations take lead in, 27; North Carolina renaissance in, 52;

the "supreme issue" of the South, 69; practical not available to white girls, 70-71; North Carolina provides Normal for Negro youths, 72; white girl overlooked in higher, 72; of a woman yields high return, 77; for teachers popular at Peace Institute, 78; widespread objection to public, 87; state should help weaker sex to, 88; institutes unique in annals of, 90; excuses for opposition to public, 91; for professions not useful to women, 92; described as social insurance, 100; a function of the state, 104; main topic in McIver home, 111-12; fashionable to be in favor of public, 112; of college grade provided for women by churches, 143-44; church plea in behalf of lower, 146; Baptists and Methodists oppose state policy in higher, 149; argument for "voluntary principle" in higher, 150; lawmakers not friendly to, 155; right of every youth to universal, 156; argument for church monopoly in higher, 158-59; higher by state a campaign issue, 160; opposition to "State Aid" for higher losing ground, 161; women's should be put on financial basis with men's, 167; given to women propagates itself, 171; as a qualification for voting, 180; legislation most needed for improving, 180; surest way to universal, 183; universal a duty of the state, 200; keynote of Aycock's inaugural, 200; of white women best field for investment in the South, 204-5; "sound logical argument" for universal, 212; new opportunities of for women, 213-14; overshadowing necessity for universal, 214; chief topic of interest in North Carolina, 215; civilization's best and most expensive thing, 244
Elon College, 152-53, 213, 214
Epps and Hackett, architects, 120

Farmers' Alliance, influential, 100; endorses training school for teachers, 112
Fayetteville *Observer,* 166
Finger, Major Sidney M., state superintendent of public instruction, 90; mentioned, 103, 105, 107, 110, 112-13, 115-16, 124, 173, 269
Fitzgerald, Ruth, 270
Floral College, trustees of want McIver as principal, 85
"Forgotten Man, The," address by Walter Hines Page, 174-75
Forney, E. J., begins association with Normal and Industrial School, 123; mentioned, 125, 139, 187, 268, 270, 272

Fort, Melville, 125
Foust, Julius I., 245, 257, 274
Fraternities, McIver's antipathy toward, 50
Freedmen's Bureau, provides schools for Negroes, 27
Frissell, H. B., 196, 202-3, 207, 210

Gant, Mrs. Joseph, 270, 274
General Assembly. *See* North Carolina Legislature
General Education Board, 203, 207, 219, 226, 252
Gilman, Daniel Coit, 207-8, 230
Gove, Anna M., M.D., 142, 190, 257
Graham, Edward Kidder, 260, 262, 275
"Grandfather's Clause," 200
Gray, R. T., 120
Greensboro College, 141
Greensboro Female College, 141, 144
Greensboro *Patriot,* 140, 166
Greensboro *Record,* 124, 136-37, 140, 142, 170, 224
Greensboro *Telegram,* 220
Guilford College, 112, 124, 152-53, 213-14
Guilford County, 176, 190

Hampton Institute, 196, 198
Harrell, Eugene G., critical of Normal and Industrial School, 136-38; mentioned, 60, 83-84
Harrington, William Dalrymple, 10, 12, 67
Henderson *Gold Leaf,* quoted, 107
Howell, J. Spencer, 267
Howell, Logan, 255

Illiteracy, a reproach to the state, 153, platform against, 214
Illiterates, proportion of in North Carolina, 69; female outnumber male, 74; high number of preventable by women's education, 170
Inner Circle, the, of North Carolina education, 53, 215
Institutes, system of authorized by Legislature, 90; McIver and Alderman chosen to conduct, 90; work of begins, 94; schedule of not conducive to good health, 101; some hardships of the, 102-6; conductors' reports of, 108-9; epochal achievement of, 109; continue erratic course, 110; model for North Carolina education campaign, 207
Isle of Skye, 3, 4, 22

Jackson, Dr. Walter C., 224, 236, 274
Jarvis, Thomas J., 56, 220
John, Maxcy L., 271
Joyner, Andrew, 275
Joyner, James Y., enters University of North Carolina, 51; member of education's "inner circle," 53; joins Winston school faculty, 61; quoted, 71, 106, 140, 173, 242; an institute conductor, 94; joins Normal and Industrial School faculty, 141; becomes state superintendent of public instruction, 215; accompanies McIver to Europe, 247; mentioned, 55, 86, 96, 104, 151, 171, 191-92, 214, 245-46, 249, 253-54, 259, 267, 275
Junior Order, United American Mechanics, 175

Kelly, John E., 30, 43-44, 49
Kenyon, Mrs. James Talmadge. *See* Buie, Fodie
Kilgo, John C., 150, 158-59, 161, 258, 272
King's Daughters, 112
Kirkland, Sue May, Lady Principal of Normal and Industrial School, 125; impresses new students, 128-29; mentioned, 137, 190
Knoxville *Journal and Tribune,* 219

Lacy, B. R., 184
Lacy, Dr. William Sterling, 39-42, 65-66, 266
Landmark, The, 76, 87
Land Scrip Fund, 145
Lathrop, Virginia Terrell, 269
Library, for Normal and Industrial College, McIver gives attention to securing, 181; Legislature makes some provision for, 209; McIver enlists help of friends to procure, 210-11; Carnegie makes offer of, 235; McIver discusses with Carnegie additional funds for, 235-36
Lincoln, President, 14-15
Literary Fund, 26
Louisburg Junior College, 144

McAlister, A. C., 115, 123
McGuffey Readers, 29-30, 47, 187
McIntyre, Edith, 125
McIver, Alex, 85
McIver, Alton, 43-44
McIver, Annie, 74, 81, 84, 111, 157-58, 186, 188-89, 221, 225, 228, 267
McIver, Archie, 27, 37, 266
McIver, Augusta Chandler, 37, 266
McIver, Catherine, 3, 5
McIver, Charles Duncan, ancestry, 3-11; birth, 12; christening, 14; Civil War childhood, 15-19; first school, 20; boyhood home, 23-24; attends school, 28-31; compositions of, 31-33; chores, 33-34; first lesson in democracy, 37; farm work and recreation, 37-38; devoted to church,

39; University course of study, 49, 53; graduates from University of North Carolina, 56; takes first teaching position, 57; casts first vote, 59; goes to Winston school, 60; becomes friend of Walter Hines Page, 62-63; meets Miss Lula Martin, 63; marries Miss Lula Martin, 66-67; elected vice president of Teachers' Assembly, 69; irrevocably chooses life work, 70; makes first speech, 71-73; accepts position at Peace Institute, 73; heads committee to ask for teacher training school, 74; persuades Alderman to favor education for women, 74; makes first formal lecture, 76; becomes one-man lobby in Legislature, 80; appointed institute conductor, 90; speaking results of, 96; humanity in letters of, 103; has singleness of purpose, 105; elected president of Teachers' Assembly, 107; helps prepare training school bill, 113; chosen president of Normal and Industrial School, 117; delivers peroration on ignorance, 119; welcomes arriving students, 128; has fatherly attitude toward Normal girls, 131; University of North Carolina awards honorary degree to, 141; halts boom to nominate him for governor, 165; declines University of North Carolina presidency, 168; becomes active in Conference for Education in the South, 197; is sought again for University of North Carolina presidency, 198; elected secretary of Southern Education Board, 207; profile of, 217; widespread popularity of, 223; pressed to become Peabody Agent, 230; declines position with Peabody Board, 234; elected vice president of National Educational Association, 239; declines to consider University of Tennessee presidency, 239; receives second honorary degree from University of North Carolina, 239; elected president of Southern Educational Association, 242; called champion of public schools, 246; sails for Europe, 248; death of, 257; funeral of, 258-59

McIver, Mrs. Charles D., sketch of, 63-68; wedding of, 66-67; an incomparable hostess, 81; helps husband with institutes, 94; teaches at Peace Institute, 100; gives satisfaction as institute assistant, 110; becomes Lady Principal of Charlotte Female Institute, 111; studies medicine, 111; carries on traditions of hospitality, 225; mentioned, 68, 70, 71, 76, 78, 83-85, 89, 102-3, 112-13, 115, 123, 125, 151, 115-57, 168, 178, 182,

187-89, 196, 205-6, 221, 230, 235, 240-41, 243-46, 248, 253, 265, 266, 269.

McIver, Charles Duncan, Jr., 83, 111, 221, 223, 234, 246

McIver, Claude, 64-65

McIver, Cyrus, 46, 50

McIver, Duncan (of Skye), 3, 5

McIver, Duncan (son of Evander), 8, 19, 21-22

McIver, Duncan (Wealthy Miller), 3-4, 9

McIver, Elizabeth (Lizzie), 36, 64, 71, 130, 248

McIver, Evander, 3-5, 7-9, 19, 21, 248

McIver, Henry, 9-12, 14, 16, 19-22, 24, 27-28, 32, 35, 38, 40, 45

McIver, J. H. (Harry), 64-67, 265, 267

McIver, John, 39, 43, 47, 266

McIver, Lula Martin, 182, 221-22, 264, 273-75

McIver, Rufus, 36, 64-65

McIver, Sarah Harrington (Sallie), 10-12, 22, 35-36, 38, 265

McIver, Verlinda Miller, 164, 221

McIver, Wesley, 46, 64

McIver, William Donald, 17, 20, 28, 33, 36-37, 40, 60, 64-65, 67, 103

Macon (Ga.) *Telegraph,* 205

Macy, Mr. and Mrs. V. E., 233

Malone, Dumas, 103

Martin, Lula. *See* McIver, Mrs. Charles D.

May School, 218

Mebane, B. Frank, 239, 241, 247, 253-54

Mecklenburg *Times,* quoted, 115

Mendenhall, Gertrude, 124, 133

Methodist Male Academy, 59

Milwaukee *Sentinel,* 271

Moore County, 11, 13, 20, 22, 33, 49

Moravians, active in providing schools, 27

Moses, Edward P., 58, 75, 84, 94, 186, 267

Murphy, Edgar Gardner, 208, 227

National Educational Association, McIver chosen vice president of, 239; McIver defeated for president of, 245; mentioned, 168, 198, 206, 219

Neatness, a McIver trademark, 51

Negroes, Freedmen's Bureau and others provide schools for, 27; Slater Fund for, 58; state provides a Normal school for, 72; are Republicans, 85; share tax benefits under dual school system, 91; place of in politics, 176; solid vote of puts Fusionists in power, 176; issue of in politics is bitter, 178; hold positions for which unqualified, 179; disfranchised in North Carolina, 200; Aycock keeps promise to, 200; Dr. McIver a friend of, 204; press reports cause difficulties concerning, 227-28; Dr. McIver credited with well-balanced interest in education of, 229

Newby, Mary, 30-31

News and Observer, quoted, 169, 171; mentioned, 82, 148, 155-56, 166, 275

Newton *Enterprise,* 140

New York *Daily Tribune,* 237

New York *Herald,* 245

New York *Mail,* 217

New York *Times,* 228, 258

Noble, M. C. S. (Billy), member of education's "inner circle," 52-53; engaged in Summer Normal program, 83; a trustee of Normal and Industrial School, 115; mentioned, 61, 86, 94, 103, 107, 118, 120, 122, 151

Normal and Industrial School, authorized, 114; purposes of, 114; five towns bid for, 114; first trustees of, 115; Greensboro chosen as location of, 117; McIver chosen president of, 117; an educational experiment, 118; site chosen for, 120; enthusiasm grows for, 120; course of study determined, 121; first faculty, 124-25; opening, 127; students represent all social levels, 130; students form self-government, 130; good relations between president and faculty of, 132; students taught self-esteem, 135; graduates first class, 140; new faculty members of, 141-42; considered unfair competition by church colleges, 143-44; has strong friends in Legislature, 155; name changed to Normal and Industrial College, 161; traditions born at, 162; is "pride of state," 173; typhoid epidemic at, 191; celebrates its decennial, 218; offers five-year degree course, 218; a great educational force, 226; several buildings of destroyed by fire, 232; suspended temporarily, 234; promised Carnegie library, 235; cornerstone laid for new domitory of, 236; gives prestige to North Carolina, 253; to award degrees in four years, 254; holds to objectives of founder, 260-63; mentioned, 138-39; 147, 151, 154, 156, 160, 186, 197, 209, 223, 241, 250

Normals, State Summer, at Yadkinville, 75-76; supersede Summer Normal at Chapel Hill, 76; at Sparta, 82; McIver principal of at Wilson and Sparta, 83; discontinued by the Legislature, 90

North Carolina, a frontier in early 19th century, 5; enters Confederacy, 15; war losses, 21; early schools in, 25-26; new constitution of silent on segregation, 27; wretchedly poor after Civil War, 34; provides no higher education for white girls, 72; attitude of toward education, 91; rabidly tax-hating, 93; educational revival in, 175; only hope for public education in, 176; vigorous campaign planned for public schools of, 212

North Carolina Agricultural and Mechanical College for Negroes, 202

North Carolina Education Campaign, planned, 215; makes education number one topic of interest, 215; opening of, 220; rallies in connection with, 220; second intensive summer of, 228; results of, 242

North Carolina Legislature, charters university, 26; rejects memorial for teacher training school, 75; McIver lobbies for educational program in, 80; fails to pass training school bill, 90; provides for system of county institutes, 90; authorizes Normal and Industrial School, 113-14; continues appropriation to Normal and Industrial School, 137; asked to aid University of North Carolina, 145-46; Baptist State Convention memorializes, 153; Populist control of, 154; equalizes appropriations to Normal and Industrial School and University of North Carolina, 160; changes name of girls' school to Normal and Industrial College, 161; appropriates $50,000 for common schools, 171; appropriates money necessitated by typhoid epidemic at Normal and Industrial College, 194; makes provision for library and gymnasium at Normal and Industrial College, 209-10

North Carolina Presbyterian, 48

North Carolina Reunion, 228

North Carolina *Teacher,* 60, 69, 74, 136, 138, 140, 269-70

North Carolina Teachers' Assembly, chooses McIver vice president, 69; chooses McIver president, 107; reappoints McIver chairman of training school committee, 112; jubilant over training school, 119; mentioned, 74, 83, 117, 136, 236

Ogden, Robert C., elected president of Conference for Education in the South, 198; begins custom of chartering special conference train, 202; becomes chairman of Southern Education Board, 203; quoted, 204, 206-8, 240; mentioned, 196, 201, 217, 219, 233, 238, 243

Oldham, Edward A., 61

Outlook, The, 76, 246, 258

Page, Walter Hines, editor of *State Chronicle,* 62; becomes friend of McIver, 62;

delivers "Forgotten Man" address, 173; quoted, 185-86, 199, 229, 258, 275; mentioned, 53, 63, 82, 115, 143, 183, 207, 210-11, 213, 227, 240, 256, 259

Peabody, George, sets up education trust, 27

Peabody, George Foster, makes gifts to Normal and Industrial College, 197; mentioned, 202-3, 219-20, 230, 233, 240, 244, 248, 251

Peabody Board, begins policy of aiding rural schools, 230; McIver declines to become General Agent of, 234; mentioned, 219

Peabody Fund, 27, 58, 94

Peace Institute, 73, 78, 86, 100, 124, 130

Petty, Annie, 270

Petty, Mary, 141, 270

Philanthropic Literary Society, 49

Presbyterian Male Academy, 57

Presbyterian Standard, The 181, 193

Pullen, R. S., 120

Quakers, active in providing schools, 27; advocates of education, 100

Randall, William George, 54, 173, 267

Ransom, General M. W., 55

Reconstruction, abuses of, 34; end of, 45

Review of Reviews, 202, 205, 258

Richmond *Times Dispatch,* 258

Robertson, Mrs. Lucy H., 141

Robinson, Ezekiel. *See* Zeke

Rockefeller, John D., Jr., 202, 208

St. Clair, D. F., quoted, 97-98; mentioned, 255-56

St. Louis *Chronicle,* 238

Salem Academy, 63

Sampson Democrat, 166

Schools, public in North Carolina, system of best in southern states, 25; collapse with the Confederacy, 25; early provision for, 26; Wiley first superintendent of, 27; maintained only in towns and cities, 27; hostility toward, 27; movement for graded, 57; Greensboro has first of graded, 58; other towns establish graded, 58; pathetic condition of, 96; average term of, 98; Legislature appropriates $50,000 for, 171; prosperity dependent on efficient system of, 171; issue of local tax for endangered, 176; McIver and Alderman "plead unceasingly for," 185; Southern Education Board agrees on vigorous educational campaign for, 212; conferences discuss rural, 217; McIver design for improving rural, 226; rural districts realize necessity for better, 242. *See also* Education

Schurz, Carl, 235, 251

Scotch Iver. *See* McIver, Evander

Scots, in Cape Fear region, 4; migration of to North Carolina, 4-5; conform to general pattern, 6; are Presbyterians, 6; write brightest chapter in North Carolina's educational history, 26

Seminaries, female, in Durham, 58; private and expensive, 70; give no practical training, 71

Shaw, Albert, 202, 205-7, 210, 219, 258

Sherman, 20

Slater Fund, 58

Smith, Hoke, 164, 204, 223, 230

Sorority, at Normal and Industrial College disbands, 165

South Atlantic Quarterly, 258, 275

Southern Educational Association, McIver addresses, 123; elects McIver president, 242; mentioned, 212, 219, 243, 249

Southern Education Board, authorized, 203; officers of, 207; aim educational evangelization, 208; mentioned, 211-12, 216, 220, 224, 226, 240, 243, 257

Spainhour, Dr. J. M., 115, 269

Spencer, Cornelia Phillips, 45, 48, 70, 155, 184, 186, 236, 266

State Aid, to higher education in North Carolina, Baptists and Methodists oppose, 144; signal for church resistance to, 144; church opposition to reflected in advocacy of lower schools, 146; principle of established, 146; church opposition to sharpened by depression, 147; church groups seek to rouse public opinion against, 149; two denominations begin organized opposition to, 149; argument against involuntary support by taxation for, 150; clerical group represents issue of as Christian education vs. Godless education, 150; church opposition continues after Legislative approval of, 158; church opposition to reaffirmed, 159; issue in election campaign, 160; opposition to losing ground, 160; *See also* Education

State Chronicle, The, 62, 82, 137, 268

Stone, Joseph J., 224, 274

Strong, Cornelia, 270, 274

Tar Heel Editor, by Josephus Daniels, 136, 268, 270

Taxes, early North Carolinians against, 27; for any purpose an evil, 92; crowds hear institute instructors urge higher, 95; McIver discusses aversion to, 99; the savage alone exempt from, 99; as social insurance, 100; growing reaction against local for schools, 152; church demands that lower schools only benefit from, 154; McIver works for increased school, 154; McIver most concerned about local for schools, 166; issue of local school endangered, 176; provision needed for local, 180; many townships without local school, 186; objection to providing Negro schools out of, 212; Southern Education Board to further principle of local, 213; teachers should point out truth in regard to, 224

Taylor Charles E., 147, 150-51, 153, 271

Teachers, few and poorly respected, 69; young women needed as, 70; pay of average, 76; part of Normal session devoted to Negro, 77; too little training for, 96; "the seed corn of civilization," 97; attendance at institutes compulsory for; 98; low pay and morale of, 98; necessity for raising standards of, 99; new professional pride among, 100; only the best good enough, 120; McIver urges Normal girls to be real, 134-35; McIver pleads for better training and pay for, 217; should point out facts in regard to taxes and salaries, 244

Teacher training school, Teachers' Assembly shows concern for, 70; Teachers' Assembly to petition Legislature for, 74; McIver credited with idea for, 75; memorial for rejected by Legislature, 75; committee to seek for third time, 84; institute conductors make strong plea for, 108; Farmers' Alliance endorses proposal for, 113; Legislature authorizes, 114

Tomlinson, J. L., 61, 64

Toon, Thomas F., 215

Trinity College, 112, 144-45, 150, 152, 161, 213-14, 258

Troy, N. C., a typical county seat, 104

Trustees, of Normal and Industrial School, 115; authorize additional dormitory and president's house, 124; reply to charges of presidential mismanagement, 138; vindicate McIver's judgment, 141; report on typhoid epidemic, 192; give thorough endorsement to president and faculty, 192

Typhoid fever, epidemic of at Normal and Industrial College, 191; deaths from, 191; attacks on school because of, 192

University of North Carolina, entrance requirements, 44; suspension and reopening, 45; 1877 commencement of, 45; costs at reopened, 46; buildings at, 47; size of student body at, 47; graduates Charles McIver, 56; Winston becomes president of, 115; awards honorary degree to McIver, 141; church resistance to reopening of, 144; requests annual appropriation, 145; clerical opposition to continues, 146; a bill to elevate to apex of state education, 147; alumni of in Legislature, 155; seeks McIver as its president, 168; Alderman president of, 169; again seeks McIver for president, 198; opens graduate courses to women, 213; gives second honorary degree to McIver, 239; mentioned, 156, 258

University of Virginia, 237

Vail, Mary, 121

Vance, Thomas Malvern, 55

Vance, Zebulon B., 45, 55, 96, 102

Wake Forest College, 112, 144-45, 150, 152, 214

Watauga Club, 213

Weatherspoon, Mrs. J. R. *See* McIver, Elizabeth

Webster's blue back spellers, 20, 30

Weekly Globe, Durham, 117

Western Sentinel, 61

White, Rev. John E., 181

Wiley, Calvin Henderson, 27

Winston, George T., inaugurated president of University of North Carolina, 115; helps prepare brief in behalf of University, 145; a strategist in church-state fight, 147-48; heads A. and M. College, 184; mentioned, 53, 60, 75, 83-84, 116, 149, 155-56, 183, 214, 259, 273

Winston Graded School, 60, 69

Woman's Association for the Betterment of Public School Houses, 216

Woman's College of the University of North Carolina. *See* Normal and Industrial School.

Women, are natural teachers, 70; needed as teachers, 70; not many occupations open to, 72-73; no illiterate children of educated, 76; proper training of strategic point in education, 77; make homes and primary schools, 77; education of surest way to universal education, 77; classical education considered useless for, 92-93; McIver believes in education for, 136; new opportunities opening daily for, 213; McIver faith in justified, 216

World's Work, 258

Young, Mrs. James R. *See* McIver, Annie

Zeke, 89, 111, 125, 158, 186, 189, 221, 248-49